Crane Island Journal Part One

Haust (Autumn)

A Memoir of a Remarkable Daily Life on a Small Island in the Salish Sea

By John Ashenhurst

Walt's Blessing

If I do it at all I must delay no longer. Incongruous and full of skips and jumps as is that huddle of diary-jottings... all bundled up and tied by a big string, the resolution and indeed mandate comes to me this day, this hour,—and what a day! What an hour just passing! the luxury of riant grass and blowing breeze, with all the shows of sun and sky and perfect temperature, never before so filling me, body and soul — to go home, untie the bundle, reel out diary-scraps and memoranda, just as they are, large or small, one after another, into print-pages, and let the melange's lackings and wants of connection take care of themselves.

From *Specimen Days* by Walt Whitman

Contents

Haust (Autumn)	1
Dedication	3
Introduction	4
One: Scavenging Firewood	9
Two: Perfect Windfall	13
Three: Foggy Dawn	17
Four: Buyer's Remorse?	20
Five: Fall Clean Up	23
Six: Unsustainable Health Care	28
Seven: Technology Options	32
Eight: Boat Troubles	36
Nine: Sailing Alone Around the World	40
Ten: Dues and Fees	44
Eleven: The Pleasures of a Splitting Maul	48
Twelve: Yvonne Visits Seattle	52
Thirteen: Ascending Turtle Knob	55
Fourteen: Otter Tracks	60
Fifteen: Island Democracy — Firing up the citizenry	64
Sixteen: Our Parents; Ourselves; Our Children — Aging and Island Living	68
Seventeen: Mud Bay Barge	72
Eighteen: Let's See What Comes Up	76
Nineteen: A Pause	79
Twenty: Dinner Guests	83
Twenty-one: Meatballs and Mashed Potatoes	86
Twenty-two: Blustery Morning	89

Contents

Twenty-three: How Heavy the Load?	93
Twenty-four: Dump Run; Exchange Visit	96
Twenty-five: Deer Harbor Thanksgiving	101
Twenty-six: Looking and Seeing	106
Twenty-seven: Salvation	109
Twenty-eight: The Damages	113
Twenty-nine: No Whining	116
Thirty: IKEA Run	119
Thirty-one: Island Transfer	123
Thirty-two: Not So Bad	126
Thirty-three: Power Watch	130
Thirty-four: Great Horned Owl	133
Thirty-five: Freezing Point	136
Thirty-six: Chocolate Pudding Cake	141
Thirty-seven: To Harstine Island We Go	144
Thirty-eight: Thanksgiving Dinner	147
Thirty-nine: Gig Harbor Field Trip	151
Forty: Home Again; Home Again	155
Forty-one: Disappointment	158
Forty-two: False Alarm	161
Forty-three: Going to Town	164
Forty-four: Some Assembly Required	167
Forty-five: Deadlines	171
Forty-six: Dinner and Music	174
Forty-seven: People Watching	178
Forty-eight: Holiday Festivities	182

Contents

Forty-nine: Everybody is Fine	185
Fifty: Bounty	188
Fifty-one: eNotator	191
Fifty-two: Bargains	195
Fifty-three: Christmas Carols	198
Fifty-four: Huginn Home	203
Fifty-five: Wet; Wet; Wet	207
Fifty-six: On the Level	211
Fifty-seven: Appropriate Technology	215
Fifty-eight: Improvisation	218
Fifty-nine: Amazing Stories and True	222
Sixty: Deer Harbor	226
Sixty-one: Run to the Lumber Yard	229
Sixty-two: Elin's Birthday	232
Sixty-three: James Comes Home	237
Sixty-four: Christmas Dinner in a Box	240
Sixty-five: Signs of Spring	243
Sixty-six: High Water	247
Sixty-seven: Christmas Eve	251
Sixty-eight: Christmas Day	255
Sixty-nine: Memories	259
Seventy: Catching Up	262
Seventy-one: More Catching Up	265
Seventy-two: Keith Comes to Visit	269
Seventy-three: Kate and Ken Visit	272
Seventy-four: New Year's Eve	276

Contents

Seventy-five: New Year's Meal	280
Seventy-six: Gift from the Sea	284
Seventy-seven: Final Details	287
Seventy-eight: Eyes Everywhere	291
Seventy-nine: Countertops!	294
Eighty: A Date at the Majestic	298
Eighty-one: Expectant	302
Eighty-two: Break In	306
Eighty-three: Moving Day	310
Eighty-four: The Father of Invention	314
Eighty-five: Water Policy	318
Eighty-six: Water Streaming Down the Walls	321
Eighty-seven: Publish or Perish	324
Eighty-eight: Piping in the Haggis	328
Eighty-nine: Kelly and Tim Come for a Visit	331
Ninety: Let the Chips Fall	335
Ninety-one: A Return to Our Routine	340
Ninety-two: Bad News from La Jolla	344
What's Next?	347

Haust (Autumn)

A Memoir of a Remarkable Daily Life on a Small Island in the Salish Sea

By John Ashenhurst

Crane Island Journal is a four-part memoir beginning with *Haust* and continuing with *Vetur*, *Vor*, and *Sumar* (autumn, winter, spring and summer in Old Norse)

Publisher: Classics Unbound

V1.00 06/01/2024

Copyright © 2024 by John Ashenhurst

ISBN 978-0-9904563-2-2

All rights reserved. Created in the United States of America. No part of this book may be reproduced in any manner whatsoever without written permission except in the case of brief quotations embodied in critical articles and reviews. For information, address Classics Unbound, 5615 24th Ave NW, #43, Seattle, WA 98107

All photographs are the property of the author unless otherwise indicated.

For more information see www.craneislandjournal.com.

Dedication

For Yvonne Lorene LaTour Ashenhurst, my companion in small adventures

Introduction

In 1997, after living in Boulder, Colorado, for more than 20 years, on impulse, Yvonne and I bought a house on Cayou Valley Road, in Deer Harbor, in the southwest corner of Orcas Island, the largest of the San Juan Islands in Washington State. I really can't tell you why.

From 1998 on we had a series of power and sailboats and explored the San Juans, Puget Sound, south, and the Straight of Georgia, and especially the nearby Canadian Gulf Islands, to the north.

By 2002 we had sold our property in Boulder and were living full-time on Orcas. As I told family and long-time friends, we had come for the beauty — and stayed for the people. In early 2007 we sold our house in the Deer Harbor hamlet and moved a mile south to Crane, a private island, at Pole Pass, a stone's throw from Orcas.

We were now in a northwest-style house with vaulted fir ceilings and big windows right on the water, on a small bluff, with our own pocket beach from which we could launch kayaks and small boats, and we got busy improving our house and property to our liking. And because we were on a private island without ferry service, we were on the water day and night, in wind, snow, and fog. Sometimes it was too exciting.

On October 19, 2010, I had an inspiration: our experiences were so different from most people's and so rewarding, I had to capture them, so the next morning I sat in a wicker chair with my MacBook in my lap next to our cozy wood stove and wrote about the day before. I wrote my Crane Island Journal daily for a year. Then that was enough.

On January 30, 2024, now living in the Ballard neighborhood of Seattle and 80 years old, I had another inspiration: it was time to share what I'd written. As I wrote and edited my words, Crane Island came flooding back. It had been a special time. Yvonne agreed.

This is that journal: *(Haust,* autumn), the first of four volumes — followed by *Vetur, Vor,* and *Sumar,* (winter, spring, and summer in Old Norse).

Introduction

Intro1: Waiting for inspiration

The San Juan Islands are an archipelago of 400 islands in northwest Washington, north of the Strait of Juan de Fuca and bordering British Columbia, Canada. Four Islands, San Juan, Orcas, Lopez, and Shaw are served by the Washington State Ferry Service. The islands are hilly, even mountainous, with Mt Constitution, on Orcas Island, the highest, at 2,407 feet. The islands lie in the rain shadow of the Olympic mountains to the southwest and experience modest annual rainfall compared to Seattle and the Olympic Peninsula, with little or no summer rain. Summertime high temperatures are around 70 °F (21 °C) and winter lows generally above freezing, with occasional snow, especially at higher altitudes.

Introduction

Intro2: San Juan Islands with Bellingham, WA to the east and Vancouver Island and Gulf Islands, Canada to the west (Raven Maps & Images, Medford, OR)

Orcas Island has about 6,000 full-time residents, with summer visitors doubling the population. Orcas Island looks like a horseshoe, with a long fjord (East Sound) dividing the island from the south. The center of population is Eastsound, at the top of the East Sound fjord. The West Sound fjord occupies the western side of the horseshoe, with Deer Harbor hamlet on a smaller bay west of West Sound. Orcas Landing, the site of the ferry terminal, is on the south side of the island between East Sound and West Sound. Moran State Park, on the east side of the horseshoe, has several lakes, trails, campgrounds, and 2407' Mt Constitution.

Introduction

Intro3: Deer Harbor bottom center, Crane Island left towards the top with airstrip and community dock, middle left at Pole Pass visible. (Photo By J Brew from near Seattle, USA - Deer Harbor, Orcas Island, CC BY-SA 2.0, https://commons.wikimedia.org/w/index.php?curid=10238328)

Deer Harbor hamlet has two marinas, one with a dock store, fuel dock, and transient moorage. WorldMark Deer Harbor and Deer Harbor Inn offer housing.

Private Crane Island partially closes the south end of Deer Harbor, with Orcas and Crane separated by only 100 feet at Pole Pass, where the Crane Island community dock is located

Introduction

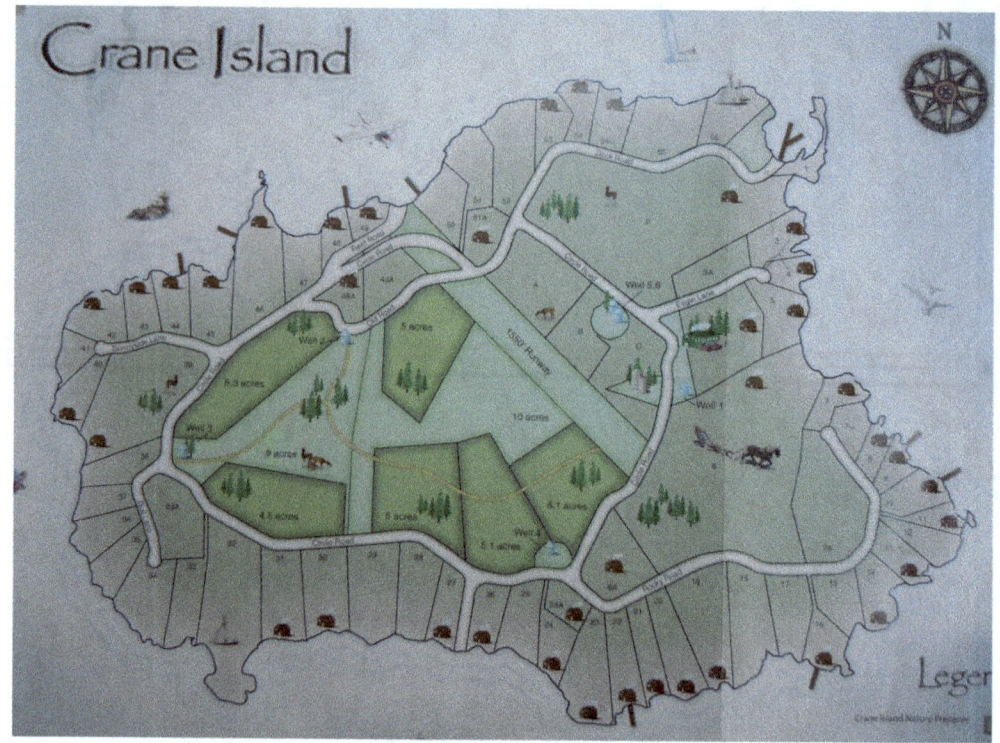

Intro4: Crane Island Lots and Roads

Crane Island was logged for the second time in the 1950s and subdivided and developed for housing in 1960. It has its own roads, airstrip, water system (wells, tank, and piping), community docks on Crane and Orcas, a clubhouse, fire engine, and a rescue vehicle. Most houses on Crane are second homes and only a few are occupied year-round. Short-term rentals are not allowed. Visitors are welcome only when accompanied by Crane Island Association members. Crane Island has no public services.

JCA, May 2024

One: Scavenging Firewood

"Before enlightenment, chop wood, carry water. After enlightenment, chop wood, carry water." — Zen proverb

For over a year, I had been thinking about a pile of tree trunks abandoned near Well House 1 in the Crane Island common area. With our F-150 pickup temporarily on the island, it made sense to consider cutting them into 16-inch sections and bringing them back to the house, about ¼ mile away, for splitting, stacking, and then burning this winter in our wood stove to supplement our inefficient electric baseboard heating.

It was a sunny October day. The grass in the field adjacent to where the logs lay was intensely green, soft, and luxurious. Why don't the island deer browse here rather than trying to find a way into Yvonne's garden?

But what about burning wood? Isn't that polluting — adding CO_2 and particulates to the atmosphere? Shouldn't the logs be allowed to return to the soil? Are they a feeding station for birds? Why not let them act as nurse logs for the next generation?

Letting the logs rot would have the same effect as burning them — releasing carbon dioxide into the atmosphere. In either case, it's certain that other trees will grow on Crane and quickly recapture the CO_2 sequestered in the logs. If the wood is burned hot in a modern wood stove, not much particulate matter is released — no visible smoke. And it seems to make sense to use a local heat source rather than electricity or propane that has to be transported long distances at considerable effort, expense, and environmental impact.

There were ten trunks, the largest being 18 inches in diameter and the smallest about 6 inches — Douglas fir, alder, western red cedar, and others — each about 10 feet long. A Douglas fir stump stood nearby, broken off about 8' up, the source of one of the trunks in the jumbled pile.

One: Scavenging Firewood

001: Abandoned logs near well house 1 waiting for someone to claim them

Where did they come from? Who cut and stacked these trunks and left them to rot? Why? At least three were deadfalls, toppled in winter storms onto the common area meadow. Perhaps Jim Johansen or Tom Temple or Gary Sale, our water system manager, had been involved. But since no one wanted the logs, they were fair game for an island scavenger.

Douglas fir, known for its thick bark and strong fire resistance, is often used for construction framing. It also has a beautiful grain that lends itself to trim, doors, and moldings. They grow like weeds in the Pacific Northwest — in the rainforest to 8' diameters and 300' high.

Alder, a brittle and easily breakable deciduous tree with gray bark, is related to aspen, birch, and beech. On the ground, they rot much more quickly than Douglas fir. Often growing in wet areas, in clumps, and in peculiar shapes, they look unkempt next to the straight and elegant Douglas firs.

One: Scavenging Firewood

Cedar trees are wonderful. Rather than spiky, their needles are flat and soft to the touch with the pattern of their bark running vertically. Cedar is particularly resistant to rot, thus its use in decks, posts, and other exposed wood.

Because I had to park my pickup 100 feet from the pile of trunks, I brought along our dock cart to carry the cut sections from the pile to the truck. With a Poulan 18" chainsaw (wife Yvonne's $105 purchase at Sears "scratch and dent" store south of downtown Seattle) and gas and chain oil, I was ready to begin cutting.

Since some of the logs had been lying there on the ground for several years, I expected some to be too rotten and unusable, and that turned out to be the case. Three fir and a single alder, wet, sporting dense, tough, clinging fungi, clearly weren't worth the effort of cutting, moving, and splitting, but the rest looked promising, if not perfect.

Besides the obvious cautions about chainsaws and bodily harm, they require a certain amount of care. When cutting wood, the blades will stay sharp through many trees, but cutting into soil, sand, or gravel can ruin a chain quickly. So cutting trunks on top of other trunks isn't a problem, but trunks on the ground can be. How do you cut them through without ruining the chain — when you can't roll or lift them?

The cedar, not surprisingly, was in the best condition, even with its bark peeling off. The alder, on the ground, wasn't usable. The fir, with an inch or two of rot on one side, looked usable.

Because these trunks had been down for several years, they were drier and much lighter than fresh-cut, live trees — and very easy to cut — the chainsaw like a knife through butter. Cutting the cedar was a particular pleasure — because it's highly aromatic — with a characteristic clean scent — perhaps what keeps insects, fungi, and microbes at bay.

But loading the cart, dragging it to the pickup, and tossing 30 lb sections into its bed made me feel stiff, weak, and old – at least for a while until my muscles warmed up and stretched out. Mostly it felt good to be outside in the autumn sunshine in a beautiful place with no one around using a very manly power tool and knowing that we would have plenty of firewood to be cozy this winter.

After about three hours of effort and two truck trips, I had a pile of trunk sections piled at the foot of our Ranger sailboat — out of the water and on its trailer for the winter. The open question remained: Would these sections split easily, or were they too soft? The concern was whether the splitting maul would bury itself in the wood rather than force it apart and break into sections.

Two: Perfect Windfall

"A crisis is an opportunity riding the dangerous wind." — Chinese proverb

Cloudy, misty, tank at 10 feet.

More than a year ago, a winter wind pushed over a 60' double-trunked Douglas fir. The shorter, dead trunk jammed itself into a big, ill-formed alder, with the longer, living trunk and crown nearly hitting the roof of well house 2, but distracted by a 20' dead fir, 4' to the east. The root ball, now half-visible, stuck up about 6', and was the source for a 24" diameter trunk. The root ball held the lower trunk about 4' off the ground. The dead fir at the other end held the crown 15' off the ground. Dead branches and spikes off the lower end also served to prop up the fallen tree.

Green for months, the wind-toppled fir eventually died and turned brown. Because its top was so close to the well house roof, held back by another, smaller dead tree, it appeared to be a danger to the well house. Because the tree floated, held up at one end by a dead tree, in the middle by branches, and at the bottom by the root ball, it looked like it might be a danger to anyone trying to cut it down and into pieces.

Our Water System Director and former sometime-arborist said he would take care of the tree, but being busy, he didn't get to it. A danger to the wellhouse and a danger to anyone who tampered with it. What's not to like? But without a way to transport the trunk sections home to be split for our wood stove, a half-mile distant, I couldn't generate much enthusiasm to tackle the project. Now, with our pickup on the island for a while and needing to set in a winter firewood supply, the double-danger task was irresistible.

Setting out about 9:00 on a sunny October day in the low 50s, I parked at the intersection of Circle Road and Rocky Road. "Road" is probably too strong, really, since both were single-lane gravel tracks that off-season didn't see any wheeled activity for weeks at a time. I walked to the nearby 8' well house cube

Two: Perfect Windfall

with a peaked roof and set my chainsaw, two-stroke gas can, and gallon of chain and bar oil on the remains of a gravel pile, one of several around the island that served as sources for filling potholes. This one was severely depleted because Jim Johansen had taken several John Deere tractor scoops from it in July to refresh a path at the Clark's, who would host the Crane Island Golden Anniversary party I made a video for a few days later.

002: Windfall bucked up for transport home

The question: could I cut the tree down without harming the well house or myself in the process? Yvonne had gone to Orcas for meetings and wouldn't be back until afternoon. As far as I knew, only Tom Temple, down Rocky Road, and Lou Falb, all the way on the other side of the island, were around, and neither had any particular reason to move off their properties that day. What if something fell on me, and I got trapped under the trunk or a branch? What if I was careless with the chainsaw and severely injured myself? I didn't have a cell phone. No one would come until too late. But I did have my Nikon camera on my belt, since I was intending to document the project. I could use the video recording feature to tell my sad story before my demise. Yvonne or someone would eventually find the video on the camera where I tell what happened and that I love everyone. Enough! Time to get to work.

I first cut through the trunk about 20 feet from the root ball, where the trunk was 5' above the ground, surmising that the upper part of the tree would drop, and the lower would hold in place. I could then cut sections in the lower part and see what to do about the upper. Since there was a chance that a cut might bind the saw between the two sections before they fell apart, I first cut a few inches from below and then cut a triangular slice from above, leaving plenty of space for the trunk to buckle into as the top portion of the tree fell away from the bottom. That worked just right.

I cut 16" (or so) sections down toward the root ball, first trimming any branches. About 8' from the bottom, at an 18" diameter, I quit cutting and left the horizontal stump. With the diameter exceeding the saw bar length and sections becoming increasingly heavy, it seemed prudent to curtail my greed for more. The summer before, transporting a big fir in sections from Chris Thomerson's house on Orcas — by truck, dock cart, boat, and then dock cart to my splitting area, I'd injured my back on the second to last section and that put me out of commission for a few weeks. And I didn't want to have the problems my son Noah was having with his back when a random twist brought him to his knees in pain and made it impossible for him to do anything but lie down or stand for weeks — until, discouraged with a pain-killer regimen, he tried a hang-board — and that did the trick.

Going back to the upper portion of the tree, I cut it about 10' along, where it was now about 5' off the ground. I trimmed branches and sliced that part of the trunk. I did the same thing two more times — on each occasion, the higher part of the trunk dropped lower so I could work on it. After pulling the crown out of the dead tree holding it, I dragged the crown and branches away from the well house to an open area under a mature grove of cedars and firs.

What a contrast! I'd been working in thick salal, sea spray, and small, crowded firs and among big branches that had broken and were hanging down from the busted big alder that now dominated the area. But 20' away, there was no understory, just clear needle-covered ground and a few rotting trunks amid big trees that captured the sunlight before it could support new life below. The old-growth forest looked elegant with its life all above. The new-growth forest, along the road and where the soil had been disturbed to dig the well and build the well house, was teeming with life in chaotic profusion. A towhee bounced along the trunk sections I'd cut looking for something good to eat. I'd seen spiders and beetles as I worked. The climax forest wouldn't support much life — not birds or deer or even many insects. Only the messy border of new growth would.

Getting the sections into the truck bed was a bit of a struggle since carrying them out of the tangle where they lay threatened to trip me, the branches hanging down from the alder wanted to poke me in the eye, and some of the sections weighed 60 or 70 lbs — (lift with your legs I said to myself). Back home I tossed the new, excellent quality Douglas fir sections on top of the pile of questionable slices I'd cut and brought home the day before from a pile of rotting trunks near well house 1. Quite a pile — certainly more than a cord once split (8' x 4' x 4') to add to the two cords already stacked and covered. We'll be warm enough this winter and I won't have to go hunting for wood until next summer.

Three: Foggy Dawn

*"In every walk with nature one receives far more than he seeks." —
John Muir*

Dawn light gathered to reveal — not much of anything. Overnight fog had crept north from the Strait of Juan de Fuca through Cattle Pass and the channel between Lopez and San Juan Islands. Orcas wasn't visible, nor Bell Island; a world with a 100' diameter. No matter; by noon, the fog would be gone, and we didn't have to go anywhere until then.

At the top of the driveway, at Eagle Lane, the large-leaf maple had shed most of its leaves, now a yellow and brown carpet over the gravel, marked with channels from a September downpour. Last fall, Yvonne raked the leaves off the lane for the compost pile and because left where they lay, autumn rains made them a slippery mass, a real problem when I tried to get the U-Haul truck out the January day we moved in.

Fog-bound, somewhere between Bell Island and the southeast corner of Crane, as it headed for Wasp Passage and Friday Harbor, moving but invisible, the *Yakima*, a big green and white Washington State Ferry, sounded its horn in warning and then again.

Just past the Community Center on Circle Road, going uphill, I could see the level indicator on the island's 35,000-gallon concrete water tank. Ten feet again today. No evident problems, small background leaks, and regular usage from the three currently occupied houses on the island.

Near Nielsen's driveway on Circle Road, I came upon Wilma Sale waiting for husband Gary, on his way in a slow-going tracked power shovel he would use to lift a new fiberglass septic tank off the truck Wilma had driven to that point and then dig out the 40-year-old failing tank and replace it with the new one.

We talked about heating systems — they had just poured a concrete floor over tubing they would circulate hot water through to warm their new barn at the homestead they were building on Orcas. One hour a day in four 15-minute periods would keep the barn at 55 degrees — a good temperature for working and keeping the place dry.

Gary came up soon in the power shovel, and we talked briefly about the two hydrants he needed to install — on Eagle Lane and on Sunnyside — as well as the coliform and cross-connect plans we owed the county. With the power shovel on the island, Gary thought it would make sense to excavate a trench from well-house 6 uphill to the tank so he could lay cable to connect a float switch in the tank to pump timers in well-houses 6 and 5. Unexpected heavy water use on a weekend last spring (many visitors) had caused the tank level to drop to its 7 ½ foot fire reserve. With no water flowing out of the tank, houses at the highest point in the system would run out of water first. Thus, the Hawkes, up from Seattle to enjoy the weekend at their Crane house, had no water and had to leave the island sooner than planned. Unacceptable.

Gary is the water manager – the homeowners association hires him to oversee the system and make required reports. I'm the board member responsible for the water system. Having a tank float wired to the timers in the two nearby and most productive wells meant that Gary could set the timers to pump aggressively but when the tank level exceeded 14 feet, the top, the pump would be shut off, overriding the timers. At times of high use, with the tank level falling, the pumps would not be interrupted, and the system could work to bring the system back to its full level.

Between Gulf Lane and Sunnyside Lane, I spied a black beetle with a brown abdomen moving around in the gravel and pine needle littering Circle Road. I often see these beetles, usually, it seemed, making a beeline to cross the road — to get to the other side, I suppose. This one moved randomly, looking for slugs to eat perhaps. But every so often it would fall over to its left. How peculiar. A six-legged creature should do better than that. I looked closer; only two legs, front and rear on its left side. What was the story behind that amputation or birth defect?

Three: Foggy Dawn

003: Mist reveals spider and web

Heading home after walking a two-mile circle. At the community dock, I started across Och's meadow, everything coated with a very fine dew left by the fog. As I had seen many times before, the tiny droplets made visible usually hard-to-see spider webs strung between the tall standing drying grass stems. The higher, bigger webs were systematic and elegant, usually with the maker positioned right at the center to feel any tugs on the web from potential meal visitors. By number, most of the webs were small, close to the ground, irregular, with denser stitching, and with no maker visible. Same goal; different technique.

The fog hides, and the fog reveals. It depends on what you're looking for. The fog creates a quiet, hushed, peaceful place, but it also causes those moving in it to speak in rich tones, sounds when vision fails.

There's the "Ashenhurst" sign Yvonne wood burned on a piece of driftwood, pointing through a copse of salal and small fir, to the path to Yvonne's bamboo north gate and home. Looking forward to a hot cup of English breakfast tea.

Four: Buyer's Remorse?

"You made your bed, now you have to lie in it" — Elin Ashenhurst

Cloudy

Corrina, our "bonus daughter," called just after noon from daughter Jeni's, in Seattle, where she was staying temporarily until she could leave for India to stay with Arjun, to see whether they were in love. He wants to come to the U.S. to study music. Corrina is applying to graduate schools in the administration of not-for-profit art organizations or something like that. Yvonne was at the Deer Harbor Community Club knitting group and also setting up for Saturday's yard cleanup there. Bonus daughter? Corrina is Jeni's half-sister, daughter of Yvonne's first husband by his second wife. Corrina began spending time with us after her mother died in 2005. We loved her.

In October 2006, we lived in an owner-built Victorian with a garage we had converted into a guesthouse/deck/sleeping porch, a boathouse/shop with my office in a loft, son-number-two Eric and I had created shortly after we bought the house in 1997. Yvonne had a big, raised bed garden, and a greenhouse, the property ringed by a deer fence. On the side of a hill with southern exposure, with scattered Douglas fir and cedar, fruit trees, native plantings, lots of deck, covered and exposed, a hot tub, a new IKEA kitchen/ dining area in a great room, one bedroom down, another up, and a family room, with a south deck and an east deck, furnished with Swedish farmhouse furniture. We'd done a lot of work ourselves and spent a lot to do things we couldn't. But — it wasn't quite what we wanted. Though we could see a little of Deer Harbor, basically we had no connection to the water. The house wasn't laid out well, the living room was low-ceilinged, there wasn't enough storage, and the crawl space was home to rats. We could make massive changes to the house but it would never be quite right.

On the way back from a yacht club trip to Sidney BC, we cruised by a house on the east side of Crane Island near Pole Pass at the south end of Deer

Four: Buyer's Remorse?

Harbor that Yvonne had seen advertised for sale. A group of kids was playing on a beach near what we thought was probably the house. Yvonne liked what she saw from a distance. We had talked with the listing agent, Al Decho, on the Sidney cruise, and we called him Monday to see the house. It was empty, and he arranged a tour for Wednesday. We loved the house and made an offer that was accepted on Thursday. Working with our friends Ken and Kate Wood, who had sold us the Deer Harbor house, we listed, had an offer, and accepted it Saturday. We then made an offer on the Crane Island house, and Dean and Iris accepted it. We were going to move.

We'd bought the house in Deer Harbor, on Cayou Valley Road, on impulse. When we visited Orcas in August 1997 we were smitten by its beauty, found the Deer Harbor hamlet charming and then bought a house with no clear plan about living there. Crazy maybe. On the other hand, though we loved Boulder and had raised our kids there, and had family and dear friends in Colorado, it seemed increasingly overrun by monied California and New York refugees and its western college town flavor was morphing into a caricature of itself, a kind of Boulder theme park. The roads were crowded, the trails were crowded, and tourists were everywhere. Too precious. We had become disenchanted with Boulder.

Something similar had happened with our house in Deer Harbor. Though we had done lots of work inside and out to make it what we wanted, it now felt inadequate. The house was poorly designed and built. It had no view of or access to the water. We had too many neighbors too close. The Crane house solved those problems or at least made those problems solvable — with a little work.

But we'd created new issues we were only beginning to become aware of. It wasn't easy to live on an island without ferry service. It had OPALCO power and CenturyLink phone but the Crane Island Association was responsible for its own docks, roads, wells, water system, airstrip, and fire and rescue service. At first I found that fascinating — lots to learn — but I was beginning to realize how much work that meant for me personally. I was on the HOA board so I had to pay attention to our common area services. And since our household was only one of three (of 45) occupied year-round, who else was going to do it? How long would we want to make the effort? What would happen as we got old and couldn't work so hard or needed medical attention or got tired of having to deal with the Washington State Ferry Service?

Four: Buyer's Remorse?

004: At some point we'll have to move off Crane

Would we make some new impulsive decision and head off in an unexpected direction?

Our dinner conversation was realistic but not very much fun and Yvonne pointed out we were getting nowhere. We can't live frequently questioning our decisions and worrying about the future. She suggested and I agreed that we table the discussion. We have a wonderful life right now. Time for a Netflix DVD and hot tub soak.

Five: Fall Clean Up

"If you want to go fast, go alone. If you want to go far, go together."
— *African proverb*

The community water tank is holding steady at 10 feet. No sign of the storm.

Because Yvonne is the chair of the Deer Harbor Community Club Grounds Committee, she is responsible for the health and attractiveness of the grass, gardens, and plantings around the Community Club building (more than a century old and once housing the Deer Harbor school) and around the Deer Harbor Post Office. The Community Club managed to buy the building from Wyndham Properties two years ago after the company refused to renew the lease for the Post Office making it almost certain that we all would have to drive to Eastsound or the ferry landing to pick up our mail. That would be an inconvenience but since our Post Office is the place where we meet one another, unplanned, to exchange news and gossip when picking up mail from postal boxes, buying stamps, or shipping presents to grandchildren, we would lose a connection with one another. Our Post Office is a stage for the theater of community.

Yvonne is a great organizer. She sees clearly what needs to be done and can recruit and direct people to accomplish a shared goal. Since it owned the Post Office site, the Community Club needed to keep it looking good as a matter of pride and practicality. The Post Office is adjacent to the Resort at Deer Harbor and just across Deer Harbor Road from the Bell Marina at Deer Harbor. The Community Club building itself is set back from Deer Harbor Road a half-mile north at the boundary of the Deer Harbor Hamlet.

The weather for the day didn't look promising. The National Weather Service predicted a strong low and high waves off the west coast of Vancouver Island, our protection from direct exposure to the storms of the Pacific. Rain and wind was likely Saturday, certain on Sunday. Yvonne had announced the fall clean up at the monthly potluck and sent emails and talked to those likely to participate — the core group that always turns out and does most of the work. As an incentive, Yvonne would serve lunch — turkey chili, cornbread, and chocolate cookies. Pam Smith would also bring a pot of chili.

005.1: Volunteers cleaning up the Deer Harbor Post Office Grounds

At the Post Office, where the cleanup would begin, later moving to the Community Club site, volunteers began to appear even before the scheduled 10:00 a.m. starting time, carrying rakes, shovels, clippers, and other gardening paraphernalia. By 10:15, 20 volunteers were on hand, raking leaves, pulling weeds, and scraping green growth from concrete cracks and joints between the roadway and retaining wall. Mostly gray-haired in their 60s and 70s, a few younger and older, all working continuously, effectively, cooperatively, happily — with intermittent conversation and news swapping.

005.2: Taking a break in the Community Club after hard work at the Post Office and here outside.

Yvonne managed the group without having to do much explicitly — other than tell people what she thought needed to be done. They worked out the details, moving in and out of roles and jobs, lending and borrowing tools. Bob Foulk brought his pickup over from his home nearby, and cuttings, sweepings, and shovels-full went into the bed.

Five: Fall Clean Up

005.3: Howard busy in the belfry

Shasta daisies, unappealing to the local deer population that likes to browse all unfenced gardens, had spread enough to obstruct the parking lot exit and pedestrian approach. Yvonne put me in charge of digging most of them out, and as I laid clumps on the adjacent sidewalk, others carried the clumps for transplantation across the parking lot to a mostly empty bed where Yvonne and I had installed two posts and signs in the spring making it clear that the parking spaces were for Post Office patrons.

With the Post Office grounds cleanup complete at about 11:45, the group migrated to the Community Club where Yvonne issued orders and began to set up for lunch. Howard Barbour, club president, had spent the morning there installing two posts, side by side with enough space between them to hold a nautical, cross-style flagpole he'd built from an appropriately sized tree trunk he found floating in and retrieved from the waters of Deer Harbor. The concrete holding the poles needed to be set a week or two before the pole could be raised. Later on, Howard scampered up the roof to the belfry where he installed a new pull rope that hung down from the bell into the front hall of the building below, used to call children to class during the years the building served as the local one-room school before the consolidation of the schools to Eastsound.

James, our youngest son, in a neuroscience Ph.D. program at UCLA, called about 5:00 responding to my suggestion that we try Apple's videophone service called FaceTime between his iPhone and our MacBook Pro. Yvonne was skeptical about the value of the service. If you talk to someone on the phone, why do you need to look at them too? In this case, FaceTime (or Skype or whatever) turns out to be well-suited to our needs. Yvonne and I could both see and talk to James and his boyfriend, Keith, beginning his Ph.D. in philosophy at USC. A more satisfying connection. And Keith could show us the Gruyère cheese pâte choux appetizers that he had prepared, and we could see the filled champagne flutes they would have with dinner shortly.

Six: Unsustainable Health Care

"The path of least resistance makes all rivers, and some men, crooked." — Napolean Hill

Some wind this morning from the predicted storm but little rain. Water tank at 10 feet.

Suzanne Olsen, moderator for the Orcas Island Unitarian Universalist Fellowship for the last two years, reported that her recent moose hunting adventure with her husband John in the Bella Coola Valley had been a great success. They had come back with a large supply of moose meat (No, they didn't bring the head). They enjoyed the friendliness of the guides and locals, but most of all, she said, she appreciated the time with John, being part of an activity he enjoyed and had mastered: hunting, which she was both ignorant of and tentative about.

The UU fellowship was formed in 2000 by Nanette Graham, a Santa Barbara refugee, and when it was clear she would have to move to Bellingham to be closer to major medical care, I volunteered to be responsible for services, to be the moderator. Nanette's style was Cruise Director Lite. The services were her party, and she made sure everyone had a good time. The congregation grew. My style is lectures on serious topics. The congregation shrunk. After five years of duty, I resigned, and Suzanne took over. Her style is poetic and intuitive. We've switched from rows of seating facing the lectern and chalice to a semi-circle, from show with Nanette to lecture with me to conversation with Suzanne. She has a gift and could have been a Unitarian minister if her life had taken a different turn.

After Suzanne lights the chalice candle, the light of truth and fellowship, and some of us come up to light additional candles, sharing a joy or concern, David Sarver, president of the Orcas Medical Center Board, fills us in on the state of health care on the island. From the outside, the system looks healthy and robust. From the inside, it's sick and unsustainable. I think about the fir I found Labor Day on my morning walk on Crane. It had broken off about 15 feet from the ground and lay across Circle Road. There was no sign of rot from the outside. There had been no wind. But the tree couldn't stand.

Until this summer, Orcas was home to five primary care physicians for a population of 5000. A more practical ratio, David says, is one doctor to every 2500. Two doctors have moved off the island because they couldn't make a living. One doctor operates within the Medical Center, a state-of-the-art facility built with donations and connected to a sustaining foundation. He is subsidized by the Medical Center. The other two doctors have their own offices and staff. One takes no money out of his practice. The other appears satisfied with low pay in exchange for living on Orcas and practicing in a low-key way. In David's view, primary care health delivery on Orcas is underfunded by $750,000 each year. Part of that deficit is made up by donations and the Medical Center foundation; the remainder by physicians out of their own pockets. That's nice for benefiting islanders — who have great care and don't need to adequately fund it, but as the doctors retire or leave Orcas and as donations dry up, Orcas may find itself in the same boat as many other rural communities — no local health care.

What is to be done? One alternative that the Medical Center has pursued is to reduce island medical care overhead (how many separate bookkeeping departments are really needed?) and redundancy (how many x-ray machines and office buildings are needed?) by encouraging the two outlier doctors to come into the Medical Center, operate independently but share the building and administrative overhead. So far, neither is interested.

A second possibility would be to create an Orcas medical care taxing district as San Juan Island did a few years ago. Orcas has one to subsidize the public library. Why not do the same for medical care? Past efforts have failed and given an anti-tax mood, David says the Medical Center Board won't attempt a referendum.

A third possibility relates to the way insurance companies and Medicare/Medicaid reimburse primary care physicians — fees for certain services. David reports that primary care physicians have to spend more time providing services they cannot collect for than services they can. They are reimbursed for office visits but not for writing and tracking prescriptions, telephone calls, and reading x-rays — even though they must do these things to care for a patient. They can't make up the difference by charging more for office visits because the payers limit the amount they'll pay for visits. Primary care physicians — family practice, internists, and pediatricians — track individuals over time and can contribute more to a person's long-term health. Specialists see patients for a specific purpose and may never see them again.

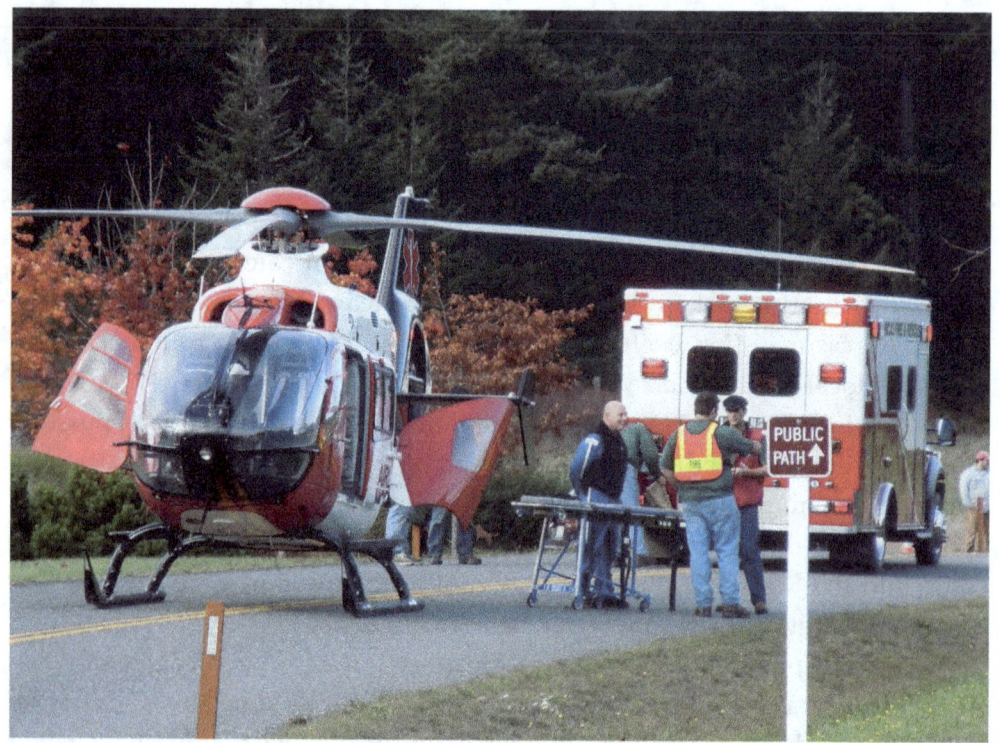

006: Emergency health care in the San Juan Islands sometimes requires an airlift

They deal with a situation, not the person. But specialists make double the income of primary care physicians on average, reimbursed at a higher percentage of costs than primary care.

Six: Unsustainable Health Care

The trick is to move primary care up the food chain. The closer it can come to the specialists/hospital world, the lower the subsidy required. San Juan Island is taking this step by working with Peace Health, a not-for-profit hospital group, to create an emergency room/small hospital in Friday Harbor. The center will house the island's primary care physicians, who will then be affiliated with the hospital. Reimbursement will be more substantial, and islanders will be able to get non-critical medical procedures without having to go to Anacortes or Bellingham. Were the Orcas physician's community centralized in the Medical Center and were a taxing district in place, Peace Health would be inclined to invite Orcas to participate in its Friday Harbor center, scheduled for 2012 operation.

But is that likely to happen? David doesn't have much confidence. The Orcas doctors value what they take to be their freedom and they're willing to sacrifice financially to have it. The Orcas population is perfectly happy with the health care they get — no waiting days for an appointment, for instance. San Juan Island came to understand they would all benefit from cooperation and shared responsibility. Maybe Orcas will get to that point once health care delivery slips as temporary, hidden, subsidies fade away.

I called Noah, our oldest son, living with his family on the water on Harstine Island, South Sound, just north of Olympia and talked first to his wife Natasha about Jonathan Franzen's new book "Freedom." She loved the writing but was disappointed in Franzen's portrayal of Patti Berglund. Too passive. Yvonne had said the same thing. No woman would act that way. Noah thought that the author's summary execution of his most interesting female character, Lalitha, was the result of fearing she would run away with the novel, as Mercutio tried to do to Shakespeare in "Romeo and Juliet." And we talked about Franzen's take on freedom.

Seven: Technology Options

"The road of excess leads to the palace of wisdom...You never know what is enough until you know what is more than enough." — William Blake, *"Proverbs of Hell"*

It is raining now, finally, but not much wind. October is usually very wet but hasn't been so far this year. Tank at 10 feet.

First, there was the cell phone question. Yvonne would be going to Seattle Friday and staying over with Jeni to go to the Bring Back Sanity Rally at Westlake. Her cell phone wouldn't recharge and probably needed a new battery. Radio Shack in Eastsound didn't have one; the phone was too old. James gave it to Yvonne as a backup when he got his first iPhone, and it was probably four years old. I had disabled Yvonne's phone by laying it on the cockpit deck of our SeaSport, which at the time was pretty wet — so we put James' phone in service.

Verizon has good service for Crane Island, with a transmitter at the ferry landing, a straight shot about two miles away. Sprint is available outside the house, as is AT&T. T-Mobile works, we understand, but their coverage other places is spotty. Might as well stay with Verizon.

We have only one cell phone. After too many business years of being tied to one, I don't want to be constantly accessible. Our current plan, 65 Plus, allowed 200 minutes and cost about $30 per month, but Yvonne never used all the minutes even when we were traveling. The Verizon service rep was very helpful over the phone. We averaged 46 minutes a month; the most in July when 14 of us convened at our family's "Borgfest 2010" reunion in eastern Washington to celebrate Yvonne's 60th birthday and visit Grandma Opal's grave at the Burnt Ridge Cemetery outside Troy Idaho, just east of Moscow.

Prepaid daily service would make the most sense. Any day we used the phone, we would pay $0.99. Any call we made would be charged at $0.10/minute. Our August charges, the highest month, would have been about $16.

Seven: Technology Options

We were now paying $30 every month. A no-brainer. I ordered a prepaid plan cell phone through the Verizon Website. It would arrive Tuesday or Wednesday. Yvonne would take it with her to Seattle Friday, stop at a Verizon store, and they'd set it up and migrate our current number to the new phone. We didn't want to risk buying the prepaid plan phone at a Verizon store because they might not have this — least expensive — phone in stock.

What about the rest of our communication infrastructure: local phone, long distance, Internet, television? Currently, we had the least expensive phone service CenturyLink offered; just a local connection with $0.45 per minute long distance (which we never used), prepaid calling cards, and iPod Skype at $3/month for long distance, 512kb DSL with Rock Island, a local ISP where we also had our email address, and DirecTV satellite cable access. Altogether, this cost about $140 per month.

My calling card was almost out of minutes, and Yvonne's would soon be. We could get refills, but that had become less convenient and more expensive. Yvonne wanted to be able to just pick up the phone and call long distance and not worry about it — and the same for guests — who probably had unlimited long-distance plans and might well expect us to have that as well — though their calls would cost us $0.45 per minute. I was less concerned about long distance since iPod/Skype calls were clearer and easier for me to understand, given my hearing loss than a telephone handset. I wanted faster DSL, 768kb, the best the local service could provide. Rock Island DSL piggybacked on the CenturyLink lines. The higher speed would cost $10 more per month.

A recent mailing from CenturyLink advertised bundled specials with DirecTV satellite cable access. Cable access now costs $62 per month. Could we get a discount or cheaper plan? Or could we eliminate it altogether and get what we wanted through the Internet for free or nearly so? Yvonne watches Seattle news when she cooks dinner and sometimes Oprah and HGTV (Home and Garden). Some evenings, when not watching a Netflix movie (DVD or streaming), we watch *The Daily Show* and *The Colbert Report* and in Season, *Mad Men*. That's it.

Seven: Technology Options

007: Landlines, cable, and cell can be problematic on a small island.

CenturyLink was very helpful. We could have unlimited long-distance, caller ID, and 768kb DSL for $75 per month and maybe get a $5 discount for having DirecTV provided we didn't have their basic plan. Though that wasn't net a lower monthly cost than we were paying for local phone, calling cards, and DSL, it did give us unlimited long-distance and faster DSL. We would have the new modem Friday. We would need to change email addresses, something I'm not eager to do — not just because we've had these addresses for maybe eight years and so many people know them but because so many Internet services use these addresses as login IDs. It's going to be a bear to change them.

The next step was to figure out cable access. Could we get everything we wanted via the Internet and use Apple TV or something else to display that content on our TV? Hulu has Jon Stewart and Stephen Colbert but with a week's delay. *Mad Men* is available through one site shortly after regular broadcast, but the quality isn't great. Seattle broadcast TV is available in bits and pieces from the stations' Websites but not in a very convenient way. A new service Ivi.tv streams all the Seattle (and New York) stations for $5/month. It seems to work pretty well but not always. Their application has some bugs. And conventional wisdom on the Web is they'll be shut down shortly by TV stations and cable operators. Yvonne says she doesn't want to watch TV on a computer. That means buying devices, including new TVs, that work in the Internet to TV streaming world. And the content isn't quite there.

So maybe we could play off DirecTV against DishNetwork. There is no physical cable on Crane Island. But it turns out that won't work. Even though there is little we want to watch, Dish doesn't offer both AMC and Comedy Central in the base package so we couldn't switch to any advantage. We would stay with DirecTV for now but very much want to dispense with cable access altogether as soon as possible. Maybe a year from now the broadcast, real-time content we want will be available through Internet streaming, and by dropping satellite cable access, it will make sense to buy the equipment it takes to conveniently watch streaming content on televisions (or whatever those devices become). It seems possible that at some point in the future everything will come through the Internet — broadcast TV, movies (e.g., Netflix), telephone, and the Web. That's going to be disruptive for telephone and cable companies but probably less expensive and certainly more convenient. Most of our Netflix watching is mailed DVDs.

Eight: Boat Troubles

"A boat is a hole in the water into which you pour money." — Boater's Lament

Windy, cloudy, 47 degrees.

This is the time of year the thermometer varies only a few degrees day and night. Thirteen years ago when we spent our first weekend in our empty house on Cayou Valley Road, we thought the big circular thermometer on the porch was broken since it seemed to hover around 48 degrees and never move. Much unlike our Boulder home, where the temperature often varies 40 degrees in 24 hours.

On Sunday, when coming back to Crane from Orcas, I noticed that the voltage indicator on our SeaSport dash showed 10 volts. It should show close to 14. That meant that the alternator wasn't working, and we were running off the twin batteries. Not good. After docking, I opened the engine compartment and looked at the V belt that was supposed to turn the alternator. Nothing obviously wrong. I felt the wires behind the alternator, and they all appeared to be connected. What was going on? Not a good situation.

We'd returned from traveling about 10 days before and had the boat repaired at the West Sound Marina while we were gone. The boat had become impossible to start after operating fitfully for a month or more. Yvonne had towed me with our neighbor Margaret's boat. Margaret was back at Ohio State for the fall semester, teaching anthropology. The problem, it turned out, was a sticky valve, and the stickiness was the result of seawater leaking through the port exhaust manifold. They'd pulled the head and had it machined. Reinstalling it, they replaced the port manifold, riser, and head and replaced the stub riser. The starter motor was clunking, so they replaced that. The forward prop was beat up, so they changed the prop and put a new zinc on it. They replaced a V belt, changed or topped off various fluids, replaced other zincs, cleaned and repainted part of the engine, and got the top RPMs up to 4200. That's good. But $3241.90 wasn't.

Well, that's how it is with boats, at least many boats in a saltwater environment. It corrodes everything eventually. It will dissolve metal unless zincs are strategically attached and can act as sacrificial metal. They are intended to dissolve rather than other necessary parts of the boat exposed to saltwater.

The $3000 hit was unexpected and unplanned for (of course). In April, we left the boat with West Sound Marina for routine servicing. They called while we were in California to tell us that the U-joint bellows, what was supposed to keep water out of the stern drive, was leaking. Ultimately they had to pull the engine, replace the bell housing, bearing, dampener, replace the trim tab cylinders — which had corroded, and on and on. That bill was $5189.80. So now almost $8500 in boat repairs.

Was the boat worth keeping? Would it make sense to continue to fix it? What was the alternative? When we lived in Deer Harbor boating was discretionary, an option. On Crane it was a daily necessity. And now the alternator wasn't charging. We were running on batteries, and that wasn't sustainable.

Monday morning I used my multi-meter to check the battery voltage. Just over 12 volts. It should have been over 12.5. So the voltage meter on the dash was probably accurate, not broken. Now what? And I could no longer ignore the starter motor. It was supposedly brand new, but it had been clanking just like the old one before we took the boat in for the latest repair session.

I called Ian Wareham, the boat repair and maintenance manager. (The Wareham family owns the West Sound Marina and is active in Orcas Island life, boats, and competitive sailing). Ian explained that a wire had probably come loose from the back of the alternator and that if it had, I could push it back on its blade connector. OK, I'd check it.

A small wire was loose, but it wouldn't be easy to reinstall. I had a hard time getting my hand to where it was needed, and I couldn't see what I was doing. I prevailed on Yvonne to lend me a mirror — not tiny but not too big. She had been very patient with me a few weeks before when I was working on replacing the electric window regulator (motor) for the front passenger side door in our Ford Freestar van.

Eight: Boat Troubles

008: Are you kidding me?

I'd never done it before (everything I do seems to be for the first time, I make lots of mistakes, take a long time, and never have a chance to apply what I've learned) and I needed to know how things were arranged inside the metal framework that held the cosmetic door panels on. She lent me a nice, double mirror compact, apparently an important beauty tool. I was very eager to get the window working because whenever I drove the van with Yvonne in the passenger seat, which was most of the time, I was subject to a continuous barrage of lower and raise the driver-side window commands. Yvonne's generous driving advice, already keeping me hopping, was now even more complicated.

In any case, I fixed the window, but broke the compact. She was so happy to have a working window that I was named hero of the day and the broken compact ignored. But now I needed another, bigger mirror that she used every

Eight: Boat Troubles

day for some purpose it's not possible for me to fathom. It would end up in the bilge so I could see up toward the back of the alternator. The bilge was wet and greasy (though I didn't tell her that). Yes, I could have it for a little while — BUT.

The mirror was wonderful. I could now see what I was doing and could see the wire with its slide-on connector and the blade it belonged on. But now everything was backward. Watching my hand in the mirror, I would move it down when I should have moved it up and vice versa. It made me crazy. Then — finally, the connector slid on. Now to see whether the alternator would charge. I started the engine and stared at the volt meter — 14 volts. Great! Once I ran the boat a bit, the batteries would be fully charged. Things were looking up.

I turned the ignition key to turn off the engine — and nothing happened. The engine wouldn't quit. I pulled out the "dead man" switch (a switch with a lanyard on it that when removed, causes the switch to depress) and nothing happened. What? Three years before I'd been blown across Deer Harbor from Crane Island because the engine stalled. I had to call Vessel Assist to tow me to the Deer Harbor Marina ($450) where I finally figured out that the lanyard holding out the switch had pulled out just enough for the switch to depress and disable the engine. But now that switch did nothing. The engine wouldn't stop.

I was bright enough not to try to pull the wire off the back of the alternator. Easy way to lose a finger. I took off the air filter and closed the choke. No air could get into the carburetor. The engine stalled. That wouldn't be a very convenient way to turn off the engine. Yvonne wouldn't go for it, that's certain.

I called Ian back. Ah, he said, for some reason there's a little resistor missing from the circuit. That's what stops the alternator from continuing to feed the engine after the ignition.

Nine: Sailing Alone Around the World

"When one door closes, another opens" — *Alexander Graham Bell*

For at least five years, five of us, now four, meet each Wednesday morning for ninety minutes of conversation over tea in Howard Barbour's one-room cabin next to his elaborate and productive vegetable garden, just above his house, shop, and outdoor brick bread oven, fenced to keep out the deer and with raspberries covered with netting to keep out birds and raccoons. Twenty-one gallons of raspberries, Howard reported, in two crops this year.

Howard offered coffee today, as well as tea, an experiment, he said, but it had no takers. Bob Harris and his wife Megan had moved to Eastsound from their longtime home on the ridge several hundred feet above, and were some of the first people we had gotten to know on Orcas 13 years ago. Bob had taught our son James to sail during our first summer on Orcas, a retired architect and then aspiring novelist, now recuperating from spinal surgery in a Friday Harbor nursing home. He'd had marginally successful knee surgery two years before and then over time was increasingly out of touch. The problem, Megan explained one Sunday at a Unitarian service, was that a constriction in his spinal column interfered with the circulation of spinal fluid. That was now presumably fixed, and Bob's mind had brightened up but his walking hadn't. An ornery, idealistic octogenarian, Bob found mingled beauty and stupidity everywhere he looked.

Howard, an Englishman, and Sheila Gaguin, his wife, had taught school in an Alaskan Inuit village just south of the Arctic Circle for nine years, coming down to Deer Harbor summers for sailing, sun, and warmth. David Sarver, a Hoosier with business and law degrees, had moved from California with his wife Maxine and was now president of the Medical Center Foundation Board. Chris Thomerson, another Englishman, had been an electrical engineer in England and later an organizational consultant here; like Howard, an avid sailor and with wife Lynn had cruised in the Broughton's this summer. Brian

Cleary, a retired Oregon Forestry professor and entrepreneur, had sailed to the South Pacific a number of times and up and down the Northwest coast, now lived alone, not by choice, missing his beloved wife Judy, who I never met.

009: Greybeards: Bob Harris, John Ashenhurst, David Sarver, Howard Barbour, Chris Thomerson, Brian Cleary (October 2008)

I had a topic: Would they be interested in doing an annotated ebook version of Joshua Slocum's "Sailing Alone Around the World?" I had a specific reason for raising the question.

For more than a year, I'd been pursuing an idea to create electronic versions of literary classics that would have a layer of annotations underneath the layer of the author's words, accessible from highlighted passages in the text that served as links to notes that provided explicitly the context modern readers lack but the author's contemporaries had. The notes would be a kind of reader's assistant, an expert at their elbow who had the answers the reader might ask as well as advice about what to look for and notice. The notes would address arcane vocabulary, the historical context within which the story takes place, and insight into what the author was up to in particular passages — and for the work as a whole. Like having an interesting literature teacher in the book you could call on at any time.

A retired literature professor who lived on Orcas and taught popular classes on nineteenth-century British literature (and some more modern, American, and German) was enthusiastic about the project. I created the software to make and manage the annotations and then convert them — with the author's text — into an electronic book for publication for Amazon's Kindle (a proprietary format) as well as the generally accepted ePub industry-standard format. After a great deal of hard work and experimentation, we published our version of Jane Austen's *Emma* in June. Seeing it in Amazon's catalog was very satisfying. Now we could test various marketing approaches and get some feedback, in terms of customer reviews on Amazon, to understand whether readers were interested and whether we had created something they could use easily.

But two weeks after publication, the annotator withdrew from the project and insisted I pull the book from the Amazon catalog. He wrote that he was ashamed of it. I didn't and don't understand. I bought a copy while it was available, have shown it to friends and family, and they find it attractive, interesting, well-written, and a snap to use. David Sarver read it and a friend of his read it. Yvonne is reading it now. All agree it's excellent. Whatever.

After this setback, David and Chris and I (they've been involved almost from the beginning) decided the idea was too good to give up on. I recruited Jens Kruse, a Wellesley German professor who has a house on Orcas, to do an annotated version of Kafka's *The Metamorphosis*, a fascinating, difficult, and popular novella. I simplified the software, with Chris providing some suggestions and sent it along with Jens when he and his wife Susan headed back to Boston in September. They would be back on Orcas for part of the winter to get a feel for whether full-time retirement might be an appealing plan for the future.

Nine: Sailing Alone Around the World

In order to recruit more annotators and get more books in the pipeline and to finally really test the idea in the marketplace we needed more books. Where would they come from? In 1895 Slocum was the first to sail solo around the world. His 37-foot *Spray* is one of the best-known sailboats of all time and a replica docked in Deer Harbor for the wooden boat festival this September. The book is well-written and tells a story almost inconceivable today when GPS, radio, satellite telephone, and Internet connection, desalinization system, fiberglass hulls in exotic shapes, and high-tech masts and rigging systems seem necessary components of any solo circumnavigation attempt. Not that others haven't and do follow in Slocum's wake, sailing simply. But he was the first, and he told the story in a compelling way.

Why couldn't we create an annotated ebook version of *Sailing Alone*? Brian, Chris, and Howard knew sailboats and blue-water sailing. I know a little. David volunteered to read Slocum and highlight the passages he'd like annotations for. Chris said he would figure out how we could use Google docs, online, to collaborate on the project. Howard said he knew someone who might be interested in doing research and writing. The goal: to publish early in the year. Rather than list us individually as annotators (with Slocum, of course, as the author), Brian suggested "annotations by the Greybeards," our way of identifying our Wednesday morning group of retired guys who like to get together and have stimulating conversations. OK!

Ten: Dues and Fees

"We must learn to live together as brothers or perish together as fools." — Martin Luther King Jr.

Almost all Crane Island Association members had responded to the invoices I sent out in late August with September 30th due dates. I was now the association Treasurer, having succeeded Mike Shimasaki, our occasional neighbor two lots down. All but three of the members had returned bills and checks; I had corresponded with two and was confident they would pay soon.

Only one hadn't responded, and I heard that the member was under water with their construction loan. They had built two years ago — actually, not built, but brought in a manufactured house by barge that was lifted onto the foundation by crane. The house was complete, and they used it from time to time but were unable to secure a permanent mortgage and had been paying 8% on the construction loan. The 2008 crash had dried up all the credit sources they had expected to use. With real estate down 10% to 15% from fall 2008 prices, they were now upside-down with their loan; it was higher than the current market value of the house. They couldn't make payments on the high-interest construction loan, and they couldn't work out alternative financing. They would probably walk away from the property — and their down payment. Dreams disappointed. Would they be able to pay their Crane dues and fees? Should the association put a lien on the property?

Crane has a community water system with six wells and a 35,000-gallon concrete water tank, a community dock and parking lot on nearby Orcas Island, a community dock and parking area on Crane, a concrete barge ramp, a grass landing strip, a community building, a pumper fire truck, an emergency rescue vehicle, and about three miles of single-lane roads that provide access to each lot. Every bit of this infrastructure requires regular maintenance at varying intervals, and all is likely to require major repair or replacement at some point. Because the entire island is private, the county is not required, expected, nor invited to play any role in our infrastructure other than regulate it, in the case of water quality, for instance.

010: The Crane community dock with Gary Sale's Mudpuppy coming through Pole Pass

Members are billed in two categories: dues and fees for use. Each member is assessed $700 per lot per year (some members have more than one lot) and those with water access (and water meters) $100 each year for the water connection. Dues are billed in advance, for the coming fiscal year (August through July), and usage fees in arrears (that is, after the usage has taken place and been reported). Fees for water, dock moorage, ramp use, vehicle use, and various kinds of storage are all due after the end of the year in which they occurred. Our bill totaled $3135.47, no small amount.

Last year the collection process dragged on until January. I didn't want that, so I got the bills out early, creating a billing list in Excel and using it as a source to merge into a billing form created with Word. I mailed paper copies to all members and sent an email with a PDF copy of their billing form attached for those who hadn't paid by the due date. I had made only one reminder call. The process had worked pretty well.

The annual bills contain amounts for annual dues, water connection, and gallons used. Members are expected to fill in the other amounts, for instance, the fees they owe for having moored their boats at a Crane Community dock. They're expected to report accurately and honestly, and that presents an opportunity for Board-level philosophical differences to arise. One school holds that member self-reports should be challenged when suspected of being inaccurate. Members should follow the rules; the rules should be enforced, and the association should get all the revenue due it. Another school believes that members will report honestly, and to challenge them on the chance that they might have underreported could cause ill-feeling and actually encourage more underreporting.

Last year a Board member who thought he had evidence of underreporting succeeded in getting the treasurer to challenge a number of members on their reporting. The effort turned out badly. They had reported accurately, at least they had good reasons for how they reported, and they grumbled a bit at having been challenged. I didn't want to go down that road, so this year my challenges were limited to arithmetic errors on the bills — bills that literally didn't add up — where the check sent didn't represent the sum of the detail the member had written on the bill. There were a few, and once I politely pointed out the error to the members, they were a bit embarrassed but paid the difference promptly.

Many homeowner associations across the country have fewer responsibilities — are not responsible for their water and roads. We are our own local government in a sense, and all the issues relating to government show up in our microcosm.

What fee structure is fair? How much should we spend on the water system? What improvements should we make? How much money do we need to hold in reserve for major improvements or repairs (like docks — which can cost $200 a linear foot)? How strictly should we try to enforce policy and association covenants?

How can we develop a culture of cooperation — since we depend on volunteer effort, and life on the island is nicer when people have a good feeling about the association and one another? What about free riders — people who take advantage of the benefits of the community without contributing any effort? What about people who have lots of money and are happy to spend it to use a disproportionate share of island resources, like water? What kind of life do we want on the island — larger and larger houses with private docks and big boats — or a low-key, smaller footprint environment? Are we a community at all really or just a group of property owners who want to serve their self-interest even if that's at the expense of others?

The association is supposed to operate as something like a representative democracy, with an elected Board of nine, with three-year terms, with an annual meeting of all members to approve the budget by majority vote. Is a formal majority vote the point, or should the Board seek consensus at Board meetings and with the association as a whole? These questions aren't theoretical about someone else or a government that we can't have much influence on. They're very real and practical. We can't blame anyone else if things don't work right. It's not about someone else. It's us. Bracing, exciting, challenging.

Eleven: The Pleasures of a Splitting Maul

"Give me six hours to chop down a tree and I will spend the first four sharpening the axe." — Abraham Lincoln

Last week, with our pickup temporarily on Crane and after cutting a number of fallen trees into 16" sections, I brought home four loads of firewood and moved them to the front yard, outside Yvonne's deer fence, ready for splitting. I already had two stacks I'd split during the summer and some leftovers from last year covered on top with tarps but open on the side so that the wood would dry out. The larger stack smelled of mink scat, and when retrieving wood to burn, I found the remains of what appeared to be mink dinners. They often crossed our yard, and last summer when I was working on stairs to our beach, a mink ran right by me up the stairs without much worrying that I might be a danger.

We don't expect to heat our house with wood but to make it cozy, raise the temperature above the 68-degree programmed thermostat setting from time to time without spending more money on our primary, baseboard, electric heating system. And since it was likely our electrical service would fail from time to time over the winter — after snow or wind or some other reason — it makes sense to have a backup heating source. But how much wood did we need? Best to prepare while we had a truck on the island to carry it.

Some types of wood burn faster than others. Douglas fir burns slowly and contains lots of heat; alder burns much more quickly and produces less heat. So how much we needed would depend on what kind we had as well as how much heat we needed to generate each day. Determining our exact firewood needs was too hard to figure out. However, I did know that in October, with temperatures in the 40s and 50s, we were using about 14 cubic feet of split wood each week. Assuming we wanted a fire in our wood stove mornings at least through May, and given some time away traveling, we'd need about 30 weeks' worth or 420 cubic feet. A cord is 8' long by 4' high by 4' deep

Eleven: The Pleasures of a Splitting Maul

or 128 cubic feet. We'd need 3 ½ cords. We had a bit less than two cords split and stacked, and it looked like at least a cord ready for splitting. It wouldn't hurt to have some more.

It took about two hours to split a week's wood and a month's kindling and to stack it on the porch. My guess is that I spent about 8 hours locating, cutting, and transporting a cord. Since a cord will last about 9 weeks, we'll use 476 cubic feet, I'll spend 68 hours splitting and stacking, and 30 hours finding, cutting, and fetching; that's about 100 hours per season. We'll save about $600 on our heating bill, which means I'm saving about $6/hour, or maybe $8/hour gross considering the withholding and taxes it would cost to net $6/hour. On Orcas, a cord costs about $200, so it would cost about the same to heat with wood as electricity. I do get exercise, and I enjoy the process. That's a plus. And we do have two sources of heat, and that's important living in the islands.

Eighteen months ago I brought a good-sized fir, in sections, from Chris Thomerson's house. It had died, it was down and cut up, and he wanted to get rid of it, so I carried it to Crane in a number of loads by pickup load, dock cart to boat, and unloading the boat, dock cart to our front yard. The lower sections of the tree were close to two feet across and weighed more than I could lift, but I did it anyway, and hauling the second to the last section out of our boat I did something to my back that took a week to recover from. But in saving the stump section I had a large, heavy splitting platform.

Last Christmas my Secret Santa (in the family, we have an arrangement so that we each give only one present — to whomever we're assigned by a friend of James' who's served in this capacity for the last five years) gave me a True-Temper fiberglass handled splitting maul to replace the wood model that was cracked and had become unsafe and nearly useless. An axe head expands to 1 ½ inches at the back; a splitting maul to 3 inches halfway back. A sharp axe can be used to chop horizontally across the trunk of a tree, creating a triangular cut across the grain, but it does poorly chopping vertically into a trunk section, with the grain, because it gets stuck easily. A splitting maul, on the other hand, does well coming down on the top of a section, and the further it penetrates the wood, the further it forces the wood apart, splitting up to at least an 8" section in one blow.

Eleven: The Pleasures of a Splitting Maul

011: Employing my new splitting maul. Where are my safety glasses?

Eleven: The Pleasures of a Splitting Maul

Cedar splits easily and starts well, so I use it to make kindling — 12" sticks mostly less than an inch on a side. Fir and alder split well too but not as easily. Other island trees, maple, madrona, and willow are much harder to split and so aren't desirable firewood.

Given section cuts that are reasonably perpendicular to the trunk, they are easy to set on a chopping block. Generally, I aim the first blow at the middle of the section. I may then split the results again — until I've got something 4" or less at its thickest point. But that first stroke doesn't always split the section. If the wood is too soft, like some of the wood I scavenged last week, the stroke buries the head but doesn't split the section. In that case, I bury the head further by hitting the back of it with a ten-pound sledgehammer until it splits. Sometimes it doesn't, and then I have to back the splitting maul out of the section by tapping the handle up with the sledgehammer until the maul head starts to exit the section. Sections that supported branches can also be difficult to split.

There is a pleasure in choosing a place to strike, sometimes based on characteristics of the specific section, then raising the maul and bringing it down hard on the wood — with the section splitting with a satisfying crack. When split, Douglas fir sometimes has a recognizable fragrance but cedar almost always does. Setting a splitting strategy on a log section and choosing where to strike, raising and then hitting the wood and the sound of splitting, the fragrance of the wood, and during today's splitting session the occasional sound of waves lapping on our beach about 100' feet away, the cry of seagulls, characteristic raven vocalization, the deep rumbling of a ferry passing through Wasp Passage, and the piercing but rich sound of a whistle from an Orcas steam-powered boat — this is my day.

Twelve: Yvonne Visits Seattle

"There is a crack in everything, that's how the light gets in." — Leonard Cohen

Signs on Circle Road indicated that Gary had finished installing a new septic tank and water line at Fisher's and had taken his power shovel off the island. Pink clouds adorned a light blue sky over a misty Crane Island airstrip bordered by firs, black in the pre-dawn light, save for a golden maple pushing through the barrier. Too dark to see its level from a distance, I walked up the hill to the water tank: 9 ½ feet. Down from yesterday or only a more accurate reading? I'll have to pay attention. At home, the sun rises right through Bell Island, half a mile east-southeast from the house, a prickly half-dome rising out of Wasp Passage and the site of frequent groundings on a well-marked reef and a non-fatal small helicopter crash with a couple from Shaw Island earlier this year. A welcome sun pours in, revealing toast crumbs on the kitchen counter.

Yesterday morning at 7:30, I took Yvonne across to Orcas so she could catch the 8:55 ferry to Anacortes and head to Seattle. She had her new Verizon pre-paid cell phone with her. It had arrived Thursday, left in the UPS/FedEx locked delivery cabinet on the north wall of the storage shed above the Crane Island community dock on Orcas, and she would stop at a Verizon store on the way to have her current cell phone number "migrated" to the new phone (with a new plan). That didn't work, and more attempts on Saturday came to naught. Told on the telephone by Verizon service that it could be done, live people in their store said it couldn't.

First, Yvonne visited her brother Ron, newly moved into his Capitol Hill studio apartment, one of Seattle's lively neighborhoods. They walked around Volunteer Park, its reservoir, old water tower, conservatory, and Asian Art Museum. In less than two weeks, Ron would start his acupuncture practice after years of schooling, exams, and preparation.

Twelve: Yvonne Visits Seattle

012: Sunrise over Bell Island

He was excited and nervous. Next, to daughter Jeni's who was just home from a long day working as a Surgical Tech in a Swedish Hospital operating room. Bonus daughter Corrina was crashed at Jeni's and would be until she left for three months in India to see a possible love interest, Arjun. In the interim, Corrina was applying to MFA/art administration programs around the country, heartened by her grandma Dotty's encouragement and offer to pay part of the cost. Her high-school friend Dave showed up later, another Pennsylvania emigrant making his way in a new city.

Benoit was hosting a pumpkin carving session at a studio art space he and his girlfriend Audrey, both French and both in the design business, rented parts of to a specialty bicycle store, and creative, non-traditional artists and craftspeople. Yvonne was very impressed with these young people — who were polite and patient with the 60-year-old grandma who enjoyed their company but really had no idea what their lives were about.

Saturday morning coffee in a nearby Tully's, waiting for Jeni and Corrina to get up and out. Rainy intermittently but off they went to Seattle's own Rally

Twelve: Yvonne Visits Seattle

to Restore Sanity. Several thousand attended, sympathetic to the Stewart/Colbert rally in Washington DC but unable to attend the big event. At Westlake Park, a large screen showed the DC scene, and loudspeakers around the venue broadcast the speeches. Local speakers overrode the intermittent musical performances in DC to address the local crowd.

Dave Ross, talk show host, encouraged the group to whisper rather than shout "Turn it down," and "Sanity, civility, discourse," adding "we should be able to debate each other without destroying each other" echoing the theme playing across the country.

Kelly and Tim had walked down from Capitol Hill and stood with Yvonne, Jeni, and Corrina in the crowd struggling to see the speakers. They had news but really weren't telling anyone yet — well maybe just a few people. Kelly was nine weeks pregnant. Married in early July at the Orcas Hotel, with John as the wedding officiant and Yvonne as ceremony traffic director, the next step happened before Tim could digest the previous, but Kelly is ready. To Perth over Christmas for a second ceremony there and eventually maybe to Zurich or Paris, with a baby, where Tim can be temporarily assigned by Google.

A little shopping on the way north, Yvonne reported that she returned more than she bought. That's good, I guess. Coming home with Marmoleum flooring for the guest bathroom where I'll install it and a new toilet in the coming months. Spaghetti, movie, hot tub, reading. Happy Yvonne is home again.

Thirteen: Ascending Turtle Knob

"I can see Russia from my house." — *Tina Fey*

Halloween and Sunday. What to do? With only three houses occupied on Crane this season, with an average age of 69, we didn't expect trick-or-treaters, so we didn't have to stay home, and if we did, we knew all we would do was work. I suggested a walk around Mountain Lake, in Moran State Park on Orcas, a four-mile reasonably flat track partway up 2400' Mt. Constitution, the highest point in the San Juans, and the same relative height as Green Mountain rising over Boulder, our last home base. Yvonne suggested Turtle Knob, a mile north of Deer Harbor so we'd spend less time driving — 7 minutes versus 35. So off we went.

Turtle Knob or Turtle Head is a mostly bare dome that joins Turtleback Mountain on the west side of Orcas Island. Viewed from the southwest, say from San Juan Island, the formation looks a lot like a turtle, with its head to the left. Five years ago the Orcas community bought Turtleback Mountain and made it a preserve. The 1578 acres had been owned by the Medina Foundation, and they wanted to turn the asset into cash to fund their good works. The Orcas community feared the mountain would be turned into a subdivision, cut by roads, speckled with mansions, and a Christmas tree at night. It's said that Norton Clapp, Medina Foundation benefactor, had bought up Turtleback in the first place so he wouldn't have to look at lights on it from his house in Deer Harbor.

The Trust for Public Land and the San Juan County Land Bank provided the $17 million needed to buy the mountain. A late summer party we attended in a sheep pasture on Orcas Road drew half the island population and raised another $1 million to go towards maintenance. It had been a beautiful day with Turtleback looming just to the west. We wrote a check we couldn't afford but couldn't resist.

Thirteen: Ascending Turtle Knob

Turtle Knob had been a nature preserve for some years before Turtleback became one, but unlike the adjoining body, there was no public road access to the trailhead. Practically speaking the only way in was to cross Jack Helsell's property. I had visited him five years before and bought some firewood and he said he had no objection to our crossing his property to get to the Knob trail provided we stayed on his road going in and then on the trail going up the knob. His sister had owned the Knob.

013.1: Hellsel's ranch, where we started our hike.

Farther up the track steepened, a moss-covered rock outcropping let in light. Higher still the track got steeper and the cedars gave way to the ubiquitous Douglas firs. Then the old logging road dead-ended to a narrow trail that broke through the trees into the meadow near the top of the knob. Not so steep now, the trail led across the knob, gaining altitude and then entering the rocky area just below the summit.

Thirteen: Ascending Turtle Knob

013.2: Deer Harbor hamlet center, Crane behind and right. San Juan Island on the horizon.

We parked in an open area below Hellsel's sawmill and walked up the road along the west side of his horse pasture, two sod-roof farmhouses visible across the way. Turtle Knob was visible above the trees straight ahead. On the north side of the pasture, we stopped to admire the six horses not far from the fence. We walked through a patch of woods and then a meadow with a seasonal pond and on through more trees to the Turtle Knob trailhead, an old logging road. The forest here was thick with big Western Red Cedars and almost no firs. Here and there a four or five-foot diameter rotting cedar stump dwarfed the newer two and three-foot trees. Discarded brown sprays littered the black soil and gray gravel trail. The trees caught all the direct sunlight so the forest floor was clear, though deep in cedar sprays with an occasional small fern struggling for purchase.

The Turtle Knob summit, at 750', has clear views to the southwest, south, and southeast. The view to the north and east is blocked by trees and Turtleback Mountain. Waldron Island, a mile away at this point, and home to a few

Thirteen: Ascending Turtle Knob

dozen reclusive souls who value being off the grid peeked through the firs to the west. The edge of the incoming tide was clearly visible on President Channel, almost as deep, below the cliff to the west, as Turtle Knob is high. Stuart Island, with its wonderful trail from Reid Harbor to the Turn Point Lighthouse, lay to the west, flanked on the left by Speiden Island, for a while a big game preserve. Vancouver Island and Sidney lay twenty miles to the west.

013.3: Memorial plaque at the summit

    The Deer Harbor Marina was visible to the south and San Juan Channel behind it silver in the afternoon light. We could see the western end of Crane Island, most of it hidden by Orcas, and Shaw Island behind Crane. Cattle Pass between San Juan Island on the west and Lopez Island on the east stood between San Juan Channel and the Strait of Juan de Fuca, passage to the Pacific and the rest of the world.

    A carved marble plaque, set into the summit, and cracked into four pieces, commemorates a World War I veteran, whose name is now indecipherable. An eight-foot circle of stones with a peace symbol inside lays below the plaque, the north side of the circle now almost invisible. Vole holes dot the summit and their tracks crisscross it. Moss and grass coexist and cover the soil among the rocks. Flecks of red, leaves of something like a dandelion, stick up tentatively here and there. A few small yellow daisy-shaped flowers hang on. The world on view — right below us, then down the mountain to Deer Harbor and our community on Crane. Then San Juan Island and another country, Canada, on the horizon, and a clear shot to Japan, China, and Russia on the other side of the Pacific Rim.

Fourteen: Otter Tracks

"Instructions for living a life: Pay attention. Be astonished. Tell about it." — Mary Oliver

Something caught my eye as I struggled with a particularly vexing problem in the ebook editing software I'd been wrestling with all afternoon. I looked up, out of my office window at the back deck and stairs to the lower studio deck. An otter, about 15 feet away — a smooth, nondescript brownish-gray coat, large eyes, two feet long with another foot or so of tail — a river otter — hop/walking left to right, pausing before taking the three-step flight to the lower deck.

Where was my camera? Where was Yvonne? "Yvonne, Yvonne, an otter on the back porch." No response — but the otter turned and looked my direction, stared, and made a decision. Deliberately but not hastily it headed down the stairs and made a U-turn under the deck and disappeared. By then Yvonne was back in the picture. "What, what otter?" I explained and we walked out onto the deck from the dining room door. Looking right, otter tracks led the length of the deck to the stairs and down. Coming back, Yvonne went down the south stairs and looked under the deck. No sign. We then traced the footprints around to the front of the house. The otter had come up the short stairs at the north end of the front deck, crossed right in front of the big living room windows, and gone around to the south, side deck to the west stairs to the lower deck where I'd seen him. Not very shy.

Yvonne had been in the bathroom at the moment the otter walked by a few feet from where she had been knitting that afternoon. She had turned her wicker chair toward the window for better light, away from the center of the room and other seating. She would have been looking right at the deck where the otter passed. Two circular knitting needles, yarn, an open knitting magazine, photocopied instructions, a coil-bound knitter's diary/journal, a plastic bag of circular knitting needles, pairs joined with cables, her pack to hold it all and a Costco "Think Green" sack – all laid out on the floor. Her iPad was tucked into the chair, against the armrest where she stored it after consulting a YouTube knitting video. I never imagined! And most importantly, what she had come into my office to show me earlier in the afternoon — a pair of knitted socks, muted fall colors, stripes — because the yarn now comes that way — an achievement!

014: Otters: sometimes too cute

"Who are they for?" "I don't know." "They're very nice. How about for me? They'd keep my feet warm." "Well, the problem is you wear your heavy socks around all the time and you wear out the heels." "Hmm."

We see otters often, though not every day and not every week. Last summer Yvonne watched five otters glide around the point that sticks out from Margaret's property next door, across our cove toward the Ochs' beach

Fourteen: Otter Tracks

and Pole Pass. They were in a playful, social mood, like teenagers using their surroundings as a stage for their ongoing psychodrama.

Every so often we'd see an otter or two hopping along the path that comes from Margaret's or down our shared driveway from Eagle Lane above, crossing our lot, heading for the Ochs meadow and beach or maybe a bit farther to the community dock and beach, where they could get into the water and head along the north side of Crane without having to struggle through Pole Pass against the tide.

Three summers ago a baby otter had come up on the deck from the north just as this one had today (maybe it was the same one), and Yvonne had gone out to look. It was making a mewling noise (lost? Motherless?), didn't back away and was clearly looking for something — love? Food? Yvonne finally used a broom to gently encourage it off the deck and down the stairs to the world to which it belonged.

We have a Costco 10' x 20' storage tent under the trees at the back of our property, behind our sailboat on its trailer, parked for the winter. Two years ago, after we moved it more out of the way than it had been, minks got in and left their scat. Before I could do anything about it, otters asserted their rights and buried the mink scat with their own. That stunk up the tent, so son James (home for the summer after graduating from college and before going south to UCLA for graduate school) and I put a wire fence with a gate around the tent, and we haven't had problems since.

But we've been lucky, I guess. Howard Block, on Crane, had otters living in his crawl space, and it was the devil to get them out. They tear the insulation down from under the floors to make cozy beds and have a habit of defecating where they dine. Mussel, oyster, and crab shells littered the crawl space, co-mingled with scat. Others on Crane have had the same problem and Orcas as well.

Otters like to get into closed spaces in boats to have their fun as well, and Howard's canvas-covered runabout was "ottered" several times, each occasion requiring extensive cleanup. They especially like to use coiled rope as a toilet, so sometimes coming back to our boat, we'd find a mooring rope buried in scat.

A few years back while working on our pocket trawler, *Gumption*, a Camano Troll, I noticed an otter sunning himself on the dock about twenty feet away. I crept out of the boat quietly and moved slowly toward the supine otter. Whenever he would put his head up and look, I'd freeze, not moving a muscle until he put his head down again to nap. After 15 minutes of inching forward in intervals and by inches, he finally realized something was going on, stared at me for a full minute working out what he was looking at (very short-sighted?), stood up, hobbled to the edge of the dock, and slid into the water. I went back to work.

    Christmas 2007 was snowy. We'd had about 18 inches, and I went out for a walk, with my camera, to take pictures around the island I could post on the Web for absent homeowners — who likely hadn't ever seen their house in the snow. Walking up our driveway, I saw a semicircular track through the snow, coming from Eagle Lane above. I followed the track all the way to Rupert Harvey's front deck. That's where it started. Was Rupert at his house? (I hadn't seen him) Had he dragged a propane bottle through the snow on its side, creating the concave track? But where were his footsteps? I continued around the island making a circle and when I crossed Och's meadow from the north, I could see that the concave track turned from our trail down to Och's beach. Aha! It was an otter slide. The next day James, home for Christmas, saw otters come down the slide but instead of crossing our lot they turned and slid down into our cove and into the water for some food and fun. They play. We work.

Fifteen: Island Democracy — Firing up the citizenry

> *"Never doubt that a small group of thoughtful, committed citizens can change the world; indeed, it's the only thing that ever has."* — Margaret Mead.

Indeed!

After enough petition signatures were gathered this fall from an inflamed public, one of the burning questions on the San Juan County November 2, 2010 ballot was whether County Council Ordinance 28-2008, "Banning All Fireworks without a Permit," should be overturned.

At its June 2, 2008 meeting, the Council had taken testimony from the Prosecuting Attorney who explained what the change would mean legally, the San Juan Island Fire Chief, who favored the ban, and another speaker who said it would benefit domestic animals and wildlife. However, it was opposed by one citizen who said the Council should delay and have an evening meeting so it could take testimony from families, another who said fireworks would be fine if their use was confined to New Year's Eve, and another who said that fireworks were an important tradition and symbol of America. The Council closed testimony, discussed the measure, and passed it unanimously. The fuse was lit.

In October, the Orcas newspaper, *Islands Sounder*, featured letters from concerned citizens opposed to the fireworks ban, rallying public opinion against it, and encouraging a no vote on Referendum 2008-2 to reject the Council's ordinance. "Fireworks ban would be an injustice," "Proposed fireworks ban goes too far," "Vote no on fireworks ban" (that is, overthrow it), and "Please reject the ban on safe and sane fireworks."

Voters approved the ban, agreeing with the Council, 3580 to 3051. My guess is that the issue will smolder like an underground peat fire until the next election when its flames will again become visible.

Fifteen: Island Democracy — Firing up the citizenry

015.1: Crane Island Fire Department and volunteers

The Crane Island Association has banned fireworks within its boundaries for many years: the worry is the possibility of starting a wildfire. The Pacific Northwest is considered a soggy place by everyone who doesn't live here. It is often wet, mid-October through May, but the summer can be very dry. On Crane, we may have virtually no rain from mid-June through mid-September. Since 95% of the island is forested and the forest floor is covered deep in needles, shed branches, and fallen trees laid out under the green canopy, the right spark could burn the island end to end no matter what our efforts.

We have a fire engine, a pumper with a 250-gallon tank capacity, and 50 standpipes around the island the pumper could connect to. We have gasoline-powered floating pumps that could supply seawater. We have a foam system attached to the front of our fire and rescue vehicle. We cooperate with the Orcas Island Fire Department on exercises and could count on their help should

Fifteen: Island Democracy — Firing up the citizenry

the need arise provided they could get over to our island. Many of us have been trained on the fire truck and rescue vehicle. Our friends on Orcas watch for inappropriate smoke appearing on Crane and report it to the County 911 system or call us directly. Many of us have first responder 911 pagers that would alert us to fire signs. All of this would help us respond to a fire on Crane, but in the summer and with wind, we might end up helpless.

015.2: On Orcas, not far from Crane, San Juan County burns a house the owner wanted cleared. It made us nervous.

In September, when Yvonne and I visited old friends in Boulder, we drove up Sunshine Canyon to observe the effects of the recent Four Mile Canyon Fire, started by blowing sparks from a campfire a resident thought he had thoroughly extinguished. An area where we had picnicked, hiked, and run was now black and brown. Chimneys left standing here and there. A sad sight.

On Crane, in the summer, fire is the devil. In the winter, in the rainy season, we often have burn piles, registered with the county and carefully watched, with a water supply near at hand.

But fireworks have a tendency to go in unintended directions, even when professionally managed, as we saw in Deer Harbor, seven years ago when a rocket from the fireworks show planted safely on a barge hundreds of yards from the shore went awry and started a fire on the palisade that marks the west side of the harbor.

Sixteen: Our Parents, Ourselves, Our Children — Aging and Island Living

"Life changes fast. Life changes in the instant. You sit down to dinner and life as you know it ends." - John Didion in *"The Year of Magical Thinking"*

Crossing to Orcas, sunrise imminent, scattered peach strokes on a blue canvas in the east, pink-topped drop biscuits above and to the west, a raven paddling north to check the dumpsters at the Orcas transfer station.

At Howard's, mugs of strong tea warming our hands, our host brings us up to date on Bob Harris, now more than a year absent from our gatherings but in our minds. Howard, David, Brian, and me. Chris is in Tucson with Lynn tending to her failing parents. Her father, at times confused but unwilling to give up control to his children, wants his wife, Lynn's mother, suffering from Alzheimer's, home, but it isn't possible. It wouldn't be good for either one. Lynn's four siblings in Tucson, paired into two competing teams who won't speak to one another, have insisted that Lynn leave Orcas, fly to Tucson, and straighten everything out.

Bob has been to Island Hospital in Anacortes again, more than an hour's ferry trip away since there is no hospital care in the San Juan Islands. Blood in his urine, a procedure, now consigned permanently to a catheter, and back at the convalescent center in Friday Harbor, another ferry trip away but in the other direction. The previous procedure restored his mind to a large extent by improving the flow of spinal fluid, and daily therapy sessions have him moving about with a sophisticated walker. But he's bored, Howard reports. He wants to go home in the worst way. But Megan, Bob's wife, tells him he needs to stay and recuperate. In her mid-80s, she can't care for a husband that can't walk. Two years ago, they had moved from their ridge-top home to Eastsound and a new, small house, a five-minute walk to the Medical Center and a 20-

Sixteen: Our Parents, Ourselves, Our Children — Aging and Island Living

minute walk to the library, market, post office, and other amenities of Orcas's main village.

016: Cedar takes root

Howard floats the idea to the group of setting up Bob to do an annotated version of Kipling's *Kim*, like what Chris and Howard are working on with

Sixteen: Our Parents, Ourselves, Our Children — Aging and Island Living

Slocum's sailing story. Bob has read *Kim* "ten times" and has his notebook computer with him. Good idea. I ask Howard to check further with Bob and I volunteer to provide Bob with the software, a *Kim* database, and training on how to use the annotation software. No telling what will happen, but it could benefit everyone involved.

David brings us up to date on an uncompleted topic from last Wednesday's session: if someone dies on Orcas on a weekend will anyone pick them up? The topic arose because one of our Unitarian friends had died a few months back on a Friday night, and the report we heard was that his widow had to wait until Monday to have him taken away. I had heard another such report about a Deer Harbor death two years before. Not so, Chris said. His widow wanted him home for three days so she could do rituals to help his soul leave his body. After doing some research, David reports that either funeral homes in Anacortes will pick up on weekends or a service they use will. He wasn't sure which. We're all happy to get the news.

Chris and Lynn are dealing with parents who can't or won't concede to reality. Megan is dealing with a husband, our friend, who won't concede to reality. Another Deer Harbor couple comes up. He in his late 80s; she younger. They skied and boated until recently, and it's a matter of principle to them not to acknowledge that they've become old and increasingly infirm. When he drives to the Post Office to pick up their mail, everyone nearby keeps an eye on the car until he's parked and then on him as he shuffles up the stairs to the door.

What about us, I ask? Will we know when it's time to make a change, to allow others to help us, even decide for us? Where will we live? Even though Lou Falb, an old man, who is losing his strength, continues to live on Crane, that wouldn't make sense for or appeal to Yvonne and me. We think a condo in Seattle or Portland might make sense. Brian and Howard have no plans to ever leave Orcas. Tom Temple, who occupies the third full-time residence on Crane, and has for the last 20 years, has studied the matter and reports that every Cranian over 75 has fallen in the water at least once.

David says he and Maxine built their house with the thought of being able to accommodate live-in help, and Orcas isn't a bad place to find some. Earned income in the San Juan Islands is among the lowest in the state; unearned income among the highest. Seventy percent of the children in the Orcas school qualify for aid. There isn't enough work, and people will work for less

Sixteen: Our Parents, Ourselves, Our Children — Aging and Island Living

to get it. Yvonne told me that 80 families showed up at the Orcas Island Food Bank, where she is Board Secretary, a new record. With twice-weekly meals and food handouts, the Food Bank serves about 5% of the Orcas population.

What about our kids? How will they cope with us as we become infirm? Will we make it easier or harder for them? Will they have to clean out our houses and cart off all our junk? Will they know or care about what we value and think they should too? Is it fair to live in an out-of-the-way place and expect remote children to be highly inconvenienced to help us? Not much response to that question, except David, who has been thinking about it. It's wonderful to live on an island, and our children love to visit us, but they don't live here, and at some point, we'll have to acknowledge that.

Seventeen: Mud Bay Barge

"To stand at the edge of the sea, to sense the ebb and flow of the tides, to feel the breath of a mist moving over a great salt marsh, to watch the flight of shorebirds that have swept up and down the surf lines of the continents for untold thousands of years, to see the running of the old eels and the young shad to the sea, is to have knowledge of things that are as nearly eternal as any earthly life can be." — Rachel Carson in "Under the Sea-Wind"

Light showed about 7:00, just a hint on the eastern horizon. The phone rang at 8:15 a.m. It was Wilma telling me that she and Gary would be bringing their barge to the concrete ramp at the end of Reef Lane, at the foot of the airstrip, rather than their preferred location at the beach at the Crane community dock, close to our house. Jansen had a big front loader he wanted back on Orcas and it was too heavy to load from the beach. She thought they'd arrive about 9:45. It wouldn't be high tide, but there would be enough water under the barge at the ramp — even with a heavy load.

Our pickup truck had been on Crane since September when we brought it over on the barge to use to haul out our daysailer and collect firewood from around the island. I also brought over a trailer Margaret, our next-door neighbor, had bought off Craigslist and towed to the Crane lot on Orcas, for transfer to Crane. Once on Crane, I towed her old trailer to Harvey's, her other neighbor, who was happy to get a trailer, on Crane, for free, even if it was old and rusty. I put Margaret's new trailer in her driveway. She'd be leaving her boat in the water until at least January when she'd be back to the island for a while. I then backed our trailer into the water at the community beach and Margaret helped me float our sailboat aboard, pull it out of the water, lower the mast and store it on top of the boat.

Seventeen: Mud Bay Barge

017: Gary at the helm bringing the front loader to the concrete landing ramp below the airstrip.

Though I'd had incredible problems backing up with a trailer in the past I finally got the hang of it this time and threaded the trees and made the sharp turn needed to put the boat out of the way under the willows.

Yvonne had been coveting the gravel on the Browne's beach at the other end of the island, very consistent quarter-inch gray/black stones with white broken shells the same size. Caroline had told her to pick some up any time. She had done that more than a year ago, taking the dock cart and two five-gallon buckets, and accompanied by her four-legged companion had, after much effort, dragged the cart back to our yard. This time we would use the truck before we took it off the island. So Friday we put eight buckets of various sizes, two shovels, and the dock cart (to carry the loaded buckets from beach to truck) into the bed of the truck and stopped to check the tank level (10 feet

Seventeen: Mud Bay Barge

— steady). We parked in the Browne's yard, tail-in, unloaded and took everything down to their beach. A cool day but surprisingly warm on the sunny beach, only about six feet deep at near-high tide. A beautiful day, small waves lapping, lapping. My guess is that we loaded about a quarter ton of gravel and got it home with modest effort and a few grunts. The buckets now stand on six inches of wood chips, a soft carpet protected by the translucent roof of the 12' x 12' rain shelter where in the summer we raise a tent for overflow guests and in winter store a wheeled wood chipper, picnic table and benches, and wrought iron table and chairs. What is the gravel for, I asked Yvonne. I'm not sure yet, she replied, but I'll put it to good use.

The converted World War II landing craft became visible as it came around Caldwell Point, a half mile to the east, out of West Sound. It would come through Pole Pass in about five minutes and head for the ramp, halfway down the north side of Crane, giving reefs and rocks a wide berth. Ilze Jones walked off and her helper drove the tractor they would use to help the regrading required for their renovation project. Then the front loader backed on and I drove up the landing ramp and then down into the barge, sitting low in the water at the stern because of the load aboard.

It was obvious to me there wouldn't be enough room but Wilma instructed me that I need only get the rear wheels on the barge and off the metal ramp. The rear end of the truck wouldn't matter. Really? I did and Wilma raised the ramp that also serves as the door that keeps the water out of the barge. She couldn't raise it all the way up because the rear bumper and bed of my truck were in the way. Then off we went. It didn't matter that the ramp wasn't pulled all the way up because the bow rode high and the stern low today and with little wind the water on our way was calm.

Gary is our licensed Water System Manager and he and Wilma provide all kinds of services to grateful Crane homeowners. We first met them when they brought our U-Haul truck over from Orcas when we moved to Crane almost four years ago, when they lived on Sucia Island, a mile off Orcas' North Beach, with their two daughters and where Gary served as water manager for the state park on the Island. Wilma had home-schooled the girls during the eleven years they'd lived on Sucia — most of the time as the only residents but with Edie in high school and Ruby soon to be, it came time to move to Orcas. Though not far away, in a wind and with an opposing tide, the reefs and shallow water that lie between Sucia and Orcas raise impressive waves, some days making passage in a small boat a white-knuckled challenge to Davy Jones. Edie had graduated from Orcas High in 2009 and was taking some time before starting college to travel in China and then teach English, living in Saigon.

Gary took the *Mud Puppy* through Pole Pass, with the community dock and beach to starboard and the red, hazard light to port, the light that years ago, Cal McLoughlin's grandfather tended as a kerosene lantern. Past the Crane dock on Orcas, around the corner to West Sound, heading for the ramp at White Beach, close to the West Sound Marina. Wilma came down from the bridge to thank me for sending them the DVD I'd made to commemorate the the 50th year of the creation of the Crane Island community. Then we talked about writing about what we know; island life, and the possibility of each making a record of our days for unknown people of the future. About an hour from ramp to ramp. The F-150 was happy to be back in a place where it could travel farther, if only back and forth the 10 miles to Eastsound rather than the 1.5 mile circle on Crane. Sure was good to have it on the little island for a while though.

Eighteen: Let's See What Comes Up

"I went to the woods because I wished to live deliberately, to front only the essential facts of life, and see if I could not learn what it had to teach, and not, when I came to die, discover that I had not lived."
— *Henry David Thoreau in "Walden"*

Mist, everything wet, droplets hanging in the air and on all surfaces. Still water, still air, quiet, soft — a muted world. Indistinct boundaries, like strokes in a watercolor that seep into one another. Not — many things, each separate from the others, but one — thing, a unity, now apparent, now visible; the universe sends a metaphor about the way it is rather than the illusion our minds project on it. A feeling of being gently held, safe, wrapped in a blanket. No rush, no problems, no time, just — now. A not uncommon Crane day, more common in the autumn but possible anytime. One of the gifts of being here day on day.

Ralph Waldo Emerson, the first American philosopher, an influence, if unseen, on everything later, everything today.

"All I know is reception; I am and I have, but do not get, and when I fancied I had gotten anything, I found I did not." Acceptance rather than acquisition of knowledge (Stanley Cavell). Rather than grasping things by concept, we find "this evanescence and lubricity of all objects, which lets them slip through our fingers when we clutch the hardest."

Reception as a form of thankfulness. "I compared notes with one of my friends who expects everything from the universe and is disappointed when anything is less than the best, and I found I begin at the other extreme, expecting nothing, and am always full of thanks for moderate goods … If we will take the good we find, asking no questions, we shall have heaping measures." (from NYR, October 28, 2010; Robert Pogue Harrison on the Library of America's two-volume edition of Emerson's Journals).

Eighteen: Let's See What Comes Up

018: Late November afternoon

"Emerson, especially after the death of Waldo, his five-year-old son, found in the sequence of days the place where life, in its intrinsic generosity, offers itself to our reception. Everything is given in and by the day ... Our perceptions, thoughts, moods, and convictions unfold with the days, which in turn unfold in the hours, so 'let us husband them.'" (Harrison on Emerson.)

"To fill the hour — that is happiness; to fill the hour and leave no crevice for repentance or an approval."

"Where do we find ourselves?" "In a series of which we do not know the extremes and believe that it has none." (Emerson). "Because the series has no endpoint, we must find ourselves in each of its successive moments...Each day is an end in itself." (Harrison.)

"To finish the moment, — that is happiness; to find the journey's end in every step of the road, to live the greatest number of good hours, is wisdom." (Emerson.)

"His days and hours gave Emerson the vast array of perceptions, experiences, triumphs, and losses that fill his journals" and his "thoughts, which dominate most of their entries. The world of thought is not the world of lived experience" and Emerson became "fully aware of that discrepancy." (Harrison.)

"I know that the world I converse with in the city and in the farms is not the world I think. I observe that difference and shall observe it. One day I shall know the value and law of this discrepancy. But I have not found that much was gained by manipular attempts to realize the world of thought." (Emerson.)

"To know that the two worlds are different is enough on which to base a philosophy. And to 'observe' that difference is enough on which to base an ethic — not an ethic of renunciation but of the 'husbanding of hours.'" (Harrison.)

Emerson trusted that "the universe is friendly to our innermost selves...Knowledge follows upon such trust; it does not provide a basis for it. If we are patient enough … that which we always know to be true, but for which experience does not necessarily provide empirical evidence, will gradually find its realization in the world we converse with in the city and on the farm." (Harrison.)

I held a skein of turquoise yarn while Yvonne wound it into a ball.

A 90-minute productive telephone call with Jens Kruse about *The Metamorphosis* project after waking up at 3:30, doing programming and documentation, and sending it to him so that he would have it before our meeting. An extensive agenda the day before to make the call focused and successful.

Splitting and stacking wood — 90 minutes. Had used about 75% of the wood split and stacked from a week before, so didn't burn as much as projected. Quality picking up after getting through most of the marginal wood. How many more sessions with the pile I picked up with the truck? Five weeks?

Nineteen: A Pause

"The mass of men lead lives of quiet desperation. What is called resignation is confirmed desperation. From the desperate city you go into the desperate country, and have to console yourself with the bravery of minks and muskrats. A stereotyped but unconscious despair is concealed even under what are called the games and amusements of mankind." — Henry David Thoreau in "Walden"

Ouch!

Friday morning I woke up a little after 3:00 a.m., and after thinking a bit about the day to come and taking 40 deep breaths in 30 minutes, I was at work at my desk before 4:00. I'd be visiting with Jens Kruse, in Wellesley at 8:00 on his progress annotating Kafka's *The Metamorphosis* and understanding and using the software I'd provided him in September when he and Susan returned to Massachusetts after the summer on Orcas. On Thursday, I had sent him an agenda of sorts, trying to collect and summarize the email correspondence we'd had over the ten days before as he began to work on Kafka in earnest after making some time in his schedule as a professor of German, with a full teaching load, at Hillary Clinton's alma mater. Though he could do annotations, he wanted to begin creating pages that supplemented the novella rather than just annotating it, such as an introduction, biography, bibliography, and so on. I had added two routines to the Annotator software but hadn't been able to fix two bugs I'd found Thursday afternoon, thus the need for a work session before our telephone meeting so that he'd have and could try out the software with me on the other end of the phone during the second part of our meeting, after going through the agenda items.

A good meeting. I promised to provide him with the ability to see complete book drafts, text, annotations, supplementary sections, illustrations, whatever, including a way to sequence the sections of the book to his liking. Our continuing goal — a complete draft not long after the beginning of the year. An end-of-week feeling now, relief after working hard on the electronic publishing project.

Then some catching up on email — including a note from Elise, the Crane Island Association bookkeeper at our accountant's in Friday Harbor. She pointed out that I had missed one member who hadn't paid and hadn't even responded to the late August billing and September 30th due date. And two members with calculation errors beyond the ones I had pointed out and already gotten supplementary checks. They needed to pay more. I reported back to her the arrangements with one member who had lost their job and asked to make installment payments until they could pay the full balance.

After a week's draw on the firewood I had stacked on the front porch the Friday before, we'd only used about three-fourths of what I had split, so usage so far is a bit slower than expected. I split and stacked another two carts full, 14 cubic feet, and will review usage next Friday. We have three sources of firewood now: two stacks of split wood and one pile of trunk sections, most cut to 16 inches or so. The plan is to split and use the pile week by week before touching the stacked wood. How long will the pile last, I wonder, before having to draw down the stacks. Maybe five weeks, it looks like, until the winter solstice, when the daylight will begin to return. Only 90 minutes this session rather than the two hours I spent the previous Friday. Less wood used, less time to prepare it. A positive trend line — but we'll see.

As I caught up on my reading, in my wicker chair by the fire, Yvonne knit a stylish neck scarf, in her wicker chair, asking me to help her with her yarn when she finished and wanted to start a new project. She needed me to hold the skein, an 18-inch loop of turquoise yarn, while she rolled it into a ball, appropriate for knitting. To work directly from the skein would invite disaster, with the yarn likely tangling and requiring hours, maybe, to straighten out. I held out my arms and held the yarn the best I could while she drew from the skein and wrapped a ball. How many times have I seen this picture?

That was Friday: work, relief, catching up, satisfying outdoor exercise with a useful purpose, relaxing by the wood stove, with Yvonne nearby engrossed in a satisfying project, a scarf for a friend.

Nineteen: A Pause

019: Mysterious carved figure growing out of a stump

Then came Saturday. I was determined not to work, to treat the next two days as the weekend and time off. So I read and wrote, bundled old magazines for recycling, and cleaned up my office, especially around the communication technology area in my office where I was expecting to be able to replace one DSL modem and service with another. Yvonne wanted to use IKEA's kitchen planning software in anticipation of a Monday trip to Seattle. Since it wouldn't work on our Macs, I opened my Windows notebook computer I was determined not to use because it had become so frustratingly slow. But Windows was what Yvonne needed, and she was able to create a tentative kitchen plan and print it. Then I spent some time clearing out the Windows notebook, removing unneeded software and files, and limiting the programs that ran at start-up and in the background. In parallel with that process, I downloaded illustrations for Slocum's *Sailing Alone Around the World*, the classic Chris and

Nineteen: A Pause

Howard were doing annotations for. That complete, I searched the Web for more Slocum pictures and then Kafka pictures.

My plan was to take time off and this was the way I was doing it. Lots of little housekeeping tasks but not relaxing and also not progressing with the bigger, more interesting projects. Sitting around; fiddling around. All the momentum I'd built up over the last two weeks drained away, a balloon with a slow leak. Saturday was becoming a day without purpose, a "what's the point?" day. Gray, sad, low.

I'm not good at hanging out. Work with a purpose is a pleasure. Time off is fine when we're traveling, visiting, entertaining, socializing. But otherwise, I get a bit lost without work. Yvonne and I have talked about being able to just be. I'm not quite sure what that means, but maybe I don't do it very well. I love to look at the beautiful view outside our windows and as I walk the island or when driving on Orcas. The northwest light, the skies, if cloudy always complex, layered, and subtly hued, the movement and patterns of the water, the calls of the ravens, and on and on. Sometimes the beauty stops me in my tracks and I'm amazed. But I take only a sip, a glance. I don't really want to stay in that timeless place; I want to keep moving, want to have the illusion perhaps that I'm going someplace for a reason.

Twenty: Dinner Guests

"The cure for anything is salt water: sweat, tears, or the sea." — Isak Dinesen (Karen Blixen)

Ken and Kate would be coming to dinner, and that meant taking them back to Orcas after dark. Our SeaSport has a spotlight with a joystick, and that helps — except in rain, snow, or fog. But when the navigation lights are turned on, mandatory after sunset, the glow from the lighted dash instruments (red) and compass (white) is reflected in the windshield, interfering with a clear view of the water. I kept a towel handy to lay across the dash and compass, but the towel would slide down onto the steering wheel. Tonight and all winter, we'd often be making commuting trips in the dark, morning or evening, so I wanted a simple but more satisfactory way to prevent night instrument glare.

Yvonne had a piece of canvas available, left over from making a sling we used to raise and lower our dog Samantha onto our Nauticat sailboat to a dingy on the water when anchored and needing to take the dog to land for a walk. I folded the canvas around a 1/4" by 1" slat I found in a scraps box in my shed/shop and laid it above the lip formed by the raised edge of the dash. Pretty good. Then I put a fuel filter box over the compass, above the dash. That would work. And, in fact, returning our guests to Orcas late in the evening, my vision was much improved. I could lift the canvas whenever I wanted to view the instruments, and I could lift off, roll up, and stow the canvas dash cover when not needed.

Yvonne baked a filet of Copper River salmon on a bed of roasted fennel, garlic, onions, and tomatoes, serving it with jasmine rice, a Greek salad, and sourdough bread, and homemade apple pie for dessert. Delicious!

Twenty: Dinner Guests

020: Dining room table relaxing in the sun

Kate was our realtor when we bought our Deer Harbor house in 1997 and helped us sell it in 2006. Ken had provided design and carpentry services as we improved the house to make it more comfortable for year-round occupancy when it became clear we wanted to live on Orcas full-time and leave Boulder, heat, cold, and dryness behind. Thoughtful, deliberate, curious, engaged people, we enjoyed being with them to hear about what they saw in the world and what they were up to in response. Both love horses, and they have four, three wild horses they bought from the BLM and brought from Oregon over several years. Kate, a rider since childhood, had progressively become more insightful about horses and their psychology and now taught her special version of training, maybe "horse whispering." She spent a year with their newest mustang, getting to know him and he her, before she ever attempted to saddle and ride him. They would go on walks together on the trails in the

Twenty: Dinner Guests

neighborhood, the mustang walking with her but independently, without a lead. He had no interest in running away. At the time, Kate had told me a bit about horse psychology, including how social and intelligent they are. They want to please, and her training was based on that insight.

Ken was now raising rabbits, a special breed that could cope with cool, wet weather, and would grow to twice the size of standard domestic rabbits. The rabbits were for eating and sale. He also bought a box of day-old chickens, shipped overnight from Minnesota. The flock, now mature, had the run of the property, and the horses enjoyed chasing them. The breed was tough and savvy and bunched together when an eagle or hawk appeared overhead. They would return to their coop several times during the day and then go back out, finally roosting after dark inside, protected from raccoons and mink. They were real chickens, not the sad substitutes raised by chicken manufacturers and sold in stores at prices Ken couldn't compete with. Ken estimated it cost $25 for him to raise a chicken. Ken and Kate described the excellence of the eggs laid by the flock. The eggs were good eating, the chickens so far less so, since the meat was tougher than what they were used to.

Their main breakthrough was coming to understand how to age venison. The San Juan Islands are overrun (some say) with deer. They ruin gardens and are a major cause of automobile accidents. Ken, raised on an Idaho ranch, learned hunting and game dressing at an early age, and in more than 20 years on Orcas, they'd often had venison. But Kate, at least, wasn't enthusiastic about the toughness of the meat. It required long, slow cooking but even then was a real chew. Wanting to be more serious about venison and acquiring a discarded refrigerator from a neighbor, Ken went about experimenting with aging the venison, hanging the four quarters at about 42 degrees, cutting small sections each day to cook and taste. At two weeks, the meat began to change significantly, becoming more tender by the day. Now at 24 days, they said the meat couldn't be distinguished from high-quality steak, in color, texture, and taste. A discovery that the best chefs already know. They'll cut the quarters into meal-sized portions and then freeze them, looking forward to venison on the menu whenever they want it for the next six months or so.

Twenty-one: Meatballs and Mashed Potatoes

"Even the longest journey begins with a ferry ride." — Anonymous

We left the house at 7:30 and because daylight savings yielded to Standard Time early Sunday morning, the sun was up, though not visible through a cloudy sky. We were headed for the 8:55 Orcas-Anacortes ferry. Yvonne piloted the SeaSport to the Crane community dock on Orcas and I followed close behind in Margaret's boat that I intended to use to get back to Crane when I left the SeaSport at West Sound Marina for a starter motor inspection.

From the dock near the end of Deer Harbor Road, the ferry landing is a 20-minute drive. In places, the roadway is narrow, curvy, and hanging on the flank of Turtleback Mountain and 50 feet above the waters of Massacre Bay. With familiarity it seems benign though blind corners and bicyclists are sobering reminders that more than one Orcas Islander has, here and there around the island, skidded off the road into space and drowned in the cold waters of the Salish sea or Cascade Lake. A fatal accident in the last two years prompted some islanders to begin carrying glass-breaking hammers in their glove compartments should the need arise to exit their cars underwater. What's happened to the hammers since? I haven't heard or seen mention in the Islands Sounder.

Quiet at Orcas Landing. We parked halfway down the second lane and walked to the nearby Orcas Hotel for something hot to drink and something a little sweet to eat. I had my usual Tazo Awake tea and Yvonne had her usual eight-ounce non-fat latte. We shared *The Seattle Times* waiting for the ferry to arrive. Compared with late spring, summer, and early fall, few were leaving the island for what the natives usually referred to as America, a place of commotion and traffic but also family and Costco. It was from the deck of the Orcas Hotel, more than thirteen years ago, waiting for the Anacortes ferry with her friend Julie after spending a moms' weekend off at the Rosario Resort, and basking in the April sun, surrounded by spring flowers, that Yvonne called to tell me that I had to see Orcas and that maybe we'd want to buy property there.

021: Homemade nut and cherry bread

Sometimes when we ride the ferry we stay in the car, napping on the way to the mainland. Today we climbed two flights of stairs to the cabin area on the lower passenger deck and found a booth with a table and electrical outlet nearby to power my MacBook Pro. Yvonne knit and I wrote. By 10:20 we were on the road, heading for Seattle to pick up Corrina at Jeni's and then on to IKEA south of the city for a reconnaissance mission to check out kitchen cabinets and countertops, with the latter on sale until late in the month.

Twenty-one: Meatballs and Mashed Potatoes

As we cruised south on I-5 Yvonne told me about a conversation she overheard from two women sitting behind her on the ferry. Actually it was more monologue than conversation. The topic was spiritual development and the weekend workshop on Orcas, hosted by a guide or teacher they thought highly of, the middle-aged women had attended. The main speaker, dissatisfied with her husband and her life, talked about weekly spiritual telephone conference calls that cost $50 a session and were wonderful. There was talk about working together to solve the problems in Afghanistan, improperly diagnosed by the uninformed, and tied not so much to politics as some connection with ascending masters who lived in caves in that suffering country. The woman, her group, and others around the world presumably, were applying spiritual energy at a distance to bring clarity and peace to the suffering country. Yvonne was familiar with the vocabulary and concepts. Indralaya on Orcas is an important Theosophist center and its devotees have spoken to our Unitarian group — some participate — but her reaction to the conversation was that she, herself, couldn't talk that way. And that led to a discussion of other language/idea systems we could describe and perhaps imitate but couldn't actually speak.

Corrina was waiting at a Tullley's near Jeni's. We were in the cafeteria line at IKEA by 12:30. Yvonne and Corrina each ordered spinach omelets and I opted for the ten meatballs, mashed potatoes, gravy, and lingonberry plate. We had three hours (three hours?!) to review kitchen cabinet door styles, colors, and wood and then check out Corian, quartz, granite, and recycled-green countertop options. Finally we'd shop for Swedish-style Christmas presents for my two sisters. Yvonne had stuffed a scrap piece of kitchen flooring and an unused cabinet door in a cloth bag to hold next to IKEA displays to check for color compatibility. Corrina pushed the cart and offered color-matching advice, a skill born of her painting, photography, and inborn visual sensitivity. The result? Two small cabinet samples and one small Corian sample we'd take home. The question? Would the proposed cabinets and countertop look good in our kitchen and adjacent dining and living areas, all carefully decorated by Yvonne using a northwest palette? Who was in a position to know? Probably not me.

Twenty-two: Blustery Morning

*"I must down to the seas again, for the call of the running tide
Is a wild call and a clear call that may not be denied;
And all I ask is a windy day with the white clouds flying,
And the flung spray and the blown spume, and the sea-gulls crying."* — *"Sea Fever"* by John Mansfield

The plan was to take the SeaSport to West Sound Marina so that Ian Wareham could follow up on the conversation we had had a week earlier; he would inspect the new starter motor he had installed — that was now making peculiar noises — and replace it if necessary or file a bad tooth on the gear it engages with if that seemed appropriate. But wind and waves discouraged both of us.

Ian said it would be a shame to waste a day like the current one on work.

The wind was out of the southeast, gusting to almost 30 mph, blowing rain ahead of it against our big living room windows facing the water. In a pinch we could pick our way through the wind and waves, were going to Orcas a necessity, but this morning it was optional. Since we were temporarily without an Internet connection, we would be left to our own devices until perhaps late afternoon. Oh no!

Yvonne and Corrina turned to the inch square IKEA cabinet material and Corian countertop samples we had brought back from Seattle the day before. I was pretty sure the proposed ash-colored cabinets wouldn't work - too gray in a kitchen and house with warmer existing cabinets, floor, walls, and trim. But now that the possibility of a new kitchen had been broached and agreed on, would we be able to step back from the impending color and style choice and look at alternatives? Yvonne wasn't convinced there were any.

As it turned out all of us were dubious about the ash alternative — and we all realized, independently, that we should have bought several cabinet door alternatives to try out and then return. We had negotiated the shoals of

Twenty-two: Blustery Morning

taste without shipwreck. Corrina commented on our calmness, rationality, and deliberateness about home improvement even when we didn't completely agree. Both Yvonne and I thrive on new home projects and it hasn't been hard to find mutually agreeable solutions. But we wouldn't start something unless we were confident about all the intervening steps — which now meant Saturday Yvonne would return Corrina to Seattle to prepare for her imminent trip to India then and pick up several door fronts at IKEA.

022: NYTimes No Knead bread

So what to do today? Corrina spent some time with my new Nikon camera to see whether she could give me some advice about how to overcome its bad color choices in certain light, especially afternoon shadow. Then she trans-

Twenty-two: Blustery Morning

ferred the 2000 photos she had taken this summer at Tim and Kelly's wedding and Yvonne's 60th Birthday — an extravaganza with the whole crew in eastern Washington — to my MacBook Pro.

At dinner, discussion turned to small-town life in Deer Harbor — where Crane Island makes the southern boundary. After restoration efforts to the tidal slough at the north end of the hamlet, and for the first time in many years, a Lummi Indian would attend the Friday potluck at the Deer Harbor Community Club to bless the hoped-for return of the salmon And that led to a discussion of Deer Harbor personalities, one of which was notorious for what at least appeared to be scams at the expense of neighbors. The story was that he had promised water to another neighbor and borrowed $300,000 from the neighbor to pay for implementation of a piped delivery system but that never materialized — with deliveries made by truck instead. The money had been spent but not on what the neighbor expected. A lawsuit was launched; there was talk of bankruptcies but now two years later nothing had changed. The legal process can be very slow and not always come to the right conclusion — but what was most interesting in this case was the willingness of the purported scammer to act without integrity in a small town where sooner or later everyone knew everyone else's business. A good name on Orcas can mean the difference between business success and failure. Why would someone knowingly besmirch their own reputation?

So we talked about the Deer Harbor gossip network, a handful of women that put Facebook to shame. Never malicious, they just know everything and are eager to share it. Yvonne had done a hike with a group the week before, with permission, through what had been the Kaiser property, in Deer Harbor but facing West Sound. Kaiser had built the Hoover/Boulder dam and ships during the Second World War and had chosen Orcas as a retreat, building a large compound to house family and visitors. The big house was elegant, Yvonne reported, in a mid-20th Century style but would never be built that way today. Looking through the windows, the ladies could see a large bar in the living room and a leather-appointed den with animal heads on the walls. Times change. Styles change. But Orcas (and Crane in its way) continues to house a collection of luminaries or near luminaries out of all proportion to its population — though by informal community agreement, neither the luminaries nor their whereabouts are shared with non-residents.

Twenty-two: Blustery Morning

The first summer we were on Orcas we bought a pickup truck from a Kaiser grandson, who lived with his Guatemalan wife and two small children in the woods. He had dug his well and built his cabin and was determined not to take any family money. He told a terrifying story about living in a jungle village and being misidentified and then beaten by vigilantes, almost dying but recovering after a long convalescence.

Twenty-three: How Heavy the Load?

"What is this life if, full of care,
We have no time to stand and stare." — *"Leisure" by W.H. Davis*

A clear night and an island walk before dawn. A load of lumber was sitting in Ilze Jones' driveway, half 2x4s and half 4x8 beams. I could see that the east part of the house, which the carpenters had opened up and removed the walls, was now protected by sheet plastic. They would be working there, it seemed, with the lumber load. Up ahead, someone was walking on Circle Road with another coming out of the woods with a gas lantern, which he then extinguished. In the gloaming, I recognized Josh but not his companion. Apparently, they were staying in Ilze's tipi, with the house now uninhabitable. We had seen Josh Monday night when we drove into the Crane lot on Orcas, where he was unloading his pickup with materials he would then take by an open boat over to Crane.

Other major construction projects in the last few years worked the same way; the workers would live on the island, often in a tent, receive material by barge but also transport smaller loads by hand, truck to dock to boat to dock to truck - or dock cart. The crew working on Waddell's project at the other end of the island lived in a tent and went home weekends. They also set up a small sawmill to create beams on-site from the Douglas fir trees cleared from the building site. That winter was cold and windy with a major dumping of snow. I'd stop and say hello from time to time and see how they were doing. Three skilled men made quick progress. They built a good-sized home and big garage/bunkhouse in about twelve months. Dave and Caroline Browne's house, south of the Waddell project, was built the same way about six years ago, by a team that lived, rustically, on Crane during construction. Building on Crane isn't straightforward and it isn't cheap - unless you do it yourself.

Twenty-three: How Heavy the Load?

023: Tank transport fun

Tom Temple has lived on Crane for about 20 years and continues to work on his property, now on a garage/shop. Jim Johansen two doors north is also building his garage/shop. Tom, now about 72, has carried everything he's needed to his site. He hasn't used a barge service — ever. That means lugging sheets of plywood and sheetrock from his dock up a path to the house site about 50 feet above the water. He carried all the masonry materials — bags of cement, sand, and gravel, concrete blocks, beams, flooring, and so on up the hill or picked them up with his tractor at the community dock and moved them the mile or so to his house. Years ago he had a small front-loading plywood barge but over time too many Cranians asked him to carry material for them, and since he wouldn't charge for the service (couldn't really because of licensing and liability issues), his only choice was to sell the barge. Now he uses a 40-foot floating dock section, abandoned when new sections were in-

Twenty-three: How Heavy the Load?

stalled on the Orcas side, and lashes it to his eight-foot Bullfrog. It's flat and plenty long, though of course, there's always the possibility that the wake from a passing boat could upset the load.

Tom says he likes to carry his load, that it keeps him fit and in shape, especially important he says because he suffered from polio as a child and does everything he can to stay strong and forestall degeneration. He often sports a generous, white Santa Claus beard. Part of the year his friend Liz makes her way from Sun Valley to live with him on Crane, and some of the time he goes there, but most of the time, he, like Lou Falb, lives alone.

For our various construction projects, we've had two lumber trucks come by barge and once brought our pickup filled with lumber. But we've carried plywood, sheetrock, framing material, posts, bags of cement, sand, soil, manure, bark, pipes, flooring, small trees, and other potted plants, and an endless supply of groceries, small appliances, electronics, cases of wine, beer, rice milk, and on and on from Orcas to our house on Crane.

The most memorable were a 10 x 20 storage tent we got at Costco that weighed 200 pounds — we somehow wrestled it home with the help of a two-wheeled hand truck — and a 450-gallon, 6-foot tall by 8-foot diameter water storage tank we intend to use to irrigate the front garden in the dry season, once I put in the gutter and downspout to feed it during the rainy season. Just the right size to fit the cockpit of our SeaSport (I had thought about towing it, floating, from Orcas to Crane), but too wide for the ramp railings on the Orcas and Crane sides, so we had to lift it on top of the railings and slide it down on Orcas and then up on Crane. A massive, black cylinder, more than 100 pounds, we trucked it across the Ochs' meadow and set it near my wood-splitting area.

A project for later in the winter since right now Yvonne wants all the rainfall coming off the roof facing the garden to go to the ground, not be sequestered. We're curious to see how well the system works and how much we can reduce our draw on the Crane Island community water system.

Twenty-four: Dump Run, Exchange Visit

"What are the roots that clutch, what branches grow
 Out of this stony rubbish? Son of man,
 You cannot say, or guess, for you know only
 A heap of broken images, where the sun beats,
 And the dead tree gives no shelter, the cricket no relief,
 And the dry stone no sound of water." — "The Waste Land" by
T.S. Elliot

It had been at least ten weeks since I packed our recycle and trash off Crane to the county transfer station on Orcas, and the old outhouse was packed full. I had help for the heavy lifting, Corrina, and she was easily convinced that the project would be interesting — and she was eager to help in any case.

The 4 x 4 x 8-foot outhouse with a translucent fiberglass roof predates the house and for many years served as a sanitary facility for the Reynolds when they camped on the lot summers and dreamed of building their retirement house. A one-seater, the moss-green structure straddled a four-foot pit the Reynolds would dust with lime from a can after use. Twice the fiberglass roof tried to lift off and blow away. I set rocks on the roof as a temporary measure and later applied roofing screws.

When we first moved to Crane, we kept our trash cans and recycle in the garage, but as we emptied the garage and then turned it into a studio, the storage moved outside. After the raccoons dumped the cans and scattered their contents, I tied the tops on with bungee cords — not a match for the resourceful raccoons. That's when we pressed the outhouse into service as a trash and recycle storage shed. The raccoons were no longer a problem, but the location of the outhouse proved to be since it was visible from the kitchen window and south deck. One day when Yvonne was in Seattle, I tipped the structure on its side onto a two-wheeled hand truck and dragged it 100 feet

Twenty-four: Dump Run, Exchange Visit

west, closer to the back of the lot and out of sight. Later, with Yvonne's help, I tipped it upright onto a foundation we made of paving stones at hand. I dumped a bag of lime into the now-open pit at the original location and filled it with soil left from excavating for the two sheds I'd built 2 1/2 years ago.

024.1: Corrina ready to load F-150 for dump run

While Corrina got herself up and ready, I dragged the plastic garbage cans, two loaded black contractor's bags, and loose items out of the shed, stomped in the cans to compress their contents, added more material to the cans and bags, and made two trips to the *Huginn*, a SeaSport (Huggin, thought in old Norse, was one of two ravens belonging to Odin, who would circle the world daily and return to his shoulder to report what they'd seen. Muninn, memory, was the other raven) at the community dock using our dock cart/yard cart to move what were now filled, compressed, and heavy containers.

Twenty-four: Dump Run, Exchange Visit

Corrina joined me for the third trip; we finished loading and headed for the Crane dock on Orcas. I unloaded the boat and let Corrina drag three cartloads up the ramp to our pickup while I packed the truck bed and arranged a bungee web to hold the four cans and two big plastic bags in place. Corrina took her coat off after the first pull up the ramp, and once the truck was loaded, commented that it was hard work and that to live on Crane you needed to be strong. The tide was high, so coming up the ramp hadn't been too bad, and the quantity and heaviness of the materials were less than it often is.

With the pickup loaded and the contents tied down, we stopped at the Deer Harbor Post Office to pick up mail and then the lumber yard to put some gas in the truck and headed back south on Orcas Road to the transfer station. I backed up to the recycle dumpsters, and we emptied two cans and the two big bags. We wouldn't have to pay the newly imposed $5 recycling fee the County Council had recently put into effect because we would be paying for leaving trash. Though I don't know statistics about recycling on Orcas, it seems to be a popular program, and the Council has encouraged it by charging for trash but not recycle. A revenue shortfall in the San Juan County budget encouraged the Council to, in effect, penalize islanders who recycled but didn't handle their trash. At some point, the county will know whether the fee for what was once free has the effect they've hoped.

The recycle goes into three large blue dumpsters near the fee station. A fourth, green dumpster serves residents who have small amounts of trash, and they pay $6 per 55-gallon can. We dump trash but not organic waste, like vegetable cuttings and coffee grounds. Uncooked food fragments go to the worm ranch in Yvonne's shed. The rest goes on to one of Yvonne's open bins that turn into soil over a six-month period.

While I drove across the yard scale so that the attendant could weigh the loaded truck, Corrina walked to the Orcas Exchange, adjacent to the transfer station grounds, to see it first hand, take some pictures, and maybe find a treasure of some kind. After I emptied the last two cans on the floor of the transfer building, a front-loading tractor plowed the trash on the floor into a huge dumpster below grade level. When the dumpsters are full, they're towed to the ferry and then to the mainland where the contents are dumped and covered with soil.

Twenty-four: Dump Run, Exchange Visit

024.2: The Exchange: incredible treasures abound

Corrina was amazed by the Exchange. Sited in a lovely grove of fir trees, castoffs piled by category fill the acre site. Some are left to the elements, like plumbing and bicycles. Most of the material awaiting recycle is kept out of the rain in makeshift tents or sheds. Skis, pet carriers, furniture, appliances, car seats, kids' play sets, books, construction supplies, dishes, cooking utensils, and on and on, a bizarre collection of discards waiting for a new owner. Nothing is priced; you pay what you will.

Twenty-four: Dump Run, Exchange Visit

024.3: You decide what to pay

We've left more than we've taken but did bring home a small bike we thought grandson Jackson could use when he visited last July. Uncle Noah cleaned it up and made it look like new. George Post founded the Exchange years ago recognizing that reuse is better than trashing and that shopping on Orcas, especially for most items inventoried at the exchange isn't possible, either because people can't afford them or they're not for sale on the island. Garage and yard sales serve a similar function, and we've made too good use of them, but usually they're not held when you need something and usually don't have what you want. The consequence is that you buy when you see a good deal on something you think you might sometime need. I now have duplicates and triplicates, even quadruplicates of tools I rarely use and materials I'll never use. From garage sale to home, age it, then take it to the Exchange.

Twenty-five: Deer Harbor Thanksgiving

"Hear the chorus, it is a grand opera,
 Ah this indeed is music—this suits me." — *"Song of Myself"*
by Walt Whitman

It felt much colder inside than outside, or at least it seemed that way as Yvonne, Corrina, and I let ourselves into the Deer Harbor Community Club at 5:15 on the second Friday in November. We carried a hot dish of stuffing, some wine, and plates, glasses, and tableware. The potluck was scheduled for 6:30; some neighbors would appear by 6:00, and we had to warm the place up. The first thing we did was to light the propane stove that replaced the old cast iron wood stove and turn on the baseboard heaters at the ends of the 25 x 40 room. This room had once had a central partition to divide the space into two classrooms when it served as the Deer Harbor public school.

The day before, the three of us had set up ten tables for diners, with eight chairs to each table. We covered them with fall-themed tablecloths, adding turkeys made of grocery bags, candles, and flattened, dried maple leaves. I folded and placed white paper napkins at each location. Traffic flow around the tables at the last potluck had been frustrating for all, as hungry people crowded both sides of a long set of tables, coming from each direction. They then had to flow through to get past one another to reach the food they hadn't yet had a chance to browse. Yvonne's solution was to set up two tables for turkey and fixings, with another between them for salads and bread. People could file down each side of the two main serving tables and then come to the center table, where they would need to spend less time. As it turned out, the plan worked well; people moved through quickly, with a minimum of delay and frustration.

025.1: Corrina at the Huginn's wheel leaving the Crane Association dock on Orcas

Pam and Steve Kyle were to help with the setup, but Pam's father was so ill she stayed in Seattle to be with him, and Steve returned during the day Friday when it looked like Pam's father might not make it through Friday night. Lynn and Chris were back from Tucson now, where they had gone to deal with her failing parents, though I hadn't seen Chris yet to find out how things went.

Twenty-five: Deer Harbor Thanksgiving

025.2: The Thanksgiving/fall dinner crowd at the Deer Harbor Community Club

Howard's flag pole was now installed to the left of the front stairs. He had retrieved an appropriate tree from Deer Harbor, dried it out, and then bolted a crosspiece near the top and mounted the pole between two posts he'd set in concrete two weeks before during the cleanup of the grounds. A maritime-style flagpole, with a conventional central line and two side lines coming from the pole to the ends of the crosspiece, forming a triangle. Tonight, American and Washington State flags flew, for the first time.

By 6:00, people were filing into the now-warm space, bringing sliced turkey and gravy. Six women in the Deer Harbor Community Club Auxiliary had baked and donated turkey and trimmings. Others brought mashed potatoes, scalloped potatoes, sweet potatoes, rice, green salad, coleslaw, bread, rolls, brownies, pie, zucchini bread, and treats I've forgotten or didn't notice. Wine was the responsibility of each diner who wanted some.

About 75 people crowded into the building, picking up their name tags from a folding corkboard at the front door, and the conversation commenced. I

Twenty-five: Deer Harbor Thanksgiving

introduced Corrina to Pat and Jack Thomas, early arrivals, and they talked about travel. Jack, a retired TWA pilot, had flown parts of the route Corrina would follow from London to India. When I checked with them later, they were talking about Greg Mortenson's *Three Cups of Tea*. When we finally took our seats later, Corrina charmed Gene Flath with her tales of travel and protracted quest to find out who she was and wanted to be. Gene later asked me to help him understand Corrina's relationship to our family. Our bonus daughter, I explained, the one we didn't know we had. More accurately, the daughter of Yvonne's first husband's second wife, who died a few years ago, half-sister to Jeni and Eric, and happily part of our growing circle of love. I understand exactly, Gene said. Wonderful.

Howard, as the presiding officer, called for everyone's attention and directed them to Yvonne, who would lead "Over the River and through the Woods," a Thanksgiving tune that boomers, at least, have childhood associations with. Then a treasurer's report from Erik Smith, a grounds cleanup report from Yvonne, introduction of guests, Yvonne introducing Corrina, a happy birthday to Bev Polis, former president and club spark plug. Finally, following a knock-knock joke, it was time to eat. Four queues formed as Yvonne had directed the group, and plate-loading went smoothly.

It turned out that Dwight sat at the end of our table to my right, and I could ask him about the progress of the Deer Harbor fire station, a project that he monitored on behalf of the fire district. With a contractor's background, he could identify problems and help solve them before construction got off track. When I asked about what appeared to be a community-compatible emerging style for the building, he explained that firehouse neighbors with interest and design skills had made a number of design suggestions, like the cupola, that were being added to the original design. The work was a bit behind schedule but pretty much on track. The new building would house one of the new, smaller, highly mobile, four-wheel-drive 300-gallon foam pumpers, a 1000-gallon water truck, and an EMT ambulance. The foam system with the portable water capacity would give the truck what was equivalent to a 15,000-gallon water supply, enough to make a major dent in a house fire. Having the ambulance in Deer Harbor, the second most populous part of the island, would save lives, Dwight was certain.

Dinner over, Bob Connor stood and explained to the group that Henry Cayou's great-granddaughter, a Samish woman who would bless the fish ladder he had built to encourage salmon at the upper end of the tidal slough, would this evening bless our building and the community. Accompanied by a Samish drummer, she described how much Deer Harbor meant to her and her people, and then chanted to the four directions. The crowd lingered, then helped clean up. A time of fellowship and sharing as neighbors had done in that building for generations.

    A dark, mostly calm night, and we headed the *Huginn* back to Crane Island, where the Christianson's had just docked, returning to Crane from Anchorage by way of other parts of the world. Yvonne would drive Corrina to Seattle tomorrow. Later Corrina would go on to San Francisco and Los Angeles and then to India. Yvonne would go to IKEA to pick up three cabinet door fronts we'd expose to our kitchen and then decide amongst for our kitchen remodel.

Twenty-six: Looking and Seeing

"And 'tis my faith that every flower
  Enjoys the air it breathes." — "Lines Written in Early Spring"
by William Wordsworth

Though it wasn't raining, the view outside our east-facing windows was mottled and streaked by the wind-blown salt spray rising from the waves striking the rocks at the foot of the point, 30 feet from the house. A stormy day? Less than it appeared. As Yvonne, Corrina, and I left the house for the dock and crossed the front yard, the wind wasn't evident, thwarted by the closely woven bamboo fence Yvonne attached to the deer fence to protect her front garden from drying out in the winter blows. At the community dock, I had to back the *Huginn* and turn carefully since the wind pushed the lighter bow faster than the heavy stern. Yvonne would return to IKEA in Seattle to pick up three cabinet door fronts to help us make up our minds about how to approach a kitchen remodel and drop Corrina at Jeni's where she'd bide her time until she could leave for three months in India.

Corrina is serious about photography and understands digital cameras and techniques in their use. Her close-up print of translucent flower petals hangs between two hammered pewter Swedish candle sconces in our dining room, and when present, she has acted as the principal photographer at our family events for the last four years. During this visit, she passed me about 2000 pictures she'd taken this summer at Tim and Kelly's wedding and at Yvonne's 60th birthday party/Borgfest in eastern Washington and western Idaho. She had helped carry the trash and recycle to the transfer station and cooked an egg in a French toast lunch. It looked like there wouldn't be time for her to help me inspect our septic system for a required report to the county. But there was time to help me understand and more successfully use the little Nikon Coolpix I got for my birthday that replaced a Canon ELPH I'd had for years.

Twenty-six: Looking and Seeing

026: Early morning on Circle Road at the south end of the airstrip with Becker's farm just over the rise

My thinking is that the smaller and simpler a camera, the more likely it will be used. I'd taken about 12,000 pictures with three generations of ELPHs, but I wanted a more powerful telephoto, anti-shake, and higher resolution in a small camera. I liked the Nikon generally but wasn't happy with the color and blurry pictures in some situations. I'd looked through the user manual but hadn't mastered the camera's capabilities. In short order, Corrina showed me how to manually set the color balance, choose a shooting context, and assign an ISO setting. What I needed was some practice.

I started before dawn the next morning. No wind, slack tide, a clear sky except over the mainland twenty miles to the east, as it often is, with the San Juan Islands sitting in the rain shadow of the Olympic mountains to the southwest. A hint of sun at the beginning of nautical twilight not long after

Twenty-six: Looking and Seeing

6:00. Interrupting my oatmeal breakfast and morning news reading from time to time, I walked out on the deck and shot a series of pictures with different settings to see what worked the best. Once I'd captured the sunrise to my satisfaction, I set out on my morning tank-level reading and constitutional, with my Nikon on my belt in its holster.

Usually, my walks are meditative, and I often can't remember what I looked at but didn't see. This day, everywhere I looked, I saw beauty. Soggy, matted leather-colored maple leaves topped with an occasional bright yellow leaf, perfect and fallen in the last hour. Ground fog rising from the western edge of the airstrip as the sunlight warmed the grass. Rich November sunlight cutting through the forest highlighting the last few leaves on a maple. A door frame and an open gate, irrelevant now because the fence around Clark's grass tennis court had been removed some years ago. An impassive face carved into a trunk, looking through rather than at me. Circle Road, dark in the foreground, bright farther on, promising a day of abundance. All submitted to the Nikon, and all looked the way they looked once housed in iPhoto, waiting for their chance to shine for others on the family website or part of a video like the one I did for Crane's 50th anniversary.

Twenty-seven: Salvation

"The pessimist complains about the wind; the optimist expects it to change; the realist adjusts the sails." — William Arthur Ward

"Salvation" came alongside at 11:15 Sunday morning just off the northwest corner of Shaw Island, at the west end of Wasp Passage. We were saved.

Six of us were scheduled to take the inter-island ferry, the *Evergreen State*, from Orcas Landing to Friday Harbor. We would take our van, so there would be a seat for everyone. The Friday Harbor Unitarian-Universalist Fellowship had invited our Orcas fellowship to have lunch with them and then join their service. After the service the six of us could visit Bob Harris, Grey Beard emeritus, and Betty Sumrall, both members of our group now staying in the Friday Harbor convalescent home. The Friday Harbor group had shared a service and bread with us in the past but Yvonne and I hadn't been to one of their services, presided over by someone who, unlike me, actually had ministerial credentials.

The ferry would leave Orcas at 10:35 and arrive at 11:15. Because it was Sunday, the return ferry wouldn't leave Friday Harbor until 5:45, arriving at Orcas Landing almost an hour later. A very long day, since we'd have three hours after lunch, service, and visiting and there wasn't anything else Yvonne and I wanted to do on a wet Sunday in Friday Harbor.

So — why not take our SeaSport? We could come back whenever we wanted. The other four declined the offer to come with us on *Huginn*, saying they had made plans that would keep them in Friday Harbor until the ferry returned, but thanks. They would be on the *Evergreen State*.

Twenty-seven: Salvation

027: Salvation on a Sunday morning

Wanting to get to the Friday Harbor Senior Center, where the Unitarian services were held by 11:30 and having to walk from the county dock space in the Friday Harbor marina, we left the Crane Community dock at 10:35, running at low speed through the no wake zone along the northeast side of Crane Island and then accelerating and up on plane heading west and then south around the west end of Crane. I held the rpms to 3600, as per the owner's manual, and the Furuno navigation system said that we were traveling about 24 knots, more than 26 mph, faster than the boat had in the past at that rpm. West Sound Marina's recent service on the engine, especially having the port side head machined to take care of a sticking valve caused by salt water leaking through the port exhaust manifold, was having a positive effect. Compression had been subpar all along. Now the engine was running to spec and we

Twenty-seven: Salvation

were cruising. What a pleasure. The $8500 we'd spent this year on the *Huginn* was well spent.

A mile from the Crane dock, the engine rpms dropped a bit, then smoke and mechanical noise billowed from around the edges of the engine compartment, and the rpms dropped to zero. We had a fire extinguisher on board and had training on how to use it but I was pretty sure we didn't have a fire. That would be very dangerous with the gasoline engine. I turned off the engine and tentatively lifted the engine compartment lid. Smoke, no fire, the bilge filled with oil. We weren't going anyplace soon. By this time it was 10:45.

Using Yvonne's cell phone I called the BoatUS/Vessel Assist help line. I could have used channel 16 on our VHF radio, monitored by Vessel Assist in Friday Harbor, but cell phoning is easier to do. The operator I reached took our information and then put us on hold while trying to reach Friday Harbor Vessel Assist. After 10 minutes on hold, she came on the line saying she would call us back with an ETA for help arriving. Yvonne hadn't charged her cell phone and the battery was almost completely depleted. Before 11:00 Vessel Assist called to say help would arrive in 15 to 20 minutes. At that point the *Evergreen State* passed our disabled boat, heading for Friday Harbor with Suzanne, Herlwyn, Babs, and Peter aboard. They had made the right decision not to go with us. We wondered aloud whether they would notice a SeaSport adrift with its engine compartment open and guess that it was us.

Little wind and current, but we were moving very slowly northwest. The depth gauge showed no value — the water was over 100 feet deep here and it wouldn't be possible to use the anchor — but today it wouldn't matter.

In the distance, as the ferry approached the turn into Friday Harbor, a boat appeared heading our direction and as it got closer I could see it had a red hull — Vessel Assist. At 11:15 the *Salvation* came alongside and we talked about the towing to come. Our rescuer would take us in the SeaSport to the West Sound Marina. We'd moor the boat and then he'd backtrack and drop us at the Crane community dock on his way back to Friday Harbor.

Vessel Assist, contracting with BoatUS, has four tow boats in the San Juans, and in the summer keeps one docked at Fisherman's Bay on Lopez and another at Roche Harbor, at the top of San Juan Island. We were tied up at the visitors' dock at West Sound Marina by noon and back at the Crane community dock by 12:15.

Twenty-seven: Salvation

Would I go to Deer Harbor Marina to pick up the Sunday Seattle Times Yvonne had intended to pick up in Friday Harbor? Of course — if they had one left. Yvonne called Renee and she said they'd hold one — so after lunch, I took Margaret's 40-year-old boat with its new Honda outboard, the mile north to the marina, picked up the paper, and came home to spend 90 minutes splitting the coming week's supply of firewood. Then I took a nap for an hour and after slowly coming back to consciousness spent 30 minutes contently looking out at a world of green gods floating in a watery world.

Twenty-eight: The Damages

"Smooth seas do not make skillful sailors" — *African proverb*

Jan, Betsy, and Ian had all been down to their visitors' dock by the time I called Ian Monday morning. Had I brought the *Huginn* in to have the starter motor checked, as I had talked about with Ian? Were the keys in the boat? Without waiting for Ian to say anything, I launched into our Sunday morning saga — the loss of power, smoke, and so on. He listened patiently and then described what he saw in his first 30 seconds on the boat: oil in the bilge and a connecting rod sticking through the oil pan. A sign of catastrophic engine failure. The engine would need to be replaced.

Yvonne overheard me talking to Ian and stomped out to her studio. Not knowing much about engines, I had hoped that the problem was a blown gasket. That would account for the loss of power and noise. But since the engine had two heads (a V6), three of the cylinders would still be operational, and that wasn't the case. I had been fantasizing a theory that might make West Sound Marina responsible — a faulty job remounting the head they had taken off and had repaired. This was my problem, not Ian's.

Why did it happen? The oil filter and oil had been replaced a few weeks before; it wasn't a lack of oil that caused the problem, as often happens. Ian suggested that the water that seeped into the engine from the corroded exhaust manifold might have caused pressure that slightly bent the rod so that over time it failed. Engines in a marine environment are subject to very inhospitable conditions and corrode faster than they wear out most of the time. A Volvo Penta gasoline engine can be expected to last 1600 — 1700 hours before it needs major repair or replacement. Our SeaSport was 17 years old with about 1700 hours on the engine. A not unlikely candidate for major problems.

Twenty-eight: The Damages

028: We depend on the Huginn every day

What would it cost to repair? Ian said he needed to do some research but it might cost in the neighborhood of $5000 to complete. There were two alternatives: the first was to get a short block, that is, a block without a head. Since we had just had a head repaired that might work. The other possibility was to get a new version of the engine that had two camshafts, the second serving to balance the engine and reduce vibration, an engineering change Volvo had made after 1993. Everything being equal, Ian said the second alternative would be the most satisfactory. They would pull the engine out, remove the alternator, starter, power steering pump, and other items, and install them on the new engine.

Is the boat worth repairing? Would we do better with something else? As long as the boat serves our needs, we're probably better off fixing and using it than getting another boat — that would likely have undiscovered problems

Twenty-eight: The Damages

we'd have to have fixed. SeaSports hold their value well so putting money into the *Huginn* isn't money lost. We'd have a hard time getting much out of the boat in its current condition. Repaired, we could sell it for at least $20,000. We had paid $24,000 four years before. SeaSports are popular on Crane: Browne's, Christiansen's, Evan's, Johansen's, Kauffman's, and Och's all have SeaSports.

Ian called back with a number: $4200 installed — with a long block (newer engine). An engine was available in Seattle and he'd have it shipped up to Orcas. When would the boat be ready? Hard to say until they have the engine in the shop. Given that we've had almost everything else mechanical fixed in the boat, the theory is that with a rebuilt engine we should do well for some years. The boat has a new cooling system, new exhaust manifolds, new outdrive internals, new trim tab hydraulics, new batteries, and a new starter.

We have to have a boat. The *Huginn* serves our purposes very well in wind, waves, snow, fog, darkness, calm, sunshine, and moonlight. It can carry six people. The cabin is enclosed and heated. It has a good GPS and depth sounder system, VHF radio, and a joystick-controlled spotlight, an FM/CD system, a V-berth area — mostly for storage. It handles well, will go about 25 mph, and looks pretty good cleaned up. It can carry quite a bit of cargo in the cockpit, cabin, V-berth, and on the bow. We could reduce our expenses with an open boat with an outboard, but we'd be miserable. So the *Huginn* is one of the prices we pay to live on Crane. Is it worth it? What's a better alternative?

Twenty-nine: No Whining

*"If you can meet with Triumph and Disaster
     And treat those two impostors just the same." — "If—" by
Rudyard Kipling*

Sitting in the hot tub Monday night, I wondered aloud to Yvonne when it might actually be possible to retire — that is, not have responsibilities and be on permanent vacation. Her reply: "When you're dead." I was feeling sorry for myself, I guess. I was retired — that is, not gainfully employed — but I was working hard every day and had less free time than I had before retiring. Does that make sense? Of course, it's what we've chosen, or made lots of choices over time to create. I believe in an abundant universe but wasn't feeling that way now. I wanted it back.

Tuesday, enjoying a stuffed cabbage hot dish dinner, facing each other across the kitchen counter as we do every night when we don't have guests, we came back to the topic of life on Crane and the future — another installment in the ongoing discussion we've had since moving here 2007.

We reviewed: If we had stayed in Boulder, like our friends, we wouldn't have to be fixing up our house to make it what we wanted. We had already done that. We wouldn't have to fight with boats and an unreliable ferry service. But we hadn't wanted to stay in Boulder living the same life. We wanted to do something different, have a new life. The past 10 years, after we sold our Boulder house and came to live on Orcas and then Crane, had been wonderful experiences we would have missed by staying in the same place. We would have traveled more, in fact, but that's very different from putting down roots and being part of a community as we have in Deer Harbor.

Twenty-nine: No Whining

029: Float plane near Pole Pass

If we had stayed in our house in Deer Harbor, boats could have been optional rather than necessary, and so causing less stress but living on Crane was the most wonderful place either of us had ever lived. We knew, coming to Crane, that our presence on the island was unsustainable, we'd be too old to do all the work an out-island requires. In ten years or sooner, I expected I'd be too old to want to deal with boat commuting and doing all it takes to take care of the house and grounds. So we knew Crane was temporary.

What seemed to be a problem was to continue to think about, worry about when we would have to leave Crane, rather than just living day to day until it was clear we'd have to make a change. I proposed we quit worrying and review the situation again in a few years. That made sense to Yvonne. She added that we put a moratorium on talking to anybody else about the possibility of moving from Crane because it made us short-timers in their minds and undercut our ability to live in the present and enjoy Crane.

That morning the New York Times described new research by Daniel Gilbert, the Harvard happiness professor, who found people are happiest when attending to where they are and what they're doing and least happy when their minds are wandering. Not surprising, but relevant nonetheless. It's what Ram Dass recommended in *Be Here Now* and what Emerson wrote about over and over. And what Francis Racey, leader of the Circle of the Spirit, a group that met every Sunday in the Deer Harbor Community Club, tried to encourage in his followers — mindfulness — Buddha's teaching of 2500 years ago.

Yvonne talked about flexibility and how it's important and how some older people don't have it, creating misery for themselves and their families. She was determined that we be flexible. When the time came to leave Crane, she'd be excited about beginning a new life, maybe in Seattle or Portland. But it was key to living here now and not being mentally somewhere else. She said she was disappointed that we wouldn't be able to live on Crane long enough for our youngest grandchildren to form strong memories of it — but that's just the way things were going to be. But we were fine, our kids were fine. We had a wonderful life and would live it without being distracted by an indefinite future.

A great talk. Now for a movie.

Thirty: IKEA Run

" He prayeth well, who loveth well
  Both man and bird and beast." From "The Rime of the Ancient Mariner" — Samuel Taylor Coleridge

Tuesday afternoon, I had an email from Nancy Johansen, concerned after seeing that there had been high winds in Seattle Monday night. What had happened on Crane? Had a tree crashed through the glass roof of their cabin? We hadn't heard anything during the night, but I had noticed one of the tarps on a stack of split wood had blown partly off. I reassured Nancy, with Jim in Mazatlán for the winter, that Crane hadn't experienced any problems. I had walked Circle Road Tuesday morning and only a few small limbs were down; almost all were dead and heavily moss-covered.

But at dawn Wednesday morning, the wind was blowing hard out of the southeast, the prevailing direction much of the year here, and kicking up a fuss on the Salish Sea. A sustained wind of 30 mph against the current can create quite a ride through Pole Pass. It was a day we normally wouldn't venture out on the water. But the plan was to go to IKEA in Seattle. "Is today the only day you can go?" I asked Yvonne. "Yes," was her answer. So off we went.

With our boat out of the water for repairs, we were borrowing Margaret's canvas-topped 40-year-old runabout, and we rocked and rolled through Pole Pass and across the quarter-mile to the Crane Community dock on Orcas. Yvonne was feeling kind of queasy. Waves in transit are one thing; docking with wind and waves another. Early in my apprenticeship with the *Huginn* on a windy day, I could only dock at the Deer Harbor Marina with the help of a sympathetic observer who refrained from laughing out loud as I overcompensated first in one direction and then another, trying to come in close and parallel to the fuel dock. Now after more than a thousand dockings, I could do it pretty well even in the wind. At the Orcas-side dock, Yvonne jumped out and held the lines, waiting for me to help. The wind was blowing too strong for her to both hold and tie.

030.1: Stiff wind drives rain against ferry windows

On the way to the ferry landing, we could see good-sized waves traveling north to the top of Massacre Bay. The parking lot at the ferry landing was mostly deserted. Not many people going to America today. After fortifying herself with latte and a muffin, Yvonne pointed out an article in the current *Islands Sounder* — the Food Bank had almost reached its fundraising goal and was now just $5000 short. Joyce Shaw could order the modular building that would be installed at the Community Church site, and the operation could move out of the crowded and inappropriate space in the Church basement.

Thirty: IKEA Run

Yvonne, as Food Bank Board Secretary, had helped with the fundraising, and we had written a check. Good news.

On board the ferry and sitting at a table on the top deck, Yvonne continued with her knitting as I clicked away on my Mac. Marion and Mic Goheen stopped by our table; Marion would have her eyes checked today, having had cataract surgery that had kept them away from last Friday's turkey potluck. The water across Rosario Strait would have been very exciting in a small boat, though none were visible, and even the ferry pitched up and down, sometimes crashing with a throaty boom and spray coming up on the lower car deck. But a pretty mild day compared to what we had seen at times in the past. Hard rain on the drive south. Yvonne had made sandwiches so we could hit the ground running at IKEA. She napped from Anacortes to Everett. We arrived at IKEA about 12:30.

The plan was to meet with an IKEA kitchen consultant, who would review and enter the order and then provide a picking list. While she did that, we found cabinet pulls we liked and dumped them in the cart and then consulted with the countertop people. They said we would need to buy the kitchen parts and then come back with our receipt — in order to get the 40% discount. The discount and the willingness of Precision Countertops to come to Crane to measure and create a template and then deliver and install made the new kitchen project practical.

By the time we had gotten through the whole picking list, we had filled five carts. The checkout clerk was very systematic and efficient. I brought the van from the parking to loading area while Yvonne monitored the process. While she went back into the store to place the countertop order, I loaded the van, trying to be space-efficient. What if it wouldn't all fit? It did, with six inches under the roof to spare. Yvonne had two countertop samples she'd take back home to decide between and call in.

Thirty: IKEA Run

030.2: At IKEA with kitchen picking list

It was a bit after 4:00; rush hour was underway. The next ferry was at 6:25 and then 8:30. We took the east side route, I-405, bypassing Seattle but exposed to the Bellevue, Redmond, and Bothell traffic. Not bad but merging onto I-5, the traffic was slow to Arlington. We were the last vehicle on the ferry and had made the drive with two minutes to spare.

Thirty-one: Island Transfer

"For whatever we lose (like a you or a me), It's always our self we find in the sea." — e.e. cummings

Low clouds, 37 degrees, but at least it wasn't raining or windy, not yet at least. Finally light, I walked across the Ochs' meadow to the dock. A raven flew west, croaking three times, pausing, repeating, talking to an unseen companion somewhere on Crane. A group of Hooded Mergansers had appeared last week and were diving between the end of the dock and Pole Pass. Small and elegant, the males mostly black with white highlights and a white crest, and the females a complex brown. A sign of late autumn. Now I could see darker clouds in the east; rain was likely soon.

By the time I began to load the dock cart from our van in the Crane Island parking lot on Orcas, a light rain had begun. The van was packed with our new IKEA kitchen, more than 100 boxes, some small and light but others long and heavy. It wouldn't be possible to keep dry what I would carry in Margaret's boat to Crane, so my first load would be mostly shrink-wrapped boxes carrying metal drawer assemblies, 31 total. Though initially disappointed at not being able to use the *Huginn* (in dry dock for an engine replacement), Margaret's boat's canvas cover actually had some advantages over the *Huginn's* open cockpit. The *Huginn's* cabin and v-berth were enclosed but with limited space.

Four round-trip cart loads between van and boat pretty well filled it. The tide was out but not far and coming in, so the ramps to the floating docks on Orcas and Crane wouldn't be steep until night. Four round-trip cart loads between the boat and our house 200 yards from the community dock. A ninety-minute process — van to house. The rain had strengthened, and water beads clung to all the boxes. Yvonne, surprised that I had already made a transfer, had thought I was out on a morning walk. She wanted to help and began to dry the boxes.

Thirty-one: Island Transfer

032: Cabinet parts in Margaret's boat awaiting transfer

After I had some tea, and we both did email chores, we cruised back to Orcas. The rain had mostly stopped so we could load corrugated cartons without having to worry that we would ruin the contents. Four more cart loads, car to cart to boat to cart to home. Another 90 minutes and now noon and lunchtime, sharing leftovers. Yvonne prepared areas in the open studio area and adjacent guest room to act as a warehouse during the kitchen construction process. The second load was mostly door fronts, shelving, and a half-dozen heavy cabinet cartons. The van was now maybe half-empty but what was left were cabinets, heavy to very heavy. The second load had

Thirty-one: Island Transfer

dragged the boat low in the water — so maybe three more, smaller loads, and carts not so full, would complete the transfer — but not today.

After lunch, Yvonne's brother Ron called. He was underway building an acupuncture practice at an alternative health clinic in Seattle, but the process was slow, and he'd start some marketing campaigns soon. He had slipped on a sidewalk steel grating and cut his leg. That was a minus but he had stopped a bloody fight at a McDonald's by stepping between the combatants and saying firmly, "Fight's over!" and it was. And when an overhead trolley cable fell across a bus shelter, he led the confused, indecisive commuters to safety. Two strong pluses. Yvonne then left for Eastsound, crossing in Margaret's boat and taking the pickup, for a haircutting appointment and some errands.

Returning when it was almost dark, she reported seeing Larry Shaw at the Island Market, where he had been a manager for many years. Larry and his wife Joyce are the primary movers for the Food Bank, where Yvonne serves as Board Secretary. Larry said the Food Bank had achieved its building fund goals and then some and had raised $140,000 of the $130,000 needed to build a new facility. Very good news. The *Islands Sounder* had done a great job over the last five weeks or so publicizing the drive, the need for the Food Bank, and its increase in activity over the last year, and we had done our part.

I had made progress during the day, adding a function to the Annotator program to allow any number of subsidiary sections to books, above and beyond the original text and annotations, for illustration albums or whatever. And when Yvonne came home with the mail, it included a check from the penultimate Crane Island Association member who hadn't paid his annual dues. Almost there. Freshly baked chocolate chip cookies and a Hal Holbrook film "That Evening Sun." More transfer action in the morning.

Thirty-two: Not So Bad

"There are always at least two sides to every story" — *anonymous*

Warmer this dawn, up to 42 degrees, cloudy but not windy, and reasonably dry. A good day to bring over more IKEA materials. During the night, it occurred to me that it might be easier to carry the heavy cabinets on our two-wheeled hand truck sitting outside next to the tool shed, where it had been for almost a year after suffering a flat tire. About 5:30 a.m., I put on my LED headlamp and went out to my shop to retrieve a tire patch kit, a compressed air carry can, and the hand truck. I removed the wheel and noticed that the pinch cap that held it on was nearly rusted through. I got my drill, a good bit, and some oil, and in about 10 minutes, had a hole through the axle I could put a cotter pin through to hold the wheel on once I had the tire repaired. As it turned out, the problem with the inner tube was at the base of the valve stem. Had I done that when removing the tube? In any case, it wasn't a location conducive to repair. I'd have to get a new tube. I wouldn't be able to use the hand truck today.

As it turned out, using two dock carts at each end, we got everything home and stashed in the studio. After lunch, Yvonne left for her knitting group at the Deer Harbor Community Club, and I got back to coding, barely noticing the outside world. Near dark, Yvonne came home and began crashing around in the kitchen. I thought it had to do with something she was cooking, but when I came out of my den for dinner, what was stored in the kitchen pantry and the west side cabinets was all stacked on two tables and the floor of the dining room. She doesn't waste any time.

032: Using our studio-from-garage studio for storage

At dinner, we talked a bit more about Tom Temple, the owner of one of the other two full-time occupied houses on the island. I was a bit irritated, perhaps unjustly. I had succeeded him as the head of the water committee, and he had retired from the Board. I was now the responsible party and had been working with the Board and Gary Sale, the Water System Manager, an outside, contracted position. But now Tom seemed to be butting in. He was going after Joe Wolford, a contractor doing some work on the Anderson property, including pressure washing, forbidden during the dry season but not now in the rainy season, and talking about checking the Anderson water meter and suggesting to Gary that time be added to the pumping cycle. Wasn't that my job? And then I was copied on an email from our bookkeeper after Tom inquired about the status of two invoices he'd sent to two homeowners for the installation of standpipes, something that I, as water chairman and now also treasurer, hadn't heard anything about. How could that make sense? Wolford was also doing some burning on the construction/clean-up site and was staying there overnight to monitor the fire, but Tom saw that he was burning old lumber and, through Dan Smith, the Island safety expert, got the county involved. Their rule: no burning of milled lumber. It would have to be taken by truck, on a barge to Orcas, and then dumped at the transfer station. How was this Tom's business?

I first met Tom on January 9th, 2007, when we moved to Crane, and he had been very helpful that day. I'd been his understudy on the water system for three years, and he'd been helpful in that role as well. But almost from the beginning, he complained about and told stories about his neighbor, two doors down, Jim Johansen. Jim cut live trees on community property without permission. He picked up rocks with his tractor from all over the island. He buried a water line without letting Gary check it first, and there had been a leak that wasted the island's water supply. He wasn't reporting and paying fees for all the concrete and other trucks he'd had come to the island. And "he has it in for" Tom. Why? Tom doesn't know. He befriended Jim when he first came to Crane, but then when Tom reported the rock thefts and it got back to Jim, Jim had been bitter since and turned against him. He was sure Jim had injured a tree on Tom's property and had put nails in his tires in the Orcas parking lot, not once but several times. Tom feared for his personal safety. Maybe Jim was a little crazy. Tom thought he had been a drug addict and that was the reason he was suffering from hepatitis C. And Jim would fly into a rage if provoked. A dangerous character. What did I know? And so I mostly stayed away from Jim and his wife Nancy, though they seemed pleasant and very helpful to the island community.

About a year ago, when Jim and Nancy were in Mazatlán for the winter, Tom reported finding a piece of 4" pipe lying against Jim's boat trailer wheel. Tom suspected that Jim had stolen it from the locked pipe shed by cutting a section off of a longer section in inventory, and when he took the piece back to the shed, the cut marks matched. Jim had a shed on skids that was a few feet too close to neighbor Doug Rosenberg's lot line, and though Doug didn't care, Tom did, and he was after the Board to insist that Jim empty it out and move it six feet away from the lot line. Because of the rocks problem, the pipe theft problem, some suspicious unaccounted-for water loss in the spur line Jim and Tom both used about the time that Jim and Nancy returned from Mexico, Tom insisted that the Board take a stand and confront Jim. Neither Jason, the Board president, nor I believe that confrontation is the best way to deal with people in a small community, but in May, Jason, Tom, and I walked over to Jim's and asked him if he knew anything about unaccounted-for water loss in the system near his property since he got back.

Jim knew what that meant. He was being accused of stealing. It became clear to me and to Jason immediately that Jim had no idea why he was being accused — if politely — and everything that Tom had told me about Jim seemed now clearly irrelevant, misleading, imagined, or a lie. I have no idea whether Jim had taken rock from community property. He probably had, but though Tom would have it otherwise, Jim is not an evil person. A week later when Jim, Nancy, Steve Kyle, and I sat outside their cabin for a meeting of the No Wake Committee, Jim and Nancy told me how Tom, once friendly, even a mentor to Jim, had turned on him and they could not fathom why. For some time they had felt isolated and guilty on Crane without knowing why or what to do about it.

In June when Tom would frequently call me complaining about Jim, I talked to a lawyer friend who suggested the Board offer Tom a choice: the Board would hire a retired judge to take evidence and render a decision he'd have to live with or he could shut up and quit complaining. I did, but Tom wouldn't decide; he just found more and more pretexts to complain about Jim — including claiming he feared for his life. Telling him that was a matter for the sheriff, not me and not the Board, and finally that I would no longer listen to his conspiracy theories about Jim, Tom backed off and cooled toward me. I was no longer useful and perhaps had become another enemy. I don't know what will happen in the future, but encouraging Tom isn't good for him, Jim, the Crane Community, or me. Island behavior? Not just island, I think. Too common perhaps.

Thirty-three: Power Watch

"A penny saved is a penny earned" — Benjamin Franklin

Our first winter on Crane, January, February, and March 2007, we spent more than $400 per month on electricity — to power and heat the house. I was in the process of converting the attractive garage — with a beamed, wood-vaulted ceiling — into a studio, loft, bedroom, and pantry. I was using halogen lamps and space heaters, so that was part of the problem, but not having programmable thermostats was probably also an issue.

By late 2007 I wanted to improve our power use efficiency, but I didn't really know where a small effort and expense could pay off best. I read about a device called TED, The Energy Detective, that would monitor house electrical use second by second, keeping a running total by day and month. TED could be set up to know the power company's billing cycle, base charge, and kilowatt-hour rates, and by the end of a billing period could show a total very close to what would eventually appear on the utility bill. At that time, there were two TED versions: the $100 model that was self-contained and the more expensive model that could feed data to a PC to allow detailed spreadsheet analysis. I decided the less expensive model would suffice.

TED was up and running in less than 20 minutes. First, I programmed the corded display unit that would be plugged into a wall receptacle, entering information from our last utility bill (billing period — the 17th to the 17th, base rate - $25, KWH rate - $0.0725). Then I had to take the cover off the circuit box to install the power monitor sending unit that would feed information to the display through the house wiring.

I spent the next several days watching the effect on current use as baseboard heaters turned on and off, the refrigerator cycled, and so on. I used the circuit box to isolate the exact source of any significant power use by flipping off breakers until the power dropped. I could see the effect of the hot tub pump versus the hot tub heating cycle. It was fascinating to watch each device manage itself through the day.

033: Calm water, extraordinary sunrise over Bell Island

Room heating was the principal cause of cold weather power use. The hot tub was relevant but a much smaller consumer. The background rate, caused by all the devices around the house, like clocks and TVs and sleep state computers used about 600 watts per hour or 15 KWHs per day, about $1 per day or $30 per month. During the summer, our electrical bill ran about $100, with $25 as a base or meter fee. That meant that when we were paying $450 per month, about $350 of that went to heating. Surely we could make a dent.

Thirty-three: Power Watch

Two strategies: install programmable thermostats and use wood heat to reduce some of the baseboard heater demand. The non-programmable thermostats, at least 20 years old, left us guessing about where we were really setting the temperature and we had to remember to go around the house setting them up and down during the day. That was a clumsy way to be more efficient. Our lot and the island were covered with trees. We had already had help taking down about ten and another 30 should be removed over time to allow more light to fall on the house, deck, and raised bed vegetable garden on the south side of the house.

The Lux thermostats cost about $42 each and it took 90 minutes to program and swap them in. During the day, most of the house is set to 68; overnight to 62. Yvonne found an 18" Craftsman chainsaw at a Sears scratch and dent store for $110. We were ready to go.

Having come to understand our usage pattern at least in general and acting on that knowledge, I put TED on the shelf until about two weeks ago. During the first round, I kept TED in the kitchen, but Yvonne found the device intrusive. This round I've got TED on my desk where I can glance at it during the day when I'm doing computer work. I've begun to keep a log to record the outside temperature, the day's KWH reading, and the hot tub temperature. I turn the hot tub up to 102 about 7 p.m. and down to 90 about 10 p.m. — assuming that is more efficient than having it stay at 102 continuously. The new cover we got last spring seems to provide better insulation than the old waterlogged cover.

I want to come to understand what the hot tub actually costs to operate per month at different times of the year. I also want to be able to measure the effect of using the wood stove on electrical usage, correlated to outside temperature. Someone, somewhere probably has all this information in general form. I want to know specifically about our house and its weather on Crane. Initial tentative figures show a 35 KWH savings at 42 outside, of about $3 for the day. Not so much. I'll know more as the winter progresses. At least one or two days I'll leave the wood stove cold and compare to days when it's going from 6:00 a.m. to 6:00 p.m. Outside temperatures are often close day to day, and the temperature may vary only two or three degrees in a 24-hour period. I'll do similar testing with the hot tub; leave it at 102 for 24 hours then turn it off for 24 hours and compare usage to the low and high daily setting pattern — with the outside temperature the same and inside usage the same.

Thirty-four: Great Horned Owl

"The family is one of nature's masterpieces." — George Santayana

Before dawn, walking along the road between Becker's field and Clark's cabin in the rising light, a pileated woodpecker, surprisingly large and elegant in his red crest and mustache crossed in front of me, right to left about ten feet off the ground, having emerged from the nature preserve forest and heading toward Clark's and then maybe Guyer's. I've seen them from time to time in our yard, and when they start on a tree, they make a racket you can hear a quarter mile away.

Passing Rocky Road, I saw and cleared a dead 10-foot Noble fir the night's wind had toppled to Circle Road. Around the other side of the island, I stopped at Brunner's camp to drain the bathhouse water system, as Matt had asked in an email since he couldn't come up from Seattle as planned because of a bad outboard engine. Some houses on Crane border on the fancy. Matt's camp is more basic: a large treehouse about 20 feet up, a platform tent, and an open bathhouse — two showers, a toilet, and three sinks. He hadn't drained the bathhouse water system, intending to over the weekend but couldn't. I opened the sink and shower faucets so the lines would drain. Four hose bibs sticking out from the bathhouse — and one with a hose connected. That didn't look promising. After unscrewing the hose, I found I couldn't turn the knob — likely it was frozen and would have to be replaced. Water dripping from a second hose bib I'd opened quickly formed an ice stalagmite below; it had been close to freezing. Before he could use his system again, Matt would need to make some plumbing repairs.

Thirty-four: Great Horned Owl

034: Soggy, fallen big leaf maple leaves

Crossing the airstrip on Old Road, I saw a Great Horned Owl come out of the woods in front of me to the left and fly across the north end of the airstrip struggling to carry something pretty large — brown I thought and probably a squirrel. Do squirrels come and go from Crane when they feel the need by swimming across Pole Pass? Were squirrels stranded on Crane when the sea rose as the massive glaciers that carved the channels between the San Juan Islands melted? Are the squirrels that come around our house from time to time their descendants?

Thirty-four: Great Horned Owl

Coming through the trees that shield our yard from the north, I saw a squirrel dart through Yvonne's deer fence and scamper up the Douglas fir that dominates our front yard. A primrose, close to the house, seemed unconcerned about the cold air but the tuberous begonias had fainted and fallen over after blooming all fall.

Grandson Jackson, five years old, called about 9:00 and told me many things I didn't understand, and then Kristin was on, and I could hear Maddie and Jackson in the background. Eric and family would soon be on their way to Santa Barbara to meet up with Uncle James, Uncle Keith, and Auntie Corrina, who was staying in LA with James before heading to India. Rain would keep the group from the zoo, and they'd see the Natural History Museum instead, after lunch together. The sad news from Kristin, and not unexpected, was that Katie, who at times would have qualified as the world's most neurotic dog, was on her last legs, literally. Sweet but crazy, over the years, Katie had destroyed furniture, wood trim, doors, screens, and windows, climbed 10-foot chain-link fences, jumped out second-story windows, and led our mild-mannered Samantha on one breakout adventure after another. After rescuing Katie from the pound, Eric and Kristin had been unreservedly loyal and paid bill after bill, but Katie's clock had run out.

Yvonne called from the ferry line in Anacortes to tell me she'd be on the 1:55 non-stop ferry. Jeni had arranged a mother-daughter karaoke night at the Bush Garden restaurant in Seattle's International District for Saturday night, first hosting the group at her Harbor Steps apartment. Yvonne and Jeni, Julie and Katie, and Kathy and Justine. Probably because of rain and threatened snow, the restaurant was lightly attended so they could sing as much as they wanted — leading off with *Do Run Run*. In photos from the event, Jeni looked particularly lovely and excused herself late in the evening for a texted-in date. Katie, by far the youngest in the group, at 23, was attracted to the DJ's nephew, and after a few drinks, she disappeared upstairs, later retrieved by Julie at 1:00 a.m. when the older people started to drag. Some video fragments await viewing on our camera — that Yvonne took along at my encouragement. While Yvonne, her childhood girlfriends, and their daughters partied, I stayed home, worked, defrosted some frozen spaghetti sauce, and watched the newest version of Clash of the Titans, the Perseus, Io, Medusa story. Great myth — not improved in this telling — but wonderful nonetheless.

Thirty-five: Freezing Point

"It is not light that we need, but fire; it is not the gentle shower, but thunder. We need the storm, the whirlwind, and the earthquake." — Frederick Douglass

I was staring at my computer screen and suddenly that's all I could see. I was having some kind of weird blackout. It was about 5:00 p.m., the wind outside was noisy though not quite howling, I was sitting on the floor with the wood stove at my back. Yvonne was in the kitchen fixing dinner, at least I thought she was but now I couldn't see her or hear the television she had been watching. I had gone into another, computer-only dimension.

Well, not exactly. The power had gone out and now Yvonne was beginning to speak up about the inconvenience. We could see no lights on Orcas or Shaw; the outage was not confined to Crane. That was good news since the OPALCO crew would be able to get to the source of the problem and they'd have plenty of motivation. Out came the candles and our fluorescent lantern. I brought in more firewood from the front porch and stoked the fire. There was no telling how long the power would be out. I put on a warm jacket, knit hat, and headlamp and towed our dock cart over to a stack of firewood outside the gate, filled the cart, brought it to the porch and replenished the stacked supply we had been using for the last week. Yvonne put on her head lamp and went back to fixing dinner, the heat source unproblematic because though the oven was electric, the stove top was propane and we had a 10 gallon backup bottle.

As I came into the house, Yvonne reported that Wilma had called and that Gary wanted to talk to me and would call a little later. Our one old-fashioned line-powered telephone had rung while I was out and it took Yvonne a while to think where and what the sound was she heard. The other phones hadn't rung because they had lost power and needed it to operate. Wilma said that Gary was concerned about the pipes in the well houses freezing. It had happened two years back, temporarily compromising the system. He had been on

Thirty-five: Freezing Point

Crane earlier in the day and had turned on the heat lamps in each well house but that wouldn't help protect the pipes with the electricity out. We ate dinner by candlelight.

036: Flicker stares into the empyrean

When Gary called he said Wilma had asked him whether he had lit the catalytic propane heaters in the well houses when he was on Crane as well as turning on the heat lamps. He said he hadn't thought of it. Would I go out in the wind and cold and light the propane heaters now? Of course. He explained how to light these efficient devices and said that a five-gallon propane

Thirty-five: Freezing Point

bottle would power a heater for five days and that some well houses had spare bottles.

Right after I hung up, Dan Smith was on the line, worried about the water in the foam delivery system perched on a platform extending out in front of the Ford Expedition Crane Fire and Rescue vehicle. The 20-gallon water tank paired with the compressed air tank could create and blow foam equivalent to 250 gallons of water, the capacity of our pumper fire truck but much more mobile. He was worried as well about the pumper — in the garage at the community center but with the garage door open. Could I open the water tank on the F&R vehicle so freezing wouldn't crack the tank and then put a light bulb under the red canvas cover that protected the compressed air foam system and close the garage door and turn up the thermostat for when the power came back on? Sure. Two sets of dark-time projects. Would Yvonne come along to keep me company? Sure — provided we drove the F&R vehicle and she could stay inside out of the roaring wind and bitter cold. Why hadn't I thought of the F&R vehicle? I imagined us making the mile-and-a-half walk around the island. Why? Yvonne asked if I would be bringing any tools. No, I wouldn't need any. I was just going to turn on propane heaters.

Before we left and while the island phone system had power I called Lou Falb, an older gentleman who lived in an A-frame at the other end of the island with his miniature wiener dog who one day had flown out the second story window chasing a dragon fly and somehow landed in the grass outside unharmed. Was Lou OK? Warm enough without power? Yes, he had a wood stove and plenty of wood — and thanks for thinking about him.

I put on my warmest parka and lighted by our two headlamps — mine intermittently even though I had put in new batteries the day before — we walked into the wind, across the Ochs' meadow to the dock parking lot and Yvonne removed the two parking cones behind F&R vehicle while I opened the hood to turn the battery switch on and we were off to the community center and well house #1 next to it. I turned up the heat thermostat in the fire truck garage and after untying the rope that held the door open to the top of the frame so the truck could exit the garage without wrecking the door, I pulled the door down to the ground and we drove on, turning into the Becker's driveway and then left to get close to well house #1. Gary had warned me that the combination lock was frozen (he had told me the combination because I didn't know it) and that earlier in the day he'd had to go through the win-

Thirty-five: Freezing Point

dow. And so did I. Inside the old structure that once housed a wooden tank on beams above the now-enclosed pumping station, I opened the insulated doors, found the propane tank and heater and got it going without much trouble. The trick of course was to create a pilot flame with the piezo circuit by clicking the switch on and off and continuing to hold the heater switch in the start position until the element in the flame turned red. Otherwise, the heater would turn itself off as soon as the switch was turned from the starting to operating position. No problem. The heater surface soon began glowing red and after a minute or so I turned the gas supply switch to a midway position and the red glow continued to grow. In business.

On to the next well house in our circuit, #4. No problem. The heater was lit. Then to well house #3 at the west end of the island. Yvonne continued to sit in the vehicle, managing the heater and defroster and saying encouraging things when I came in out of the wind and cold, like "Great!, Where to next, Cap'n?" As I fumbled with the combination lock on the well house door on the backside of the well house, away from Circle Road, I saw a glow of light through the crack between door and frame. During our odyssey, the island power had come back on. Great! But I would light the heater anyway. What if the power went off again? Inside I tried to light the heater but it wouldn't start. The tank, too light, was empty. And I couldn't hook up the spare because — I didn't have any tools.

On to well house #2, up the hill on Old Road and across from the Hawkes'. Another empty tank and a full spare I couldn't connect. On to well house #6 — but it requires a key — no combination lock. The key, I remembered was in the water supply room in the community center building. Well house #5 was 50 yards away and I lit the heater there. Batting 500. Back in the F&R vehicle, Yvonne suggested I take her home so she could work on protecting her worm ranch in her shop (they needed at least 40 degrees to thrive and without heat on a night like this would likely freeze to death) and she needed to move and cover some of her plants. The winter crop of lettuce was already toast.

I grabbed two large adjustable crescent wrenches from my shop, headed back to the water storage room to get the key to #6, drove to #3 and then #2 to swap empty for full tanks and start the heaters. At #6, after starting the heater, I found I couldn't get the key out of the lock to return to the water storage room. Oh well, it wasn't likely anyone (who else was on the island besides

Yvonne and Lou and me?) would try to break in. My hands were very stiff and cold but didn't hurt the way they would have when I was younger. Small mercies. Home again I left the F&R vehicle close to a power supply post in the yard, got a trouble light/extension cord from Yvonne, and found an incandescent light bulb in the supply of inefficient bulbs I'd replaced with fluorescent versions all over the house last spring, screwed it into the trouble light receptacle and left the lighted bulb under the CAFS on the front of the F&R vehicle and then called Gary and then Dan to report the completion of my tasks.

Yvonne wanted to watch a documentary on John Lennon. I fell asleep halfway through. Out to the hot tub in the icy wind with an icy deck underneath, Yvonne hooting from stimulus overload. A bright moon and a long cigar-shaped ghostly white cloud directly overhead moving ever so slowly south. The north wind, Boreas, roaring through the grove of pencil-thin forty-foot firs outside the deer fence waving like tall blades of grass with tasseled ends. Were we in any danger, Yvonne asked. I don't know but isn't it wonderful?

Thirty-six: Chocolate Pudding Cake

"Little by little, a little becomes a lot." — *Tanzanian proverb*

At my desk at 3:42 a.m. Cold outside, 21 degrees, but the wind had lessened a bit. TED read 159 KWH used since midnight. That wasn't possible. The two-hour power loss yesterday followed by a 10-second loss late in the evening must have scrambled TED's memory, and it didn't know a new day had started but was carrying over accumulated use from the day before. My goal was to create a Kindle version of the annotated Slocum book Chris and I had been working on to give to David for his Kindle before he and Maxine left Orcas to get the train to Portland for Thanksgiving. David could read the book — with annotations — and critique their usefulness and clarity — and make suggestions for additional passages that could profit from annotations. By 7:15, I had sent the ebook file to David and to Chris and was off the critical path, where I prefer to be most of the time.

While I sat by the wood stove in the living room catching up on my email and web news reading, Yvonne did the same in her studio. The day before, when I was programming most of the day, Yvonne had emptied more of the kitchen drawers and cupboards, stacking everything on tables and the floor in the dining room. Easier to find things when they're all sitting out, visible, but not very attractive. When she removed all the cream-colored kitchen cabinet doors, the dark oak frames and shelves were exposed, making the kitchen much darker and by evening, in the artificial light, some of the shelves were almost invisible in the gloom. Clearly, the kitchen needed light, not dark cabinet door fronts — exactly what Yvonne had picked out at IKEA.

Later in the morning, I bundled up and went out front to split firewood. I found that the tarp had blown off the northernmost wood stack, and part of the north layer had fallen to the ground. Mischief wind. I had brought one cart full — picked from a stack of split wood — to the house the night before when the power had failed, and I was concerned about having to heat the whole

Thirty-six: Chocolate Pudding Cake

house all the time with wood. I split and filled another cart — so that made two since the last porch replenishment ten days before. I noticed or thought I did, that the wood was easier to split at 25 degrees than it had been at 40 or 50.

036: A little nap is always a good idea

After lunch, Yvonne sat on the floor in the living room by the bay windows facing the water and worked on a sewing project. Two fabric patterns — she said she needed a third. She cut sections from a Kwix Sew pattern and ironed them on the carpet to make them flat. She had two patterns, one for granddaughter Opal and one for Opal's American Girl doll. A Christmas present in the making.

Thirty-six: Chocolate Pudding Cake

I sat, again, in my favorite chair by the fire and caught up on the news online and found myself dozing. To the couch for a real nap — while Yvonne continued with her sewing project. What a pleasure.

At dinner, we discussed the kitchen remodel project — which would begin in earnest after we returned from our Thanksgiving visit to our son Noah and family on Harstine Island, on the Olympic Peninsula. I thought we might be able to start the remodeling on the north wall first — since it was independent of the rest of the kitchen — and then put away what belonged there. Then the west wall, with the refrigerator, the east wall with the range, and the south wall with the sink and dishwasher last, since we wanted the least possible disruption to our water and cleanup functions. That made sense to Yvonne. We both looked forward to getting started. A tentative goal — a usable new kitchen by the holidays when James and Keith and maybe Jeni and others would be at the house. Perhaps we could have the measuring for the countertops done by then, though the countertops installed would be well into January if not later.

Chocolate pudding cake for dessert. All is well in the world.

Emails from Chris. He had been reading our new version of Slocum's *Sailing Alone Around the World* and was eager to begin revising his annotations. Could I send him the database and the software to make changes and create new versions of the book to review? Yes, but I'd have to make some changes to the software, for instance, to make assigning annotations a type optional rather than mandatory. By 8:00 he had his kit, and Yvonne and I could watch the *Oxford Murders* streaming from Netflix, in bed after warming up in the hot tub. The WiFi was too slow in the bedroom, so I connected my computer via an Ethernet cable to the DSL modem. By changing to CenturyLink, we had supposedly improved our Internet transmission rate by 50%, but it was still much slower than what people in the cities are used to. We were running on a telephone line, after all, not on coax or fiber. An interesting movie, the opening scene, a lecture by John Hurt playing a professor talking about Wittgenstein, just my cup of tea.

Thirty-seven: To Harstine Island We Go

"Over the river and through the woods...." — *Lydia Maria Child*

We left the house at 7:00 for the 8:55 Anacortes Ferry and managed to carry everything without needing a dock cart. I had set all the thermostats down to 62, turned off the water at the meter, and closed the propane tank. Light but cloudy and wintry. At the ferry landing, Yvonne got some coffee and a day-old danish. I had a cup of tea and a day-old scone. Yvonne picked up the *Seattle Times* and *Islands Sounder* at the Orcas Village Store, and I got a sandwich for lunch. Not many people on the ferry today, the day before Thanksgiving.

In the weak morning light as the ferry cruised toward the Lopez Island ferry landing, Orcas Island, to the north, was black and white, green firs and cedars absorbing what light there was and giving none back, and snow-covered open patches, meadows, giving almost all the light back. East Sound and Olga to the right; Obstruction Island and Peavine Pass farther to the right, and then the mass of Blakely Island, a private community with its own airstrip, and so like Crane Island but on a different scale. A barge carrying a fuel truck with a trailer cruised along south of our ferry.

The front page of the *Islands Sounder* featured the successful Food Bank building drive and included a photo of Hillary and Larry and a percent-of-completion meter. Now within AT&T signal range, I attempted to re-subscribe to AT&T on our iPad but had apparently forgotten the password. We'd have to stop at Starbucks in Anacortes where I could use my Mac Powerbook to pick up an email from AT&T giving me a new password. After digesting the newspapers, Yvonne turned to her knitting, and I to my writing.

As I drove south, Yvonne napped until Everett and then put together the lunch provisions. Entering the ferry line at Edmonds at about 12:10, we were a few minutes late for the 12:05 to Kingston, but with the ferries running about every 40 minutes, the next one wasn't long in coming.

Thirty-seven: To Harstine Island We Go

037: Crimson sunrise over Bell Island

We had a shopping list for Safeway in Belfair, about 35 minutes north of Harstine Island, and while Yvonne shopped, I got the oil changed across the street, an efficiency not possible on Orcas. North of Bremerton, we had seen trees down, flattened by Tuesday night winds. In the voicemail Yvonne picked up from Natasha in Edmonds, our daughter-in-law told us that the Washington State Department of Transportation road status web page had shown slowdowns for Route 3, on our route to Harstine. When Yvonne checked with the iPad, Route 3 had all been cleared up. More patches of flattened trees south of Belfair. Later I would see scavengers with chainsaws and trailers picking up the firewood that would heat their homes — conveniently available along the highway.

Once we left Route 3 for Harstine Island, the road turned icy but had been sanded. At Noah and Natasha's house on Pickering Passage, Morgan and Natasha helped us unload the car. A warm, welcoming house, fire flickering from the woodstove, the kids laughing, playing, hugs all around. Yvonne made a spaghetti dinner and then chocolate pudding cake. Opal told us stories non-stop. Noah and I talked about house projects, and later the adults caught up in the living room but by 9:30 could barely keep our eyes open.

Thirty-eight: Thanksgiving Dinner

"For each new morning with its light,
  For rest and shelter of the night,
  For health and food, for love and friends,
  For everything Thy goodness sends."
  — *Ralph Waldo Emerson*

Out of bed a bit after 8:00 — a longer sleep than I'd had in years. A bustle of activity downstairs, the aroma of turkey roasting. Son Noah walking the dogs. Nine-year-old grandson Morgan on the computer wearing earphones and watching skateboarding videos. Overnight the temperature had risen into the mid-30s. Yvonne began working on the stuffing. At 9:30, I left for the Bremerton ferry to pick up Jeni and Yvonne's brother Ron who would be on their way over from Seattle. The ice on the road out of Harstine Island had softened overnight and wasn't as slick as it had been the evening before. A good sign.

Four huge aircraft carriers were parked at the Puget Sound Naval Shipyard in Bremerton, imposing presences next to the road coming into the city from the south. Looking more forlorn and abandoned than impressive and threatening, the carriers waited patiently for the attention they weren't obviously getting. A busy Starbucks next to the quiet ferry terminal. Jeni, in a yellow and gray flowered coat, and Ron in a dark overcoat and Tam O'Shanter with red trim soon walked up the gangway, standing out from the more conservatively attired arriving passengers. I got updates from each, hearing about Jeni's plan to work part-time at Northwest Hospital assisting Dr. Bloomquist, who was leaving Swedish for an environment he felt was more favorable to his patients. Adrienna was back in Seattle for the holidays and had another semester at Carnegie Mellon in the International Studies master's program. Childhood friend Kirstin would be coming from Colorado for several days to visit Jeni in the Emerald City. Ron talked about the business development,

Thirty-eight: Thanksgiving Dinner

marketing efforts he would initiate soon to build his acupuncture practice at the clinic in Seattle he had signed on with.

Back on Harstine Island with Jeni and Ron, Natasha's brother Justin arrived with five-year-old Hope and three-year-old Hunter, now with the legal custody he had sought and won but also overwhelmed by the practicalities of managing the day-to-day welfare of two small children while struggling to make ends meet. Natasha's brother Seth arrived not long after, from Bend, Oregon, with 16-month-old Taylor, his dark-haired, pink-cheeked daughter he now had legal custody of as well. Less equipped than Justin even, Seth was determined to do well by the daughter he hadn't expected to have. The two mothers, off and on lost to drugs, couldn't be trusted to care for their children, and the young men stepped up to duties they hadn't sought and for which they had little preparation. Then Natasha's father Gene and partner Laronge and then Natasha's mother Jan arrived.

A solid turkey dinner, mashed potatoes, rolls, cranberry, stuffing, and salad, with some helping themselves to seconds or maybe thirds, and the kids to dessert. Justin left temporarily to take Hope and Hunter to their mother for a visit. The rest of us put on our shoes and coats, and we headed out the door for a settling walk to the State Park half a mile away. Noah with McKinley, a huge black mixed breed, and Sugar, a bull terrier on their leads, Morgan on his bicycle wearing his Orcas Island Camp Orkila billed cap. Still some snow here and there, ice on the roads, very quiet, with no cars or a sign of other people.

In the camping area at the state park, an open area, once an orchard, five deer — two does and yearlings, and a single doe, stood under the apple trees, one dangling hundreds of green and red, frosted over treats. The deer didn't budge, even with the dogs nearby. They wanted something, and Morgan was the first to try to get it for them. First, he tried climbing the tree carrying the most bounty, then pulling low-hanging branches. Gene and Laronge joined in, and soon a handful of apples dropped to the ground. Morgan tossed them in the direction of the deer, who had backed about 30 feet out of the way, and they quickly went to work on their Thanksgiving feast. More bough shaking and more apples down and served. The group flowed down to the path to the park dock in the cove. Morgan and five-year-old granddaughter Opal looked for sea tubes while the others milled idly on the dock. Across the way at the marina, smoke rose and trailed from a green-hulled sailboat where someone was serving Thanksgiving dinner.

Thirty-eight: Thanksgiving Dinner

038: Deer at their Thanksgiving feast in Jarrell Cove State Park

Justin returned soon after the rest of us, now with enough room for dessert: pumpkin, apple, and chocolate cream pie and whipped cream. Before dinner, Opal had us each write down our answer to the question, "What are you thankful for," and now she directed us to read the answers, drawn randomly from a wooden bowl. Three were especially poignant: from Justin, Seth, and Natasha. The young men acknowledged the love and help of their family; Natasha, the joy at having a niece and nephew to care for three days a week while Justin worked, and for Morgan and Opal.

Thirty-eight: Thanksgiving Dinner

In the living room, it was time for "Hide the Dime," a game I remembered from Cub Scouts and began to share this September. We had a wonderful time playing it with Noah, Natasha, Morgan, and Opal when we stayed with them on our way to California. The dime must be in plain sight, not hidden in any way and not requiring anything to be moved for anyone to spot it. When you see the dime, you delay sitting near the hider so the rest of the group can't guess where you saw the dime. If the search drags on, the hider can give clues. Yvonne saw Natasha's dime first, so she hid the dime next, then Opal, then Morgan. Ready to try something else, Morgan brought blank sheets of paper and pencils to the living room, and we did two rounds of "He Said, She Said," a game Natasha had introduced to us a few years ago. At the top of the sheet, you write a man's name or a male character's name that everyone would know and then fold the paper over so that the name isn't visible. When everyone is finished and folded their sheet they pass it to the person on their right, who adds a female name, folds the paper, and passes it on. Then a place is added, what he said, what she replied, what he said next and then what she said. The finished sheets, now folded to thin strips, are passed once more and then read, one by one, by whoever holds them. The names and phrases, written without an overall plan, have an uncanny way of turning into amusing stories more often than unrelated lists. Everything, if you look hard enough, is a story.

Yvonne had talked briefly to James, who with Keith, had Kiri, Lauren, and one of their friends up from San Diego for the holiday. Their turkey was taking a long time; 90 minutes longer than James had planned. His first turkey. Yvonne advised up to 20 minutes per pound. No reply from Eric, Kristin, and family hosting three other couples for the day.

Then I drove Jeni and Ron back to the Bremerton ferry, Jeni carrying a foil-covered paper plate with leftovers back home to Harbor Steps and looking forward to sleep and some weekend fun with her friends. Back on Harstine, the day trippers gone, Noah, Natasha, Yvonne, and I talked about the day, family and friends in Colorado, politics, gold and silver, the predicted collapse of the global economy, men as single parents, and Franzen's *Freedom*. Eyes slamming shut, we dragged ourselves upstairs and to bed.

Thirty-nine: Gig Harbor Field Trip

"An hour with your grandchildren can make you feel young again. Anything longer, however, and you start aging quickly." — Gene Perret

At about 9:30, we loaded Morgan and Opal into the van. I had vacuumed it at Yvonne's suggestion and then put the middle seats back in place after having removed them the week before to make adequate space for transporting the kitchen cabinets from IKEA) and headed for Gig Harbor, about 45 minutes away in the direction of Tacoma. Cloudy, occasional sun breaks, and more often intermittent rain.

Opal quickly got us started with the "I spy with my little eye something" fill in a color "inside/outside the car." Yellow, green, blue, white, black, red, orange, in endless succession. Sometimes hints were required. The successful guess won making the next challenge. After 15 minutes, Opal announced a change: we would now say a letter, the letter being the first in the word describing what it was we spied. She had added a spelling dimension to the game — our five-year-old granddaughter. After only a few rounds, both Opal and Morgan were stumping us with their puzzles. Even with hints, Yvonne and I failed to come up with the answers.

In Gig Harbor, we quickly found the Harbor Museum, first on our iPad and then in the flesh. Opened in September 2010, it is a first-class area historical museum and the kids were as interested as we were. A special exhibit described the history of the Tacoma Narrows bridges, especially "Galloping Gertie," at the time the world's third-longest span suspension bridge that twisted itself apart in a 40 mph wind a few months after opening in 1940. We especially enjoyed understanding how Europeans began coming in the mid-1800s, living peacefully beside the Puyallup, first logging and creating mills, then fishing and shipbuilding, and farming, with Puget Sound the water highway that connected isolated settlers with one another. A one-room school on-site

Thirty-nine: Gig Harbor Field Trip

and the Shenandoah, a retired wooden fishing boat that had frequented the San Juan's a century ago and its then bountiful fishing banks.

039.1: Yvonne, Morgan, and Opal exploring Gig Harbor Historical Museum

We drove up and down Harbor Drive letting the kids make their choice for lunch, which turned out to be Spiro's, a family-run Italian restaurant. They wanted pizza and ate a whole small four-cheese pizza between them. Well, actually Yvonne had one piece. At the theater, in the new mall, a few miles away, we settled in to watch "Tangled," an animated Pixar musical retelling of Rapunzel, in 3-D. We loved it. Then ice cream at Ben & Jerry's and the drive home. This time we played the alphabet game, trying to find the letters of the

Thirty-nine: Gig Harbor Field Trip

alphabet in order as the first letter in a word on a sign. By the time we got close to the turnoff from Route 3 to go to Harstine Island, the group had resorted to cheating. Yvonne wrote an "X" on a piece of paper, and then pulled out her driver's license and Morgan made a "Z" with his fingers.

039.2: A little treat

The new Highlander was gone! Noah and Natasha weren't home yet, and a note inside said they were on an adventure, couldn't predict when they would be home, and that we should go about our business and not worry about them. The opportunity Yvonne and I hoped they would take. Yvonne got out the leftovers, and the kids helped me start a fire in the wood stove, the house's source of heat, and find food for McKinley and Sugar. Then the front door opened, and Noah and Natasha were home. Why should they spend money and go out to dinner, Natasha said, when there was delicious Thanksgiving turkey, gravy, mashed potatoes, and rolls at home. We were all happy they were home.

After dinner, Morgan demonstrated some new skateboard moves he was perfecting after having reviewed videos on YouTube. Then it was time for "Crazy 8's," Opal's first exposure to the game and to playing cards and suits. Noah and I tied for the lowest scores, especially satisfying because Yvonne and Natasha are merciless card players. A round of "Pig," and then "Spoon," its sibling. For both games, a deck is created of as many fours-of-a-kind as players and then dealt. The dealer calls "Pass" every so often when everyone is ready and each player passes on a card to the left, trying to create a four-of-a-kind in her hand. The first player with four-of-a-kind puts her finger to her nose, subtly, and the other players do the same as they see the move. The last person with a finger to nose is Pig. Spoons work the same way except after the deal spoons are laid on the table, one less than the number of players. The first with four-of-a-kind grabs a spoon. The player without a spoon loses.

The kids to bed and then conversation as we slumped toward bedtime. Tomorrow we would be going home to Crane Island.

Forty: Home Again, Home Again

"The magic thing about home is that it feels good to leave, and it feels even better to come back." — Wendy Wunder, *The Probability of Miracles*

A happy morning household. Natasha thought they'd spend some time with her mother, Jan, probably shopping. Morgan was last up. It's hardest for him to get up and he'd been up late. Opal was singing and dancing as usual. Somewhat reluctantly we left their warmth and headed north to Kingston for the ferry to Edmonds. On the ferry I wrote and drank tea in the galley and Yvonne stayed in the car to knit. Did I detect the odor of urine in the galley. I tried to ignore it while I tapped on my Mac's keyboard.

Costco was next, for Christmas presents and supplies to take back to the island. With limited shopping on Orcas more planning is required than where a variety of stores is close by. I dropped Yvonne off at the door and filled the Freestar's tank, an important strategy because gasoline cost about $.75 per gallon more on Orcas than at Costco so we always tried to have a mostly full tank when we got on the ferry. Costco was crowded, but Yvonne said less so than other Costco's. Lines formed at some of the food sample stations. It was noon but Costco made sure no one had to interrupt shopping to sustain themselves.

In the ferry line, I read our first draft of *Sailing Alone* and took notes about what we needed to fix and what additional passages might benefit from annotations. Yvonne took a nap. On the ferry, I got back to my writing and Yvonne her knitting.

Suzanne Olson appeared, like us, on her way back from America and we talked about the Unitarian service the next day, with Larry Shaw and Tom Murdock coming from the Orcas Island Food Bank to explain its role, needs, and the current building fund drive. We also talked about our sagging attendance and energy. The UU's would be responsible for the Food Bank lunch Tuesday, which happened every fifth Tuesday of a month, and Yvonne, the

Forty: Home Again, Home Again

coordinator for our group, had little response to her email asking for help. Maybe the UU group couldn't manage to continue providing Food Bank lunches beyond next spring.

040: Stormy sunrise over Bell Island

In near dark in the Crane dock parking lot on Orcas we saw Gary's truck and then Gary with a dock cart full of empty or near empty five-gallon propane tanks. He had turned off the catalytic heaters I'd turned on Monday night and was taking the tanks in for refills. He wanted to get a few new tanks so that there would be at least two in each well house. Good idea. What about the possible leak that seemed to show up in last month's water usage report, an unaccounted-for 12,000 gallons? Lou Falb had some plumbing problems that were being fixed but needed pipe cement — but that wasn't the problem, Gary said. A contractor had somehow used or wasted 10,000 gallons. Though I didn't say so at the time, that was a problem but not THE problem since that water had gone through a meter. The problem was accounting for water that had been pumped but wasn't in the tank and hadn't gone through a meter. Once Wilma did the meter readings Wednesday and Gary reported them we could see whether November had a similar loss to October. Then we would have to figure out what to do about it.

A little light lingered in the western sky. We had left the clouds behind when we passed Thatcher Pass and entered San Juan County. We could see clouds to the west, south, and north. We were in the rain shadow of the Olympics today for sure. It must have been a beautiful day in the islands. Heading away from the Crane dock on Orcas, the calm water, reflecting the sky, made it unnecessary to use the spotlight on Margaret's boat until we neared Pole Pass. One cartload and some to carry and we got everything home, except the tarps we had bought at Costco to cover the kitchen cabinets we'd begin removing and store next to the house on the covered walk to the front stairs. We hoped someone on the island would want to take them. There was no way we would carry them off Crane.

I turned on the water and propane and took the thermostats off their 62-degree hold settings, raised the hot tub setting to 102 and added some shock and chlorine. Yvonne fried some potatoes and made a cheese, tomato, green onion, feta cheese omelet — and then I finished the chocolate pudding cake we'd left covered on the counter before heading south. We were home again.

Forty-one: Disappointment

"The meaning of life is to find your gift. The purpose of life is to give it away." — Pablo Picasso

A beautiful late November morning. A walk around the island shows the effects of wind — someone has cleared a tree from Circle Road. Small branches — alive and dead — litter the ground, noticeable in our yard and on our decks. Last week's cold weather has decimated Yvonne's fall planting. The lettuce, that looked so good ten days ago is withered and comatose. I moved the Fire and Rescue vehicle from our yard back to its station by the community dock; its compressed air foam system water reservoir no longer needed a 100-watt bulb lit underneath to keep it from freezing. The island water tank level, after Gary had put more time on the well #5 and #6 pumps was up to 11 1/2 feet, more cushion against an unexpected gang of visitors or other heavy use.

Sparse attendance at the Unitarian Universalist Fellowship service focused on the Orcas Food Bank — in part probably because some people were still gone for the Thanksgiving holiday but also because fewer people could attend or wanted to. Tom Murdock, Food Bank board member, who was attending with Larry Shaw, Food Bank president told me before the service that the Episcopal Church in Eastsound had a similar problem. Time was taking the older members, and young people with families tended to go to the Community Church, which because it was non-denominational, could serve, without much controversy, people coming from a variety of Protestant denominations.

Yvonne introduced Larry and Tom to the group, providing background to our congregation. Larry focused on numbers and Tom on the need for a maintenance fund for the new building. In 2010, 268 families had asked for and received aid at the Food Bank, about 10% of the Orcas Island population, a shocking number. Each week about 80 families were served compared with 25 per week a year ago. Since the Food Bank isn't the exclusive source of food for the island's hungry, the real number of struggling families may be much higher.

Tom repeatedly quoted the Bible and Buddha, sprinkling his text with the word God, not often heard in our Unitarian Universalist group. When he talked with Yvonne beforehand and it was clear he didn't know anything about Unitarianism, she told him he could use whatever language he wanted. She did not try to explain that Unitarianism has no creed and most Unitarians are theists, atheists, or agnostics as those theological positions are normally understood. His view was that Americans all had the same god; she didn't argue with him.

In the car driving back to the Crane community dock, Yvonne and I talked about our reaction to Tom's language at our meeting. It seemed peculiar. Why? What she heard was defensiveness, not toward us, because Tom didn't understand our perspective but an attempt to justify the Food Bank to Christians. He was giving us the same presentation he had given to Christian groups on Orcas and had felt a need to justify making efforts to feed the hungry because not a few Orcas Christians were adamant in their opposition to the Food Bank and public and private charity generally; it was a moral hazard, making people lazy and irresponsible. If people didn't have money and food to eat that was their fault and it shouldn't be condoned in any way. The Food Bank does no means testing; there are no hoops to jump through. Anyone who comes to the door will be fed. So some Christians considered it suspect.

Back to our kitchen remodel.

After lunch, we started on the north wall of the kitchen, and in short order, the existing desk and cabinet above it and the large pantry to the right were outside under the portico leading to the front door. We brought in one of two IKEA cartons with tall cabinets that would be the new pantry and Yvonne could see right away something was wrong. The parts were for a 24" wide 80" high 24" deep cabinet. Two would make a 48" wide pantry, but Yvonne had planned for a 30" wide installation. "I'm so disappointed." The woman who had entered our order had picked the wrong width. We couldn't make a new pantry today. We were stymied.

Forty-one: Disappointment

041: Orcas Unitarian Universalist Fellowship — May 2009

While I assembled the 36" wide floor cabinet that would go on the north wall next to the pantry, Yvonne assembled everything that would have to be returned, and it was quite a pile. A check of everything else we'd carried to the island was positive. Only the pantry was wrong. We'd load the car on Wednesday and Yvonne would take the ferry and then drive back to Seattle and IKEA on Thursday, return the too-wide cabinet kits, and pick up the models we needed. That would take all day. On Friday we'd carry everything to Crane and be in a position to complete all the cabinets on the north wall.

Forty-two: False Alarm

"The only way to make sense out of change is to plunge into it, move with it, and join the dance." — Alan Watts

I was in the kitchen removing cabinets from the west wall, and Yvonne had some troubling news; the washing machine had filled with water but then wouldn't start washing. A replay of a problem we'd had two years ago?

We've got a circa 1988 Maytag apartment-size dryer over/washer under unit that's located in a convenient spot in the master bedroom walk-through closet. Three years ago, the belt on the dryer broke. The new belt I ordered online appeared in the Crane delivery shed at the Orcas-side dock, and with some effort, our son James (home from college), and I pulled the unit away from the wall (then realized we didn't need to), replaced the belt, and the dryer was again operational.

Sometime later that summer, Yvonne reported the washer was filled with water but wouldn't wash, and an error light had come on. I downloaded a user manual from the Internet and, in reading it, found that for some reason, the unit's computer system thought that the tub door was open and wouldn't start agitating until it was closed. But it was closed. I found a washing machine expert on San Juan Island who worked a day job but was available odd hours - but not to come to Crane Island. I wasn't eager to buy and bring in a new unit. They were heavy and awkward and not inexpensive. His advice was to keep the old Maytag machine if possible. None of the newer machines were as well-built, including Maytag, which had become a division of Whirlpool. I did get the washer running but only after accidentally cracking a connector that James and I taped into place.

The fix didn't last, and then we were without a washing machine. Margaret, our part-time next-door neighbor, home from Columbus, where she taught, invited us to use her washer-dryer, but that wouldn't be a long-term solution. A few days later our Swedish cousins arrived for a visit. Once I de-

Forty-two: False Alarm

scribed the problem to Lars-Erik and Janne, they wasted no time in removing the washer circuit board and wrapping it tightly with wire Janne carried with him wherever he went. That worked and Janne left his spool of wire with me to use to solve future problems. Solvig and Ann-Sofi weren't surprised their husbands could fix the washer; it was their habit in Sweden to be self-reliant. Yvonne and I were amazed.

But now the problem had apparently returned. I was in the middle of remodeling the kitchen, had a Crane Island Association Board meeting coming up in a few days I needed to prepare for, and was working with Chris on the annotations for Slocum's *Sailing Alone* and Jens on Kafka's *The Metamorphosis*. Maybe we could use Margaret's machine (she was back in Columbus teaching) — but then we'd have to turn on her water, worry about another cold spell, and so on. I decided not to think about it and took a shower — and heard the washing machine start and run. Yvonne had tried a different setting, permanent press, and that had worked. She could live with that level of inconvenience. The problem wasn't a recurrence of what the Swedes had fixed. It was a new problem with the circuit board itself apparently. We'd leave that for another day.

Late morning the pest control service arrived and sprayed around the perimeter of the house for carpenter ants. Years ago, according to the service, the house had been infested, and they'd been called to solve the problem and had been protecting the house ever since. Four times a year they'd fly to Crane from Friday Harbor, spend a few hours making their rounds spraying for ants at several houses, and then fly back. I hadn't researched carpenter ants or their preventive measures, which involved spraying something toxic. Noah and Natasha's house on Harstine Island, on the Peninsula, had been infested a year ago and after tearing off wallboard to get at the ants and vacuum them up, Noah applied a non-toxic, homemade spray that would keep them away. Too much for me to think about.

Later at work on our kitchen remodel and removing the wall cabinets, I noticed how much warmer the temperature was high on the wall compared to low. Maybe we needed a fan. Then when I pulled out the under-cabinet heater/fan unit, I decided we really didn't need a source of heat specific to the kitchen, the warmest room in the house.

Forty-two: False Alarm

042: Yvonne enters IKEA hive mind

Every morning, at 6:00, the kitchen, dining room, and living room baseboard electric heat would come on for about an hour to warm the house from 62 to 68, while the fire I had started in the wood stove in the living room caught up and took over warming the house. But maybe that didn't make sense. It would be better to remove the kitchen heater and set the thermostats for 7:00 instead, so that's the current experiment. It may make the most sense to leave the thermostats set to 62 and let the wood stove carry the house higher all day long. I can live with 62 while the wood stove raises the temperature and Yvonne won't know the difference because she doesn't like to get up before 8:00 and the house should be comfortable enough by then. We'll see.

Forty-three: Going to Town

"A community is like a ship; everyone ought to be prepared to take the helm." — Henrik Ibsen

It was the fifth Tuesday of the month, and Yvonne had enough Unitarian friends as volunteers to serve lunch at the Food Bank that she wouldn't need my help, so when we left the house on this blustery, sometimes rainy morning, we could each have our own itineraries. She would stop to pick up a hot dish from Sheila and then head to the Community Church basement.

We hadn't been to the Deer Harbor Post Office since before Thanksgiving. As I retrieved mail from the Crane Island Association box and our box, I could hear Pat's new assistant chattering and wondered how Pat, used to relative quiet, was coping. As I arrived at West Sound Marina, their two boatyard dogs greeted me — the Golden Lab coming up for a friendly sniff and the speckled Black Lab mix standing back and giving me two woofs. Betsy told me the engine for our SeaSport would be delivered the next day and would be installed and operational within a week. Good news, since Margaret would be back on the 18th so we would no longer have her boat available to borrow. On the way out, I saw a green-hulled 19' SeaSport on a trailer in front of their new storage shed. Since there aren't many that size, I was surprised and then realized I was looking at our boat, in dry dock awaiting an engine transplant.

On the drive to town, I fiddled with the heater control in our F-150 pickup, a problem since it was broken into in Seattle, and the radio/CD system stolen six years ago. It was a pleasure driving north on Orcas Road, along the eastern side of Crow Valley with Turtleback Mountain to the west and Mount Woolard to the east, where Rachel and Marilyn now lived in their new sod-roofed house that resembled the one they had built and lived in on Crane for 20 years.

In Eastsound, at NAPA, Ray reported that though they normally stocked the inner tube from our hand truck I had with me, they were out of stock. His

Forty-three: Going to Town

wife Kathy had told me Ray couldn't make last Sunday's Unitarian meeting because he had to work. Ray suggested that Crescent Service might have a tube the right size. They did and could fill the 10-gallon propane tank I had with me and install a new tube in the hand truck wheel — and have them ready for pickup in about an hour. I filled Margaret's second five-gallon fuel tank for her boat — we had used that much gas since she left in September.

043: Pole Pass warning light on Orcas, once a lantern

At the Orcas Medical Center front desk, a sign encouraged me to get a flu shot, my reason for coming in while I passed time before returning to Crescent Service. Within 15 minutes, Carol came to find me and led me back to one of the examining rooms. Her son had moved to Austin, where some of his friends lived. Yes, Tony, the clinic doctor, found being on call all the time sometimes a burden since Tom left, but the winter wasn't a busy time, and it looked like he'd have some help by spring. She told me to encourage Yvonne to come in for a shot.

Harold said hello at Ace Hardware, where I stopped to buy three heavy-duty extension cords I'd be using for the remodeling project. At the Library, I opened the envelope from Pat, filled out a blank deposit slip I'd brought with me, and made photocopies. Phil, the library director, came out to the front desk, and we walked back to his office to chat. They had two candidates to fill the Board position being vacated by Lois, but he didn't know much about either. Checkouts for the last six of seven months had set a new record, impressive since the Orcas Island Public Library was already one of the most heavily used libraries per capita in the State of Washington. The Sunday hours experiment this year had been well-received, and it was in the budget for next year. They were within budget for this year, and staff would get a small raise for next year but not a cost of living increase. His nursery at home was doing well, but his garden hadn't worked out so far because he just didn't have time, no one else in the family was interested, and the grass he'd dug out to make space for his crop was coming back.

I made a Crane Island Association deposit at Keybank with the clerk who had sympathized with me last time I was in and had forgotten to bring a deposit slip with the account number on it. Because I didn't show in their system as a signer on the account (I didn't know why), she couldn't tell me the account number to write in, but she held the deposit and completed it when I called from home later with the number.

Back at Crescent Service, I picked up the propane tank and hand truck wheel, the mechanic telling me how he had used a hand truck in a past job moving 800-pound 55-gallon drums of toxic liquid. Hmmm.

Back at the dock, the rain had increased, but the wind was slowing and would abate by evening. Home again, with the wood stove stoked, I took a break for lunch in our topsy-turvy under-construction kitchen. So much excitement!

Forty-four: Some Assembly Required

> "She walks in beauty, like the night
> Of cloudless climes and starry skies"
> From "She Walks in Beauty" by Lord Byron

Three Northern Pintails dallied in the water a few feet from the stone breakwater that connects the rock that forms the south side of Pole Pass and Crane Island and protects the community dock from the prevailing southeasterly winds, a female and two elegantly plumed males with orange-brown heads and white highlights. A perfect late fall island morning; air calm, complex gray sky and gray water, a translucent emerald green near the shore where it reflects the evergreens in this Evergreen State. And though we'd had cold weather and snow that had partially flattened the chest-high grasses in Och's meadow, everywhere the ground was a lively green where soil covered the basalt out of which Crane Island was formed.

Only Brian, host Howard, and I attended today's Greybeards session, to drink tea or coffee and share experiences, observations, ideas, and fellowship in the tiny summer cabin on the hillside above Howard's shop and house and looking out over his elaborate garden and netting-covered berry patch. David was in Minneapolis, where his client of many years had died recently. Chris was especially busy this week, practicing with the Orcas Acapella Choir every day for five hours in preparation for a holiday concert. The choir had performed several times abroad and together with visiting choirs, including one composed of Swedish young people six years ago. Six of the young men had stayed with us in our house on Cayou Valley Road, and it was mild enough in the early spring that Chris, Howard, and I could take the young men and five young women from the choir to Stuart Island in our Camano Troll pocket trawler for a picnic and walk.

The tea, as usual, was strong, and kept hot with a tea cozy, habits Howard brought with him when he emigrated from Britain in 1977, at age 34, seeking more opportunity and a better life than he could cobble together as an agriculture teacher at a small college in England. There he couldn't afford to make payments on a small house as interest rates rose on a variable-rate mortgage, couldn't afford a safe and reliable car. His had rusted so badly that it wouldn't pass inspection, and he was getting around on a motorcycle he drove illegally down back roads. Not so long afterward, with a teaching job in Oregon, he was making twice as much money with about the same cost of living, and the credit union was eager to help him buy a house, much improved from where they had lived in England. America was a wonderful place.

From time to time, the topic was the younger generation, sometimes to admire and sometimes to wonder, and I turned the conversation to Natasha's brothers Justin and Seth and how they had taken responsibility for their children when the mothers were lost to drugs. That led to a discussion of the variety of forms families now took and the socially acceptable choices men and women now had to arrange their lives and work that they hadn't had when we were forming families. Brian talked about how family was his most important priority and when work at Weyerhaeuser had made it impossible for him to spend adequate time with his family, he quit. I agreed about the priority of family and talked about how being self-employed had meant long hours but with a flexibility that let me walk my four-year-old to pre-school. That led to a discussion of the rise of home economics and other practical classes in high schools in the last century and that to the role of marketing in the creation of life expectations and family roles and what groups benefitted from the changes and why, recounting how Sigmund Freud's nephew Edward Bernays organized what he described as a women's rights parade in 1929 and had hired models who lit up Lucky Strike cigarettes, successfully linking women's freedom with smoking. And that led to the question of whether the desire for accurate information could overcome people's desire to believe something, anything, even if nonsense. I thought probably not very often.

At home, Yvonne and I worked on kitchen assembly most of the day, taking a break in mid-afternoon to transfer the rest of what she would be returning to IKEA the next day from the studio by dock cart and boat to the van, parked in the Crane parking lot on Orcas. At the Orcas dock, we saw Lou, returning from his regular Thursday trip to Eastsound for socializing, doing his wash, and replenishing supplies.

Forty-four: Some Assembly Required

044: Yvonne with her favorite tool

He had a big bag of birdseed, bird-watching an avid avocation for him. Tom was helping him load his boat and then helping us cart the heavy 80" x 24" cartons up the ramp and slide them into the rear of the van. Would he be going to Ketcham to see Liz? He said she had been on Crane a lot and was now being treated for the early stages of dementia. They had been to Walnut Creek, California, over Thanksgiving to see her daughter and family. We reviewed the water situation, and I thanked him for his continuing attention to the system even though he didn't need to since I was now responsible. I had felt that Tom was unhappy with me because I had told him I no longer welcomed his, I thought, paranoid complaints about Jim — or felt that I was unhappy with him. On a small island, it is very important that people get along and cooperate, no matter how peculiar they think one another. If the social fabric was tearing between me and Tom, I wanted it patched, and I let him

Forty-four: Some Assembly Required

know by engaging him, being friendly, appreciative, and interested, and he did the same. A good thing.

As I watched Yvonne install drawer sliders in floor cabinets and doors on wall cabinets I was struck — again — at how graceful she is with her body, her working a kind of dance and a pleasure to watch. When I told her later as we settled into bed with our books after having warmed up in the hot tub, she said she consciously put her whole body into her effort, engaging every part of it in the task. I understood that. She told me I was amazing at the way I could make things look good, right, being accurate and precise. Well, sometimes I could, I said. It's really, really important not to rush, to check again and again and not go on until it's right. And that was an implied response to her suggestion in the hot tub that rather than have the countertop measuring people come in two weeks, as scheduled, that we try to be ready in one week. No, no, let's not torture ourselves. It isn't necessary.

Forty-five: Deadlines

"It's not enough to be busy, so are the ants. The question is, what are we busy about?" — Henry David Thoreau

At my desk at 4:30 a.m., working on software I've created to publish enriched versions of *Slocum's Sailing Alone Around the World* and Kafka's *Metamorphosis* and then other classics that can benefit from an electronic reader's companion, a click or touch away. Every sailor and many landlubbers read Slocum — for the story — the first person to circumnavigate the planet solo — and the excellent writing — but his vernacular was now inaccessible to many modern readers. Chris researched and entered the Slocum annotations through Google Docs. I wrote a routine to import the text and annotations from Word HTML output into the Annotator software database, but the quick and dirty routine left residual problems that needed correction by software and by hand. Our tentative goal was to publish Slocum by year-end. At the other end of the country, in Wellesley, Jens had prepared some annotations and the beginnings of an introduction and chronology for Kafka's novella, one of the most well-known, widely read, and puzzling stories of the early twentieth century, and I had scheduled a telephone meeting for the next day to introduce him to a new version of the software, discuss his writing, and what we wanted to accomplish for the reader, and a plan for next steps for a late winter publication. Chris was waiting, and Jens was waiting. I was on the critical path and wanted to be off it.

At 7:30, I left Yvonne at the Crane dock on Orcas so she could return to IKEA and swap the too-wide pantry cabinet parts for the right size. The day before, she had talked with the countertop people and scheduled December 14th to measure and December 28th for delivery and installation. The former date meant all the floor cabinets would have to be installed, perfectly level, and ready to receive countertops (and thus be ready for measurement). The latter meant that Gary and his Mud Puppy barge would need to be available on the 28th to bring the countertop truck and installers to Crane from the ramp at West Sound when they arrive on the Anacortes ferry and return them late afternoon so they could catch the ferry and return to Seattle.

045: At the computer — 2008

Back inside I spent two hours adding links to illustrations for the Slocum book and finally sent a copy to Chris to review. It looked pretty good. I heated up some leftover soup for dinner and picked Yvonne up about 8:00 at the dock on Orcas. We were both happy she was home. Tomorrow we would transfer what she'd brought and continue the kitchen assembly process.

Forty-five: Deadlines

In two days, I would be hosting the Crane Island Association Board of Trustees for our December meeting and needed to be ready to report on the association's finances and the state of the water system. Yvonne wasn't happy at the prospect of having guests when the house was a construction zone with what belonged in cupboards stacked on tables and the floor in the dining room — next to tools and parts in use for the project — as well as assembled but uninstalled cabinets here and there. I needed to finish my work in preparation for the meeting, and we needed to do some more installation so we could unclutter the house.

About 1:00, Yvonne called from IKEA in a panic. She'd returned too big parts and loaded the right-sized parts but had a sense that the car wasn't riding correctly, looked at the tires and saw that the right front was nearly flat. What should she do? Go to the Les Schwab store close by, and they would fix it for free — and they did. Somewhere the tire had picked up a nail. She could drive to the ferry and come home. By 3:00, it was clear that I couldn't finish what I needed to for Jens for our scheduled telephone meeting the next day, so I sent him an email, with an apology and a suggestion that we reschedule for a week later. Then I picked up the splitting maul, sledgehammer, and two axes, put them in the dock cart, wheeled it outside the fence to the unsplit woodpile and spent the next 90 minutes enjoying myself splitting and then stacking two cart loads on the front porch. I noticed that the head of the splitting maul was starting to crack, probably because when a stroke sinks but doesn't split, I use the maul as a wedge and whack it with the sledgehammer.

Forty-six: Dinner and Music

"I went out to the hazel wood,
  Because a fire was in my head,
  And cut and peeled a hazel wand,
  And hooked a berry to a thread;
  And when white moths were on the wing,
  And moth-like stars were flickering out,
  I dropped the berry in a stream
  And caught a little silver trout."
  "The Song of Wandering Aengus" by W. B. Yeats

As we left the Crane dock, parts of the Spring Point hills on Orcas to the northwest were glowing in the early morning light. Deer Harbor and its western cliffs where David and Maxine lived were ablaze with light and though more than a mile away, close enough to touch. Boats moored at the two marinas, the marina store, the resort, and houses — many housing people we knew — had a kind of hyper-reality as if becoming visible after a hundred-year sleep. Puffy clouds, every shade of white and gray, with wispy stringers, opened here and there to reveal the world's cerulean ceiling. A seal crossed Pole Pass toward Crane Island, watching us as we turned right to enter the pass. South, in Wasp Passage, a half-mile away, next to Shaw Island, a tug heading east struggled with a quarter-mile-long log boom bound for Anacortes and the mainland milling and plywood mills. Years ago, a boom had come loose on the north side of Crane in a storm spilling hundreds of logs against the rocks at the barge ramp, and Marilyn had gone log walking. Yvonne and I talked about this day's light — a late-in-the-year low in the sky light, crystal clear, bringing everything close, and bathing it in beauty.

As we docked, I recalled to Yvonne my meeting with a mink on the Orcas ramp two days before when returning from Howard's about 9:30 in the morning. A 150' fixed wooden ramp, at high tide, 15' above the water at the land side, descends gradually and then connects at a right angle to the 20' metal movable ramp with its lower end riding up and down on the floating dock below as the tides rise and fall. At the highest high tide, the movable ramp is almost horizontal. At the lowest low side, say a minus three, the ramp is so steep it's sobering to walk down — and then carefully, holding tightly to the railings — and very difficult to drag a loaded dock cart up. As I started down the wooden ramp, I saw a mink bouncing up the metal ramp, wanting to come to land the easy way — not to raid Warren's chicken coop because after losing too many, Warren had given up, and the chickens were gone — so the mink was on some other errand. The mink was now off the metal ramp and on the wooden ramp headed toward me, oblivious. Near-sighted surely, but couldn't it hear me coming? About 40 feet away now, it paused and did some calculations. No, it wouldn't make sense to jump from the ramp into the water ten feet below, so it turned and retraced its steps down the metal ramp, and I kept coming. Now what?

At the bottom of the metal ramp, now on the floating dock, it scampered to the end of the section right under the ramp and considered slipping into the water. No, the threat wasn't imminent, and it didn't want to go into the water; it wanted to use the ramps to get to land. It waited on the section of the dock under the ramp out of sight while I came down and walked to Margaret's boat to unzipper and unbuckle it for my trip back to Crane, and the mink, confident again, made its way up the ramps to finish its morning errand perhaps muttering about how the two-leggeds are always getting in the way.

The transfer was easier this time because the tall cabinets were narrower, and they and the drawers weighed less and took up less space. By noon, one cabinet was standing in the kitchen on its four adjustable legs more or less where it belonged. I'd need to cut away a strip of sheetrock to slide it under an overhang that had been created for the original cabinets. Yvonne went off to her Friday afternoon knitting session at the Deer Harbor Community Club, and as it turned out, Bev was the only other knitter. They sat by the heated stove — it was cold in the old, uninsulated building — and talked about Africa, comparing notes. Bev and Dave had almost the same itinerary we'd had ten years before, including a balloon ride over the Masai Mara, the high point of an extraordinary two weeks among charming, graceful, and happy people and beautiful, dramatic, and revelatory wildlife.

Forty-six: Dinner and Music

046: North wall arrangement

By the time Yvonne returned, I was ready for her to help me raise the second tall pantry cabinet. I had tentatively installed the hanging wall cabinet to the left. And then it was time to quit for the day. We headed back to Orcas as the sun set to have dinner with Joyce and Larry and attend the Celtic Christmas Concert at the Community Church as their guest. Though the Madrona Bar and Grill had been open for more than a year, this was our first visit. While living on our sailboat at Cayou Quay Marina while studying for his oriental medicine exams, Yvonne's brother Ron had eaten dinner frequently at the Madrona Grill, looking for a good meal and company and he recommended it. The Grill occupies the back portion of a building of shops, converted from a gas station and convenience store. Christina's, a four-star restaurant, had filled the second floor for many years, but she had retired and sold out to a Seattle chef who renamed the restaurant Allium, reduced the prices, and was serving modern American and organic meals. The Grill, behind what had been the gas station, had served as the auto repair shop, the room rustic, all stained wood, and surprisingly attractive for what had functioned as a garage overlooking the water of Eastsound. The original plank floor, once supporting vehicles in for oil changes and clutch repairs, had been sanded and buffed. Overhead, the rough-sawn trusses, cut from Orcas Island fir, supported a vaulted wood ceiling. What mechanic would have suspected in 1960 that the space would be a restaurant 50 years later?

Enjoyable dinner conversation about food and family, not the Food Bank, a business topic. A good meal, then off to the Community Church for the concert. Howard was among the crowd of several hundred, looking for something to do while Sheila was in Florida with her 88-year-old father whose surgically installed defibrillator had started malfunctioning, delivering jolts to restart his heart when it wasn't necessary, and surgery might be required to repair it. Dick, the minister, and a great friend to the Food Bank that was housed temporarily in the church basement, said hello to Yvonne and to me. I had been part of an informal Orcas clergy meeting for a while, a Unitarian representative, and we'd had some useful discussions about the churches and island needs — one being the Food Bank.

Flute, violin, and keyboard music, variations on familiar themes in a Celtic style, the audience lending their voices several times. A full house, warm, friendliness, a sense of peace. We could see why the Community Church had the largest island congregation. The more I knew about the church, the more impressed I became with its orientation — actions were more important than words. Unfortunately, though not of primary importance, the words were not our words. It couldn't be our church.

Forty-seven: People Watching

"I have learned that to be with those I like is enough." — Walt Whitman

The Crane Island Association Board meeting, our first since October, was scheduled for 9:00 a.m. at our house, and as treasurer and water committee chair, I had a good deal to report on. Gary had sent me his November meter readings spreadsheet Thursday night, and Elise, our Friday Harbor bookkeeper, had provided current, tentative end-of-November financials, our fiscal year running August to July. Those documents would serve as the source for some of what I needed to report on. At my desk by 4:30 a.m., I updated a member billing and receivable report and then analyzed budget versus actual revenue for the fiscal year. The results were encouraging. Though some sources were under budget, others, unanticipated, had appeared to make up almost all of the difference. For the January meeting, I'd study and report on expenses. Gary's water report showed an unaccounted for loss of 26,000 gallons, up from 12,000 gallons in October and 3,000 gallons in August and September. Tom and Liz had found two leaking hydrants last winter, when the system had high unaccounted-for losses, and the background leak level plummeted. Another hydrant? Seeing these results, Gary had switched pumping from well #5 to #6 to see if the problem was the pump meter. We'd have to see.

I set up the association speakerphone in the living room, where we would have the meeting, and though the dining room and kitchen were in disarray, the living room remained a very pleasant place to be. Yvonne put out tea and cookies and then took Margaret's boat to Orcas to be part of the Deer Harbor Community Club annual Santa Ship celebration. About 100 people, half expectant children, spread out over the Deer Harbor Marina dock to welcome Santa coming from the North Pole by boat, to hand out presents and goodies at the Community Club after making his way there in Santa's taxi, Terry's red and

Forty-seven: People Watching

green vintage dump truck. Yvonne and the women of the Auxiliary would try to keep the excited children and their parents from falling into the water.

Jason, Board president, had sent me an early morning email. He wouldn't be attending; something had come up. At 9:00 I dialed into the conference call number hoping someone would be there; no one had come to the house yet. Martha, Dan, Dave, and Kate were in the conference; good, we'd have a quorum. We hadn't mustered one for the last meeting. Then Pat and Blair were at the door. We were seven; only Jason and Tim, who called late, after the meeting, were missing. Pat and Blair would get the cookies and tea. Yvonne and I both favor short, effective meetings, and when we have a chance each run them that way. We were done well before 10:00 and had our action items for the January meeting. No one seemed distressed that the meeting was brief and teleconferenced, a change I suggested and helped implement last year. It was an effective way to include people who, in the past, wouldn't have been because they hadn't come to Crane for the meeting — by choice or necessity.

Back to the kitchen project, with Yvonne's help, I got the pantries and wall cabinet installed and ready for the installation of drawers. We had come to realize that I had installed some drawer rails in unacceptable locations, where they would conflict with yet-to-be-installed door hinges. We knew where the top and bottom hinges would fall but because we didn't have the doors — because with the tire problem, Yvonne had forgotten to pick them up from a special location at IKEA — we couldn't be certain where they'd be located. A call to IKEA and the kitchen department and a friendly young woman helped us understand exactly where the center hinge needed to be installed. Yvonne could now remove all the drawer rails, put the hinges on the pantry, reinstall the rails, assemble the drawers, and slide them in — while I went to take my turn serving tea and coffee at the Orcas Island Public Library Holiday Tea.

Though not eager to interrupt my kitchen project work, I had become dimly aware that I was spending too much time on Crane, away from the larger community of Orcas. Yvonne kept up her connections; I tended to ignore them when I was engaged in a project. I needed to see and talk with more people. As Library Board alum, this would be an opportunity to visit with people I hadn't seen in months.

Forty-seven: People Watching

047: Story time at Orcas Public Library 2008

After a short training session from a pretty high school girl who explained patiently to the white-haired gentleman how to operate the silver sugar cube grasper and the rest of the silver tea and coffee set, I took my place at one end of a table covered with homemade cookies, candies, cakes, sandwiches, and brownies — and some nuts for protein. The sugar cubes reminded me of how my Swedish grandfather Carl drank his coffee. The sugar cube would go in his mouth, not in the cup, and he would drink from the saucer, where he poured coffee from his cup.

The Library was crowded with babes in arms, little children who probably came to Nita's story hour once in a while, older children, and high schoolers, many wearing red vests and helping fill, consolidate, and clean the serving table. Adults of all ages, into their 80s or maybe 90s — it's sometimes hard to tell — appreciated the food, and many were customers for Tom, the other pourer this hour, currently still on the Board, and me. By 3:30 nearly all the food, coffee, and tea had been consumed. Two hundred cups of tea and the same for coffee had been brewed. Since probably fewer than half requested the caffeinated beverage, opting instead for punch, it's likely 800 people attended the Tea during the afternoon. They came for the music — some of the kids were performing — to see friends, enjoy the food and to share the warmth of the season. Howard appeared at about 4:00 having run errands in town and happy to be fed, if in a not particularly nutritious way, while Sheila was gone to Florida.

I especially enjoyed talking with Martin Lund, an LA studio musician who could play every wind and keyboard instrument and who I had met when he first came to Orcas years ago when his dog bit me on the leg while I did my morning walk by Dennis and Candy's house in Deer Harbor, where Martin was house sitting. Martin was the new band teacher at the Orcas school and finding it a challenge. "If they're disorganized," he said generously, "that means I'm disorganized." We talked about the issue of tone-deaf students playing non-digital instruments like trombones. His half-time position took all day.

Andrea looked good, and I was happy to see her. An island artist and Unitarian transplant from Palo Alto, she had lost her husband, Hugh, to heart failure a few months before. She talked about her trip to Houston for a family Thanksgiving and her appreciation for the seasons of the Northwest and the general interest and enjoyment of the outdoors. The changes of the seasons made her feel part of a larger cycle of life and that it was all right, as it should be, and tears came to her eyes. We hugged.

What I noticed immediately on sitting down at the table, the silver tea service in front of me, and then a table covered with food, and surrounded by people — talking, hugging, greeting, laughing, enjoying one another's company — was how the world of nature, no matter how beautiful, awe-inspiring, calming, isn't enough. I do love to be in the middle of hubbub, people bustling, in moderation, to talk and listen, and to observe, to watch and wonder, the great pleasure of an urban, rather than insular, rural life.

Forty-eight: Holiday Festivities

"Maybe Christmas, he thought, doesn't come from a store. Maybe Christmas ... perhaps ... means a little bit more!" — Dr. Seuss, How the Grinch Stole Christmas

With the pantries, other north and most west wall and floor cabinets installed, lined up and leveled with a makeshift plywood countertop, Yvonne could begin clearing the dining room of most of what had been temporarily stored there, a great visual and organizational improvement. The microwave was now on its own shelf, off the countertop. The refrigerator was pushed back into the slot where it belonged. In short order, she moved food and other stuff to its new home.

Adjusting the big IKEA drawers had taken some experimentation. In retrospect, the characteristic IKEA line drawing help booklet had the right information, but seeing wasn't the same as doing. Ultimately, the drawers looked pretty good but not quite right — since IKEA designs and manufactures to high tolerances, anything that doesn't look right probably wasn't installed right. When we first slid the drawers in, there was a big gap between the bottom and middle and an overlap between the middle and top, so I moved the drawer rails down a notch and adjusted as best I could. Yvonne finally realized that the drawer in the middle belonged on the bottom and the bottom in the middle. They were different sizes.

The IKEA drawers are all metal with lots of parts. Yvonne spent an hour assembling the first drawer while I was on Orcas. She said she had to enter the "IKEA hive mind" before it all made sense, and assembly then went much more quickly. IKEA is a collection of ideas and processes that incidentally deals with physical objects and is the result of decades of small improvements. Smart engineering and manufacturing, always practical, always about value. IKEA was born in the province of Småland where my grandfather claimed only children and rocks would grow. That made the Smålanders resourceful, clever but never fancy. Småland is home to thousands of small businesses that compete globally and sometimes operate out of barns no longer needed for agricultural purposes.

048: Some disassembly required

At 4:00, just at sunset, we crossed to Orcas to attend Al and Sue's holiday open house, as we had for the last seven or eight years. Sylvia was back from Seattle where she was helping take care of a newborn granddaughter while her daughter, a consultant, adjusted to the change, difficult because her husband, also a consultant, was away weekdays on a project. Gordon was happy to have his wife back on Orcas. And suddenly, there was Judith, also a retired

Forty-eight: Holiday Festivities

Orcas Library trustee, whom I hadn't seen in a year or so while she and her partner Barbara taught in Portland. Barbara was at a conference in DC. Maybe they could come over for dinner before they had to leave Deer Harbor for spring semester. I told her the story of publishing an electronic, annotated version of Austen's *Emma* only to have to withdraw it at its editor's inexplicable request. She wanted to read it. I would send her my copy, one of four sold through Amazon before I pulled it off their electronic shelves.

I'd known that Al and Sue had grown up in Chicago, I in the suburbs, but was surprised to learn that Jim and Sarah also come from Chicago, the city and Evanston, immediately north. We talked about the early days of Second City, and Jim mentioned "It's Here," a folk music venue, where one would sit on the floor on pillows and drink non-alcoholic beverages and where it turned out we'd each spent happy times during the early to mid-'60s. And I had a conversation with Judy while we ate together sitting in the living room about children, grandchildren, and travel. Two years before they'd done some hiking in the Pyrenees part of the time on the Camino de Santiago de Compostela pilgrimage route (the Way of St James), something Yvonne and I have talked about doing, and that led to telling Judy about our 17 years of walks to the El Santuario de Chimayo in New Mexico with our Boulder friends.

Some of the people at the party we see rarely and in some ways have little in common with — we have different backgrounds, politics, and views on religion, but it turns out to be more important that we live in the same place by choice and have similar day-to-day experiences. All these people are generous, care about the community, volunteer, put their time, and sometimes money in, and are completely dependable.

Forty-nine: Everybody is Fine

"We are stuck with technology when what we really want is just stuff that works." — Douglas Adams

First, there was the problem of the 15-month-old, post-warranty microwave, sitting proudly on its new shelf and powered by its own circuit, the power source hidden behind the adjacent refrigerator. After stopping on its own occasionally over the last two weeks, it now wouldn't complete a timed cycle and displayed an error code on its LCD readout after a few seconds of operation. An internet search told us the problem was serious and would require professional intervention. I called Panasonic, was instructed to try plugging into another power source but had the same result, and then was given the name and phone number of a Seattle repair shop. A diagnosis would cost $22.50, and the repair probably another $80. The microwave hadn't cost much over $100; it wouldn't make sense to take it to Seattle. It was totaled, junk, and was soon sitting next to the trash and recycle shed, waiting for the next trip to the transfer station. Yvonne assigned me the task of making her oatmeal, which she now couldn't do in the microwave and wouldn't be hard for me since I had recently converted from microwave to stovetop oatmeal preparation (more trouble but more tasty), and I could make a bit extra at 6:00 a.m. when I had breakfast, two hours before Yvonne usually had hers. We'd get a new microwave during our Thursday trip to the mainland to pick up a new dishwasher.

A row of three cabinets was hanging from a sandwich beam over the east countertop and range and under the wooden vaulted ceiling that separates the kitchen from the dining area. Along the bottom of the cabinets and inside an oak valence, plastic lattice-covered fluorescent lights and a fold-down television provided counter light and cooking company. It all would have to come down so the new, glass door IKEA cabinets could be hung from the beam. The existing floor cabinets and countertop would provide a place to stand while working on the hanging cabinets.

049: Ready to hang and position new cabinets

The outer edge of the first and third cabinets rested on 1/2" indentations in the sheetrock at each end of the counter, and threaded 1/2" rods descended through holes drilled through the plywood spacer between the two 2x8s that made up the beam then down between the cabinets and through a 6" 1x4 and bolted. The indentations and bolted 1x4s held the cabinets up. A clever approach. We'd need to be careful removing the cabinets or find them crashing onto the countertop or us.

The bottom of the cabinets was a little over 30" above the countertop, so Yvonne suggested we put three assembled IKEA floor cabinets on the countertop, under each cabinet, and add shims to make up the difference. It worked like a charm, and the old cabinets were soon outside under the portico leading to the front door, waiting for transfer to the rain shelter and then perhaps installation in my shop out back.

The three new cabinets, in total, were three inches shorter than the originals and would need spacers between, but they were also all the same length, and the originals weren't. That meant I'd need to drill new holes to hang the rods, and the longest 1/2" drill bit I had was six inches. I could drill down and then up, as Dean had done, but that was likely to result in a larger hole, as it had for Dean, causing play in the rods, and that's not what I wanted. Yvonne would be going to Eastsound the next day for a Food Bank Board meeting, and she could stop at Ace Hardware, get some help from Harold, and pick up a longer bit.

Eric, second son, aerospace professor at CalPoly, and living with his family in Los Osos, Central Coast, California, had called the day before to catch up when we were at Al and Sue's Holiday open house. After a chili dinner by candlelight in our usual places on either side of the yet-to-be-removed countertop, with no cabinets and no light above, Yvonne called Eric, who continued to enjoy a much more satisfying tenure as department chair with the new dean in place and the power of the departmental disrupters removed or at least weakened. Everyone was fine. Dave had officially proposed to Eric's sister-in-law, wife Kristin's sister, Lauren at Thanksgiving dinner — Yvonne could see the scene in her mind's eye. Eric would take five-year-old Jackson skiing at Sierra Summit soon, and the whole family would go later. Grandma and Grandpa wouldn't be expected to attend — snow, chains, cold, and even skiing no longer high on our desirables list — especially after last winter's trip to the ski area. Forty degrees was now our lower acceptable temperature limit and 80 the upper. The way it is.

Fifty: Bounty

"There are two ways of constructing a software design: One way is to make it so simple that there are obviously no deficiencies, and the other way is to make it so complicated that there are no obvious deficiencies." — C.A.R. Hoare

A mild day in the 50s. No kitchen work today. Time to catch up in other areas. Yvonne went off to do errands in Eastsound and attend a Food Bank Board meeting, and she was sure she would be back before dark. She hadn't yet piloted a boat in the dark. She called from ACE Hardware, where she was talking with Harold about drill bits and wanted me to hear the options. She explained, and when I said I had no idea what she was talking about, she put Harold on the line, and he and I agreed that a 12" long 3/4" bit would be the best choice given what they had in stock — but it would cost $30 — a bit much to drill two holes.

About 3:00 the wind started to blow — hard. About 3:30 I positioned myself sitting in the living room facing east with a view of the Crane dock on Orcas. I was concerned about Yvonne coming back in the wind and the rising darkness. About 4:00 I could see Margaret's boat heading away from Orcas, and I put on my shoes and coat and walked quickly down to the Crane community dock in the wind. Yvonne came through Pole Pass and turned south to come in behind the breakwater. The wind from the southwest wanted to push the boat into the dock, so she turned the bow into the wind, moving the boat at a 45-degree angle along the west side of the dock until she got it out of the wind. A nice move — which she said she had no choice making or she'd be bashed into the dock. Yvonne was very happy to see me and grateful I could tie up the boat without her having to get out and struggle with it.

After Yvonne had left for Orcas, and while I ate lunch, I sat at the kitchen counter reading articles on the Internet, and the MacBook Pro got slower and-slower and finally wouldn't do anything — not even Shut Down (from the

Apple menu) so I turned it off by holding down the power button, but then the computer wouldn't start up again though it kept trying. Chris responded to my email for advice with a FaceTime prompt, and we talked about the problem. He suggested booting from an operating system disk. I did but had the same result: repeated, unsuccessful attempts by the computer to boot up. Chris suggested I bring it with me when I would see him the next day. Yvonne's response when she got home and I described the latest technology failure — "Everything's breaking. The boat engine, the van flat tire, the microwave, and now our kitchen computer."

050: Early December sunrise through living room windows

I had spent the whole day doing programming, beginning about 4:00 a.m., and had made good progress. I would be meeting with Chris the next day and Jens by telephone Friday and needed to add the functionality they needed to complete the annotated ebooks they were working on. I added a routine to structure a book out of its elements in any order, another to create subsidiary tables of contents, a third to add text to table of contents pages, a fourth to manage images, and a fifth to make it easy to insert images into annotation text. And I simplified the directory structure the program uses that had grown by ad hoc accretions. Lots more to do over time but useful improvements.

At dinner, Yvonne reported on the Food Bank Board meeting: the capital fund drive was significantly over the goal set in the summer. The community had come forward with more generous donations after Thanksgiving. Besides the new building, the Board would have adequate funding for continuing maintenance, making the new building a long-term realistic project. Though the Food Bank Board had some success raising funds, a special citizens committee with the cooperation of the Orcas Island Community Foundation and the informal clergy committee (and their churches) made the big difference. Orcas Island has a significant group of people who are in danger of going hungry in these bad economic times. But it also has a population of people at the other end of the economic spectrum: 200 units had contributed — from $10 to $10,000.

Fifty-one: eNotator

If you have an apple and I have an apple and we exchange these apples then you and I will still each have one apple. But if you have an idea and I have an idea and we exchange these ideas, then each of us will have two ideas." — George Bernard Shaw

Thirty years ago, John Lennon, Yvonne's favorite Beatle, had been shot and killed outside his and Yoko's building in New York City. Yvonne and I were newly married, though Noah, half the time, and Yvonne, Jeni, and Eric, had lived together for two years. It was a warm day in Boulder, and the next afternoon, a Tuesday, we sat together on the deck in silence. On Saturday, October 6, 2002, a beautiful fall day in New York, after attending an anti-war rally in Central Park's East Meadow, where one protestor held a sign with the word "Imagine," we walked over to what came to be called "Strawberry Fields" in 1981 and walked around the Imagine mosaic and then over to the Dakota. A poignant time. On that trip, to attend a party celebrating Euan and Bethany's wedding, we spent time at Ground Zero, Ellis Island, and a service at All Souls, presided over by Forrest Church, who talked about how Unitarianism is sometimes described as empty and limited when, in fact, it's rich and inclusive.

When I left the house to go to Howard's for Greybeards, the wind was blowing, and the rain was coming down in buckets, but the mild temperature carried hints of spring, in my mind at least. A very high tide, 8.6 feet, covered almost all the rocks of the Crane community dock breakwater and came up to the grass along the beach. The Salish Sea was full to the point of overflowing, more being added from the skies. In the time it took to unfasten Margaret's boat's canvas cover and shove off, my Levi's were soaked. With Sheila gone to Florida this week to attend to her failing father, Brian, Howard, and I were in the house, rather than the garden cabin, so I could stand next to the oil stove and dry out. Howard talked a bit more about coming to America in 1977 from

England. After a two-year wait in England, he was granted a Green Card, in part because his wife was American, and their first stop was Los Angeles, where her parents lived. Knowing they didn't want to raise their daughters in southern California, Howard and wife toured Oregon and Washington, and he found a job teaching at the Dalles on the Columbia. Brian reported he was moving slower because of Parkinson's, the medication, and his back. David was in Las Vegas apparently, and Chris was not present, but I would see him shortly.

051: King tide floods Crane Island breakwater protecting community dock

Back to the Crane community dock to pick up Yvonne, with her box of homemade cookies for the Garden Club Holiday Tea and program, where she presided over the welcome committee and was honored as one of the past presidents of the organization, presented a table flower setting, used for the program — red roses among greens in a shallow box — that she admired and appreciated.

Chris and I met in his living room, Lynn reporting that a satisfactory arrangement had finally been established for her parents in Tucson, where her failing mother would have full-time care and might not last through Christmas, and then Lynn retired to another part of the house. I had brought my old MacBook Pro, and Chris had the same problem I had: it wouldn't boot — even from an operating system disc. I would leave it with him, and he would try to diagnose the problem. If only a hard drive failure, it could be fixed; otherwise, the computer was toast.

I transferred the latest version of the Annotator to his Mac, along with the Slocum database and a test database, and walked Chris through the new program features and their rationale, mostly not important for *Sailing Alone* but necessary for the *Metamorphosis* and other literary works. His sense was that *Sailing Alone* was at the simpler end of the spectrum of books we would publish. Our task, his task really, since he was doing the annotations, was to decipher Slocum's argot, not to delve into various levels of meaning, since Slocum's story had only one, the one he told, very well.

With his annotations virtually complete, we needed to create a punch list of what we needed to do to publish on Amazon and Barnes & Noble, to start with at least. We agreed it made no practical sense to read-test the book before publication with whomever we could convince, friend or family, to read it and then critique Chris' added content and my formatting. The simplest approach would be to offer it for sale and learn from reader reviews. Amazon offered a free version of *Sailing Alone* and several other editions, virtually the same, offering no value-add, were priced at $3.00. The paper *Annotated Sailing Alone Around the World* annotated by Rod Scher, was priced at $13.67. A $4.99 price for Chris' ebook offering seemed reasonable. We had struggled in the past with a title for the annotated *Emma* (that we had to withdraw from publication at the request of the editor and had ended up calling it "Emma (in Context)." That wouldn't work for Slocum's book. The prior fall I had registered ClassicsUnbound.com, intending to use that as a publisher name, and we had incorporated as Classics Unbound, Inc. but in January I discovered that another group was publishing Jane Austen and other Kindle books using the name

Fifty-one: eNotator

"Classics-Unbound" so for *Emma*, after much research and discussion we had chosen the name, BookDoors.com but having given that name up to the *Emma* editor, it wasn't available and didn't seem appropriate anyway.

Chris said he had been thinking about our using something like "eNotation" rather than "annotation" as the core word in the publisher name and book title. I liked the idea, and we both did Internet searches and were reminded that "E notation" is an engineering and science convention for formatting large numbers. We eventually decided that didn't matter — we would extend the use of the term. "enotatedclassics.com" was available, so I registered it. We already held the domain name "annotatedclassics.com," and we would use it to direct browsers to what would be our main site, eNotated Classics. A new concept, adding a layer of help behind the main text accessible to the reader at the touch of a finger or click of the mouse — and so a new word. The new concept, derivative from annotation, and the new word, derivative from "annotation" — but also indicating a connection to ebooks. Chris would look at writing an introduction. I'd finish the program code to create Kindle and ePub book formats out of the database, and we'd both think about what a cover should look like. And as occurred to me later, the Annotator software program should probably become the eNotator program. A very productive meeting.

Fifty-two: Bargains

"I'm a great believer in luck, and I find the harder I work the more I have of it." — Thomas Jefferson

Though we weren't early for the second ferry, only eight cars were already in line, and we parked on the drive leading from the laned waiting area down to the road and ferry loading area below. Yvonne walked down to the Orcas Village Store while I cut through the woods to deposit outgoing mail at the Orcas Landing Post Office. Catching up with Yvonne at the store, I could see that the addition project had progressed in the last two weeks with the upper story now framed. Carpenters were at work; everything was soaked from two days of rain, and Ron was consulting with the contractor about some aspect of the building. Coffee and a muffin for Yvonne, tea for me, and the *Seattle Times* and the *Islands Sounder*. The big news in the Orcas newspaper: a challenging winter predicted and the Barefoot Bandit's mother says she promised her son flying lessons, and when she couldn't deliver, he taught himself by stealing and crash-landing planes.

First stop, Lowes in Burlington to price dishwashers (for the kitchen remodel) and microwaves (to substitute for the Panasonic that died). The knowledgeable sales clerk explained feature differences and American versus European approaches to drying. With prices and some understanding in hand, we drove a mile south in Mount Vernon to Anderson Appliance where we'd bought a fancy Electrolux side-by-side refrigerator out of their scratch and dent area a while back, saving $900 in the process. They'd been helpful to me when I was trying to diagnose why the refrigerator that came with the house quit cooling, and when after loading the new refrigerator in our pickup, Anderson himself helped secure it to the truck so it wouldn't tip over. The next day Gary and Wilma had taken me and the pickup by barge to Crane, helped us get the new refrigerator off the truck and into the house, and the old one out and onto the truck, and then got me back to Orcas so I could leave it at

Orcas Sanitation for recycling. Today Anderson had a Blomberg dishwasher on sale, like a Bosch but less expensive. That's the one Yvonne wanted, so we bought it. Though they didn't have a microwave that fit our needs, we learned from the clerk that Sharp was reliable. Back in Burlington at Costco, we found the right-sized Sharp on sale and got it, along with a new kitchen faucet. All told, we had saved almost $300.

052: Christmas present project for Opal and her doll

We were in line at the Anacortes Ferry Landing well before the 3:30 departure time, and while Yvonne went to get a treat, I fell asleep reading from my Kindle. We'd get home before dark. On the ferry, I wrote, and Yvonne read. Cabot appeared and said hello. He and Cynthia were stopping by Crane to enjoy their house for a few days. They were away from Anchorage so that he could have minor inner ear surgery in Seattle and had done that in the morning. What time would the sun set, he asked? About 4:00, though the sky would be light for about another hour, depending on cloud cover, but there wouldn't be much of a moon. He was concerned about taking their SeaSport in the dark to Crane from the West Sound Marina where they had it moored. Cabot disappeared downstairs, and Cynthia appeared, Cabot having told her we were aboard. She wanted to talk to Yvonne about gardening on Crane, a subject they'd discussed in the past. Cynthia knew that Yvonne was a Master Gardener and had created an attractive garden behind deer fencing around our house. Cynthia didn't want to fence but did want to plant. What wouldn't the deer eat? How about rhubarb? Yvonne recounted her experience. Deer didn't eat rhubarb, except for Crane deer, who had consumed one we had been given and had transplanted from Orcas. Cynthia made a few more suggestions, and Yvonne told her that, in her experience, Crane deer would eat them as well. Cynthia then said she thought she would plant blackberries. Deer don't eat the plants because of the thorns, and she wanted to be able to pick blackberries in the fall. The thought of planting blackberries confounded Yvonne and me as well as I sat typing and overhearing the conversation. There are few blackberries on Crane but some very large patches on Orcas. They are highly invasive and will drive out everything else. Once they get a foothold, they are very difficult to remove. We each had the thought — why would anyone want to deliberately introduce blackberries to Crane and to their property? Nothing but trouble for Cynthia, whoever buys their house next, and for the whole island. But neither of us said that. What Yvonne did say was that blackberries grow where they want to grow, and if they're not already on Cynthia's property, it's because they don't want to be. I thought that was well said, but Yvonne later told me that Cynthia doesn't listen, only talks, a trait Yvonne doesn't admire. When we got back to Crane in Margaret's boat, there was no sign of the *Kelper*, Cabot, and Cynthia's boat, even though we had stopped at the Post Office, and I expected them to precede us. We had brought over the microwave, faucet, and other Costco purchases but would get the dishwasher, perhaps the next day. Yvonne made a quick dinner, we watched a movie, enjoyed the hot tub, and went to bed looking forward to significant kitchen remodeling action the next day.

Fifty-three: Christmas Carols

> "I sing the body electric,
>   I sing the soul located in the body,
>   I sing the mechanics that upheave the earth,
>   I sing the railroad made of iron,
>   I sing the whistle that responds to my whistle,
>   I sing the engineers who run the trains."
>   From "I Sing the Body Electric" — Walt Whitman

Visible in the slowly rising morning light, the hard rains had eroded the driveway a bit where it started its upward climb to Eagle Lane and the interior of the island. Farther along on my morning walk, I could see that the island water supply tank level had fallen by half a foot from its level two days before. A leak? I'd have to keep track of it. Rainwater filled occasional potholes on Circle Road, our one-lane track through the Crane forest, packed gravel with a center strip of grass and edges of salal. Though there was virtually no wind, as I passed one fir with low-hanging branches, it saluted in greeting, showering the puddle below with conserved raindrops, disturbing the puddle's surface and the picture of the tree and gray sky above it that it had held seconds before. Signs of the rising sun could be seen in the pink and white of higher clouds and blue sky visible through gaps in the thick gray to almost black layer closest to the earth. Ghostly wisps of ground clouds tangled with trees here and there in Spring Point across Deer Harbor on Orcas. Small rocks fallen from Matt's property above littered Circle Road as it ascended from near sea level to the airstrip. Two browsing deer were visible on the west side of the airstrip a quarter mile away near its south end, the other end of the cord the airstrip forms connecting two sections of Circle Road. Lights on at Ilze's house, Josh already at work on what looks like an atrium, where the roof has been cut away and posts rise on either side of the section above the front door. No sign of Cabot and Cynthia's boat at the Crane community dock. The path that cuts across Och's meadow as it runs down to the rocky, gray beach, finally looking like its winter self, soggy, water running slowly across from soil unable to absorb more.

053: Bigleaf maple leaf enters recycling process

Our firewood stack on the front porch was nearly depleted, and I wanted to split more rather than take from what had already been split and stacked, keeping that as a backup. Still, there wasn't time given what we had to accomplish with the kitchen. The floor counters needed to be in place and level by Tuesday for the countertop measurer coming from Seattle and the south, sink area with dishwasher as well as the east area, with the range and open to the dining room needed to be completed. Once Yvonne was up and had her breakfast and coffee (I had made her oatmeal again, forgetting that we again had a microwave and she could and would prefer to make her own), I started to disassemble the current sink and its attachments, a disposal and an instant hot water heater. We didn't want either. Disposals can be hard on septic systems, and septic system problems can be expensive, especially on Crane, and calamitous if a new drain field is required. To dispense hot water instantly, the heater needs to be turned on, and that uses, or from my point of view wastes electricity. Both systems would go — Yvonne suggested to the Deer Harbor Community Club for its rummage sale she expected to help organize in the summer.

The new countertop would have a built-in sink. We wouldn't have that until the 28th, more than two weeks away. My thought was to pull off the sink, remove the old cabinet, put in new IKEA cabinet, cover it with plywood that could be removed for measuring, and then return the plywood so we would have temporary counter space. I would cut a hole in the plywood countertop, lay in the old sink, and reattach it for the interim. While I worked on the sink area, Yvonne finished assembling the drawers. She had assembled everything and put doors on and slid drawers into everything that was installed, except for the pantries — where the doors were waiting at IKEA.

At 11:30, I took a break to have a telephone meeting with Jens in Wellesley. I had sent him a new version of the Annotator software on Wednesday after I had gone through it with Chris. I had included a test database that provided examples of some of the new functions. Besides technology, Jens had some questions about the writing samples he'd sent me, asking whether I thought they were appropriate for our potential market. Most importantly, the new functionality would let Jens add to and structure *Metamorphosis* in any way he chose and then see a finished complete prototype of the book. A good session. We'd see each other in January when he and Susan came out to their Orcas home, and he took a semester sabbatical.

One of our concerns about the new kitchen arrangement was whether the south (sink location) and west (refrigerator location) cabinets would clear one another's handles when one or the other was opened. Yvonne had measured and knew it would be tight but was confident it would work. Once I placed the small cabinet that would stand next to the sink cabinet — that was constrained by where the existing one was located and where the dishwasher would have to be — it was obvious it would not be possible to open the top drawer from the south-most floor cabinet on the west wall. The drawer would collide with the handle from the west-most floor cabinet on the south wall. A potential solution would be to slide the west cabinet a bit north and snug it up against the refrigerator. That worked. There was a 1/4" to spare. By 5:00, the sink cabinet would slide in after cutting through the back panel to allow for the now overly complex plumbing. More tomorrow. It was time to go to the Deer Harbor Community Club Holiday potluck.

Walking to the Crane dock in darkness, punctured by our headlamps, we noticed the *Kelper* parked behind Margaret's boat and that the spotlight was on though dimly. It was obvious the boat's batteries were nearly depleted. That would be a problem for Cabot and Cynthia. A year before, we had helped them jump-start their boat from one of the batteries in our SeaSport when they were rushing to make a Kenmore float plane flight to Seattle. Being the association dock steward at the time, I got approval from the board to buy a rechargeable jump-start unit and put it on a shelf above the dock cart in the association shed just off the beach, next to the dock, to provide help in this kind of eventuality. From time to time, Cranians needed to jump-start their boats or cars parked in the community lot next to the dock. Cabot and Cynthia had had water problems as well, twice, when they were gone and they hadn't turned their water off at their meter, six or seven thousand gallons had been lost, in one case because of a poorly installed frost-free yard faucet and in another because the house drain had been left open to prevent freezing.

About 50 people at the potluck, and everyone happy to enjoy the holiday time together. Carol wanted to talk with me about our commuting back and forth to Crane in the dark and about streaming movies from Netflix. She and Terry didn't have a television and most of their married life hadn't. Terry and I then talked a while about Swedish mystery writers; he was a fan of Mankell and on his recommendation I had read *Dogs of Riga*. I described Larsson's *Millennium Trilogy* as engaging but at times too violent for my tastes. Judith appeared; we had saved a seat for her. Don, in Howard's absence (he was in Oregon visiting his daughter while Sheila was in Florida tending to her aged father), called on Gene for a blessing, and everyone lined up for food. My conversation alternated between Judith, across the table, one seat to Yvonne's left, and Pam, on my left, and Erik, on Yvonne's right. Somehow the topic of philosophy had come up between Erik, a Dane, and Yvonne, and I was drawn into the conversation. Erik had read Ouspensky, studied him for seven years, continued to be interested but dropped it to get on with this practical life. I had read Ouspensky as well and apparently was the only person Erik knew who had besides himself. I had a lot to say but tried not to talk too much. I did talk about Gurdjieff and his concept of the Fourth Way, an approach to enlightenment, as understood by Gurdjieff, that Ouspensky had written about in his book on Gurdjieff. That led to a discussion of religion and Erik's skepticism of the organized variety, and Yvonne talking about Unitarianism, a creedless, congregational, unorganized religious group that provides a community of like-minded people without commitment to any particular belief system. Pam had grown up a Lutheran, like Yvonne, and had appreciated the ritual and community.

Don called on the committee chairs for reports: Erik — a new septic system was affordable and in the works, Judy — the Auxiliary Santa Ship had served 100 children the previous Saturday, and she thanked everyone for their help; Yvonne reported that Grounds was dormant, and everyone laughed. Which, someone asked, the committee or the plantings? Both, Yvonne replied.

Becky had invited Martin to lead Christmas carols, and he had brought an accordion and alternated between it and the Club's upright piano. We sang until hoarse, Martin lending his jazz skills to his playing. Once home, I called Cabot to alert him to his dead battery. He said he had a backup and thanked me for the warning.

Fifty-four: Huginn Home

"Change is inevitable. Growth is optional." — John C. Maxwell

Another mild morning, 43 degrees at 5:36 a.m. Over the past week, the temperature hasn't been below 40, getting as high as 48 one day. A typical 24-hour temperature range: 43 to 45, bizarre for someone who lived in Colorado for 25 years and was used to 30-degree changes dawn to mid-afternoon. On my morning walk, I noticed that the community water system tank level had dropped by a foot, twelve to eleven feet, which meant that the island had used 2500 gallons more than had been pumped. Assuming Gary hadn't changed the pump timer, four occupied households had used more than 600 gallons each — not possible. Something was going on.

While Yvonne finished assembling the last of the kitchen drawers, I worked with the sink cabinet, attaching it to its neighboring cabinet and binding it to the wall, being especially careful that all the floor cabinets that would be part of a continuous countertop around the west, south, and east parts of the kitchen were level in all directions and exactly the same height. Even with my reading glasses on, I had a hard time seeing the bubble and lines in the level. My headlamp, which I wore almost all the time now working on the kitchen and which I found extremely helpful, didn't help. I needed a digital level with a large readout.

Because I'd taken the kitchen sink out the day before, we were without water in the kitchen, an undesirable situation, so with the new sink cabinet installed, I could put the old sink back in temporarily — to take out when the countertop measurements were done in a few days and then put back and use until the new countertops were installed two weeks later. I retrieved my supply of sink plumbing parts from my shop, some I'd had for twenty years or more, and finally found a combination that worked. We now had running water again and a sink but not a countertop around it so in her concern not to splash water on the new floor cabinet, Yvonne suggested that we wash dishes

Fifty-four: Huginn Home

in the sink in the studio pantry, 30 feet away. That would work for the immediate future.

Betsy called from West Sound Marina. Our SeaSport, the *Huginn*, was ready for pickup, its new engine installed. They'd be open until 3:00 but had left the key in the boat's ignition should I need to come later. We'd leave the house at 2:00.

054: Huginn at Deer Harbor Marina December 2007

Having finished her assembly work, Yvonne retired to her studio to continue her sewing project — matching outfits for Opal and her American Girl doll — and I began work on removing the floor cabinets from the east side of the kitchen, on either side of the range, the counter on top, and the bookcase that backs up to cabinets and range and faces the dining area and where Yvonne keeps her cookbooks. I couldn't slide the bookcase out from under the countertop because I had raised the floor level in front of it when I had installed a new laminate floor in the dining room, kitchen, and hallway and I couldn't lift the bookcase over the lip of the floor because of the countertop above. So I applied my circular saw to the countertop, having adjusted the blade depth so as not to cut into the cabinets below — that we wanted to keep and repurpose — and cut the existing countertop into three pieces and removed it. I could now move the bookcase out of the way and then remove the floor cabinets — which were fastened to the floor with angle brackets at the back. The east side of the kitchen was now completely open, and I could begin the process of installing the new floor cabinets, a larger one now to the right of the range and a narrower one to the left, which meant the range would have to shift to the left about three inches.

Yvonne dropped me at West Sound Marina, and I talked to Betsy about what I needed to be careful about with the rebuilt engine in the *Huginn*. She told me I should not run the engine at the same speed continuously but vary it from time to time — and that I shouldn't run at top RPMs. It was a bit before 3:00, and the rain was starting, as Cliff Mass had predicted on his weather blog. Betsy alluded to the coming rain, a classic Pineapple Express, a rise in temperature and heavy moisture coming across the Pacific from the southwest. She raised the topic of Lou Falb and the coming bird count on Crane. I repeated what I'd told Howard: I'd be happy to help and walk around Crane with a counter, but someone needed to call Lou first, as a courtesy.

In the *Huginn*'s cockpit, I raised the engine compartment cover and saw what looked like a brand new engine. What a pleasure! The engine started easily, and running it had a different sound than the original, more mellow and with less vibration because of the second camshaft in this model. The throttle was stiffer but smooth as I took the boat to plane and dashed south the length of West Sound. Slowing down at the No Wake buoy between Bell Island on the south and Caldwell Point on the north, I headed toward Pole Pass, less than a mile away to the west. South of the Crane dock on Orcas, I could see that Margaret's boat was still docked there. I had gotten there faster than Yvonne, who had come the longer route by car. I pulled out my walky-talky and called Yvonne, who it turned out was just coming down the ramp. "Want to bring the dishwasher to Crane now?" Good idea. We loaded it on the *Hug-*

Fifty-four: Huginn Home

inn, the rain now stronger, and in two boats returned to the community dock on Crane. Yvonne went ahead, and I brought the dishwasher home on the hand truck, now with two properly inflated tires after I had one repaired a week before. We could complete the cabinet installation process and be ready for Tuesday's measurements — pending needing some new parts for installing the dishwasher.

Jeni called in the late afternoon, and Yvonne had a wonderful time talking to her. Jeni had hosted a going-away party for the oral surgeon she often worked with, moving from Swedish to Northwest Hospital, in part to be able to charge his patients lower fees. The party room on Jeni's floor at Harbor Steps above the waterfront in Seattle had been remodeled and at least from the pictures Jeni had sent, was very attractive and a perfect place to host the party — with about 40 guests and catered gourmet food. Jeni was getting to know JC better and thought it was almost time for us to meet him. Kirstin was coming from Boulder, and Adrienna from Pittsburgh between semesters to stay with Jen for a few days. Jen would be on Crane for Christmas. Maybe she could come back with her two friends on New Year's Day when James and Keith needed to return to Los Angeles. Jeni has been Skyping with Corrina — who was very unhappy in India — with Arjen and the place — so Jeni told her to come home. Yvonne was very happy Jeni called.

Fifty-five: Wet, Wet, Wet

"No rain, no rainbows" — G.K. Chesterton

Yesterday's Pineapple Express deluge continued this morning until about noon. A raincoat wouldn't be enough; I'd take an umbrella as well and was glad I did. Crane rain is usually gentle, more drizzle than rain and usually doesn't require a raincoat. While not a downpour as I'd seen in Colorado, this rain was substantial and by 8:00 had been coming down continuously for seventeen hours.

Yvonne's water-feature pond, just outside the garden fence on the south, is overflowing, the water draining out toward our cove and then stopped by the raised path. Water flowing down our driveway from Eagle Lane and then turning toward our cove where it creates many little waterfalls, streaming down the ten-foot bank face onto what's left of the beach — the tide close to high. The ditch on the south side of Eagle Lane filled and flowing east, spreading out across the road and then down our driveway. The excavation for Gary's unfinished standpipe replacement project filled with muddy water. Puddles everywhere, some on Circle Road three or four inches deep. At well house #3, a small torrent exits the forest and the higher ground on the Crane interior and the nature preserve and fills the ditch along Circle Road, rushing downhill and then turning into a patch of foam where it ducks under the road and across what we all still think of as Rachel and Marilyn's pasture.

Farther on, at Skip's, water that's come down from Brooke's, 50 feet above, enters an unseen culvert and streams out the other side intent on escaping to the Salish Sea. So far, no erosion and I began to notice how when the roads were scrapped out of the rocky island in 1960, it was done following a design some engineer, now forgotten, had done. The section of Old Road, once part of Circle Road until a new section was cut at the base of the airstrip, and very steep, has no water flow.

055: Fyo and Leo

Why not, I wonder. Fifty feet to the east I can see water flowing down in a grassy ditch; that's the explanation; a water diversion was created when the road was built. A good idea. But the new section of Circle Road, below the airstrip, has eroded, two channels, each six inches wide and four inches deep, zigzag down the road, cutting into the smooth, finely graveled road surface Skip generously had put in a year ago. I later alerted Pat to this new erosion problem by email; he is Crane's new "road commissioner." He explained that we could build a catch basin or put water bars into the road, the latter being his recommendation.

Rather than continue straight ahead, at Becky's, I turned right, continuing to follow Circle Road. I wanted to see how much water was coming from the Island's interior and how the road had been designed to handle it. I discovered two culverts, accepting water from the roadside ditch, filled with fast-moving water, joined by rivulets emerging from the forest. The water crossed under the road and flowed onto Och's land. How much water was escaping the island's interior and how much was retained? I was curious because presumably, Crane's retained rain feeds the aquifer source of the Crane water system.

Backtracking, I turned right onto Dock Road and could see that Och's retaining pond was full, and below the dam, the level-setting pipe, spurting water. Just before the community dock parking lot, ditch water was flowing the wrong way, toward the beach. The culvert here must be clogged and should be cleaned out. The path across Och's meadow was awash in the water I saw cross under Circle Road a few minutes before, undeterred in its return to the sea. We'd had more than three inches of rain in a few days, a deluge since we average only 25 inches annually. We were now at 29 for this year with half of one of the wettest months to come.

Without too much trouble, I finished installing the new dishwasher and started it through a cycle just as Yvonne returned from the Cal-Clarina bench dedication ceremony at the Deer Harbor Community Club. Mike had built the bench and also organized the effort and today acted as MC. Clarina had died in March and had been widely admired in the community she grew up in. Cal's grandfather had come to Orcas in 1877, vowed to return, and did ten years later, buying more than 200 acres on the Orcas side of Pole Pass facing west and had maintained the kerosene warning lights at the Pass, now a red flashing beacon right across from the Crane Community dock. About 50 people had shown up to honor Cal and Clarina, including their three daughters. Eulogies delivered, a photo period followed, with various arrangements of people seated on the big, strong bench that will sit outside the Post Office, an association property. Yvonne came home and made her report and then began filling new cabinet drawers and convinced me to consolidate the tools I had scattered all over the dining area and move them off the living area carpet where they might create grease stains.

On the phone, son Noah reported that our granddaughter, Opal had suffered a reaction to a live flu vaccine but was now recovered. She, with her cousin Hope, and mother, Natasha and grandmother Jan, had seen Olympia's *Nutcracker*, and Opal had loved it. Our Grandson Morgan attended a Christmas party with a dozen happy, screaming children. The host's parents excused Noah when he volunteered to help, so he went Christmas shopping. Son

Fifty-five: Wet, Wet, Wet

James sent more pictures of the kittens he and partner Keith had adopted. All four of them were having a wonderful time. The kittens would be Leo and Fyo (Fyodor), heavy-duty literary names for little kittens Natasha had suggested, and James explained, because the kittens were Russian Blues.

Fifty-six: On the Level

"Measure twice, cut once" — *English proverb*

Before dawn, I put on my headlamp and went out to one of the covered stacks of split firewood outside the deer fence to fill a basket to start the morning fire in the wood stove because I'd been too busy to split and stack wood on the porch. Fog, usually only over the water, had invaded our precinct, and as I walked into it, I was dazzled with millions of glowing dots, a swarm of minuscule stars moving in unison in some extraordinary cosmic dance. I'd never seen fog visible this way before. Fascinating.

Later, as it was getting light, the inter-island ferry foghorn sounded somewhere to the south in Wasp Passage between Crane Island and Shaw Island. It sounded again and again at 30-second intervals as it made its way east in the dense fog heading for Orcas Landing.

Minutes before sunrise, the fog lifted to the east and south, Bell Island in the foreground and Shaw Island in the background became visible, and above them what had been a formless gray, transformed into a complex layer of gray and white clouds and through them, here and there, windows opened to a higher level of peach-colored, sunlit clouds and blue sky. As I looked east to north, toward Orcas, form yielded to formlessness, water, land, and sky merging into one indistinguishable gray nothingness, richness to paucity.

Straight ahead, in front of the house, below the deck and a few feet from the edge of our point above the water, two brown aluminum lawn chairs with plastic strapping we sometimes sit in to admire the view lay on their backs, blown over by a gust during one of this fall's storms. Later, when Yvonne was stringing Christmas lights along the deck rail, she would notice the overturned chairs and walk down to the deck stairs to right them, only to slip on the wet moss covering some of the point's rocks ending up unhurt but on her back after doing the splits on the way down. I comforted her by pointing out that she hadn't gone over the cliff edge onto the rocks or water below. And I

Fifty-six: On the Level

would have laid there for hours because you wouldn't have noticed, she teased. Probably not until dinnertime I replied.

056: From the dining room

During the night, I had worried about the bookcase installed by the original owner facing the dining area that provided a back to the kitchen cabinets and range. Its top edge was about an inch lower than the new cabinets, with a smaller difference in height at the south end than the north. In other words, it wasn't level. I didn't mind the gap between the top of the bookcase and the countertops-to-be because that would allow the bookcase to be raised above the level of the new floor I had installed a year and a half ago so it could be removed, and the area behind, which included the range, made accessible. But

Fifty-six: On the Level

the bookcase not being level was disturbing. Since we moved into the house, my sensibilities had been offended by the countertop and floors not being level and some walls bulging or not being plumb. I had made an effort to level all the cabinets, easy to do because they sat on adjustable legs, one of the smart features of the IKEA system, but I was stymied at first because level cabinets left gaps with the walls and the gaps meant the cabinets would wiggle a bit even though screwed into the wall. Screwing them tight distorted the shape of the cabinets and pulled them out of level. I finally realized I could shim the cabinets and retrieved some cardboard sheetrock shim from my shop and inserted pieces into the cabinet top/wall gap and then tightened the screws to the wall.

I wanted to go through the situation with the bookcase with Yvonne and started to explain it to her as she made her coffee and oatmeal but it became evident she wouldn't be able to focus on kitchen questions until she'd enjoyed her breakfast. When I finally explained and demonstrated how the countertop and bookcase below with a gap in between would look, she was appalled. Fine with me, not with her. She wanted the space filled; but if filled the bookcase wouldn't be removable. (Actually, it wasn't quite that simple). The solution: raise the bookcase so that the top was even with the tops of the cabinets on either side of the range. Over Yvonne's objections, I removed the bookcase and put in a series of shims, resetting it several times until the top was level and even with the cabinets. Then I could re-screw the bookcase and cabinets back together to form a rigid base for the new countertop to rest on. The bottom of the bookcase was now slightly above floor level. It would be no problem to remove it should that be necessary. But another problem was that the cabinets were too close, on either side of the range, to open freely and I couldn't make IKEA's drawer front sideways adjustment work properly. We'd have to pull the cabinet on the north side of the range farther north and then the range but that meant the north side of the cabinet would extend farther north than the bookcase behind it. That wasn't acceptable. Yvonne suggested pulling the bookcase a bit farther north. A good idea and possible because the bottom of the bookcase was now shimmed to be slightly above the level of the new floor, up out of the hole it had been placed in when I installed the new laminate floor over a worn parquet floor. Level and tops and ends even. Great!

During the day I had a conversation with the Precision Countertops installation manager. What ferry would the installer coming to take measurements be on? Did he know how to get to the Crane parking lot on Deer Harbor Road? The installer would call me to coordinate a pickup time at the Crane dock on Orcas. He did. I explained how to find the Crane Island dock parking lot and made arrangements to be there at 9:00 the next day.

Late in the afternoon, I cut plywood to make a temporary countertop while Yvonne continued to put away what she had taken out from the kitchen and stored in the dining room. All that was left were the dishes stacked on the dining room table pushed against the east windows — with three wall cabinets standing nearby to house them once hung from the beam above the bookcase, cabinets, and range. She consolidated my tools into a small area in the living room laying on flattened cardboard boxes that had housed cabinet pieces. The sink was working — with a plywood counter on either side Yvonne had covered with contact paper. The house looked spacious again, with nothing underfoot, leaning against a wall, or waiting for disposal. The back deck was littered with the old dishwasher and torn-out trash, and the front walk was stacked with old floor and wall cabinets, drawers, and cut countertop. It all had to be moved, but inside the house, it looked good, felt good, and the kitchen worked. Progress.

Fifty-seven: Appropriate Technology

"If the only tool you have is a hammer, you tend to see every problem as a nail." — Abraham Maslow

Richard was walking down the Orcas Crane dock ramp as I ascended, carrying a box to put into our van for Yvonne when she went to the Post Office later, when returning Richard to Orcas for his return to Seattle. Richard, an installer for Precision Countertops, would measure for our new countertops today and then install them in two weeks. He turned around, and we walked up to the parking lot together so I could deposit the box in the van and so he could fetch what he needed for the morning. It wasn't much: a clipboard with our order, ten pieces of corrugated cardboard, 24" by 72", and ten more, 6" x 72", an electric glue gun, and glue sticks.

As we made the short trip in the *Huginn* to the Crane community dock, Richard talked about the storms he had driven through this morning on the way north from Seattle to Anacortes to catch the ferry; heavy rain, even hail — we hadn't seen anything like that and didn't expect to since our weather is almost always milder than Seattle's. He hadn't been to Crane before but had been to Orcas the week before and had been "all over" in his 11 years as a countertop installer, his first and only job, and not a likely candidate for outsourcing. I commented on the challenge of measuring for, fabricating, and then installing something in the real world — irregular and inconsistent. His countertops had to conform to the kitchen as it is, with all its construction errors. He would install something that was manufactured and perfect into something that wasn't. The IKEA cabinet system involves installing something manufactured to close tolerances into something that may be off by half an inch. The adjustable legs under the floor cabinets are one interface between the perfect and the blemished; the hanging rail and its adjustments another.

One way to measure for countertops would be to make numerous measurements with a physical or perhaps electronic tape measure. But how many measurements? Thousands? The walls against which the countertop would sit can vary inch by inch, swelling and receding. Forty-five-degree angles might start out that way and change to something else. Richard's way of measuring was to create a template out of cardboard that perfectly matched the reality of the place where the cabinets would be installed. He cut and glued sections of cardboard together, in multiple layers that exactly fit the cabinets below and the walls on the side. After first reviewing what we wanted and answering questions, the template creation process took less than an hour, and when he left with Yvonne, who would take him back to his car on Orcas, he took all his cardboard with him, even the scraps because, he said, he knew if he didn't take the scraps off Crane we'd have to, and he had created them. He'd take the templates back to the shop and discuss the job with the fabricators who would cut the Corian and backings to exactly match the cardboard picture. An analog solution to an analog problem.

In the afternoon, Yvonne and I attached handles to all the new cabinet drawers and doors, and that made the kitchen, other than the temporary contact paper-covered plywood countertops, look finished and handsome. And the process went well; after we decided in general about where the handles should go, I drilled the holes and Yvonne installed the handles. When we had installed the IKEA kitchen on Cayou Valley Road ten years before, I drilled four too many holes — these in the panels above the doors and below the sink — which didn't need any. No extra holes today. When I'd done that kitchen, I made a template out of cardboard to locate the holes consistently on the doors. In the interim, I'd found a plastic template perfectly suited to locating drill holes and used it today — so that all the drawers and doors are visually consistent. More detail work to go. I'd leveled the drawer fronts but was having only occasional success shifting them right or left — even after calling IKEA to confirm that I was turning the right screws the right way. The cabinet door needs adjustment, spacers need to be installed in two places, and the over-the-east counter cabinets need to be hung from the overhead beam.

Fifty-seven: Appropriate Technology

057: Great simple tool: template for drill holes

Yvonne got her Colorado-bound box of Christmas presents mailed off at the Post Office. We talked about and contrasted that experience with the one we usually had at larger Post Offices — long waits. Yvonne completed her doll and doll's mom clothes she was making for Opal, held it up, and I took a picture. Very cute — but she observed that the arthritis in her hands made it impossible for her to sew as well as she wanted. It just didn't come out quite right. Just like my carpentry, I offered, but I don't have arthritis.

Fifty-eight: Improvisation

"Nothing is Plumb, Level, or Square" — Alan Dugan

A Great Blue Heron emerged from the willows at the water's edge and took flight as I approached the community dock, startling me. The day before, a solitary Canada Goose noisily flapped out of the shelter of the metal ramp into safer water ten feet away. To the left off the end of the dock, about twenty Buffleheads and on the other side five Hooded Mergansers. Crossing to Orcas, a Brandt's Cormorant flew left to right in front of me with wingtips almost touching the water. In recent weeks I noticed pieces of what looked like twisted light yellow translucent tubing. I had also noticed gulls paddling along the floats of the Orcas dock here and there, pulling at something attached to the black plastic flotation chambers. The flotation chambers had been covered with a variety of anemone, clams, and Turkish Towel seaweed, and now it was all gone, and I don't know why — except that it's likely the gulls were feeding on the anemone and left pieces on the docks. Broken clouds over Anacortes, invisible behind Blakely, with a little color beginning to show. It wouldn't rain today.

Brian, Chris, and I arrived at Howard's simultaneously and let ourselves into the house where Howard stood with a pot of tea. We sat down around the table happy for the warmth of fellowship and the radiating oil stove. Over the next 90 minutes, our conversation moved from topic to topic and then circled back to pick up dangling threads, some political, some personal. We talked about the Franklin dimension to American culture — thrift, hard work, perseverance, continuous improvement, inventiveness, and community-mindedness — and noted that David Brooks had recommended it becoming an import-export to the rest of the world and its growing middle class. We talked about the wisdom of simple technology, now sometimes lost or replaced by unnecessarily complex and expensive technology — or simple technology invented now for a purpose — like countertop templates made of cardboard.

Fifty-eight: Improvisation

Brian raised the topic of burning garbage to produce electricity on Orcas, solving both the trash removal and power problems. I cited the article in the *New York Times* about Kristianstad in Sweden doing that, and Chris, president of the local power co-op board, pointed out that the return on investment was 50 years. Fortified with fellowship, we went our ways.

After some experimenting, I was finally able to arrange the power plug-in behind the range to be accessible and not in the way of cabinets or range, but in the process had to disassemble the bookcase, cabinets, and range peninsula. Putting it back together, I noticed that nothing was adequately plumb and level — though I thought it had been. Was I mistaken or had I settled on an arrangement too soon? In the IKEA checkout weeks before with six carts filled with kitchen cabinets and other supplies, the customer behind us offered that it had taken him three months to adjust everything in his kitchen, and he finished only by abandoning the effort. I had dismissed him as an incompetent, but he was right. The cabinet tops needed to be perfectly level and the sides perfectly plumb for the drawers and door to line up. That meant adjusting and adjusting until converging on just right, but even while wearing my reading glasses (which kept falling off) and my headlamp, I couldn't see the bubble and level lines well enough. A sorry state. The most important thing for now was to make the kitchen functional for Yvonne, who would be home about 4:00 after a Food Bank meeting. So I gave up on perfection, realizing I'd have more chances before the countertops arrived for installation, and went out to split firewood. My porch supply had run out almost a week before, so I'd been carrying armloads as needed from one of the stacks I'd split last spring, assuming I'd get to splitting soon — but I hadn't. I guessed I had taken one cart full in small loads. Today I would split and bring to the porch two cartloads, a supply that would probably last a week.

I had almost destroyed my fancy fiberglass-handled splitting maul, a secret Santa gift from a year ago, by using it as a wedge and banging on its head with a sledgehammer when I couldn't split a log section in one stroke, and it wasn't intended for such use. A crack had formed in the head, and the first application of the sledgehammer chipped out a section of the steel. If I kept that up, I'd soon be without a maul. I had another, the precursor to this new one, with a heavier though less effective blade and a much heavier head — but its wood handle was cracked and held together by hose clamps. Replacing either or both meant a trip to Orcas. I didn't want to spend the time or money.

Fifty-eight: Improvisation

I needed a solution using what I had on hand. A hypothesis: if I don't split a section in one stroke using the new but head-cracked maul, I'll use the heavier maul with the cracked handle as a wedge, leaving the new maul in the wood and extending the crack it caused, if any, with the old maul-as-wedge — and that will allow me to split without further damaging either wedge. And that's what I did. I should have been doing that all along. Having two blades in the wood worked better than one: I could split faster while using the tools as intended. Learning by almost destroying.

058: Morning sun on Huginn's bow

At dinner, homemade lentil soup, Yvonne reported that the Food Bank was continuing to receive donations — for its building project and for 2011

Fifty-eight: Improvisation

operations. The more than 200 donors needed thank-you notes, and Yvonne had volunteered to help with the writing, convening a group, including Joan, at the Orcas Island Community Foundation to handwrite the appreciations. Enjoying tea with Joyce afterward, Yvonne learned that Larry, George, and others had made a nervous presentation to the Building Commission but had received full approval.

Fifty-nine: Amazing Stories and True

"Storytelling is the essential human activity. The harder the situation, the more essential it is." — Tim O'Brien

One major kitchen remodeling task remained: hanging, from the beam over the range, the three side-by-side 39" by 12" horizontal cabinets with doors that opened upward. Underneath, a counter with plenty of space to the cabinets above, would provide a place to sit and eat. Yvonne and I worked closely together on this and were receptive to and took one another's advice. She discovered right away that if the south cabinet was hung exactly as its predecessor had been, the door wouldn't open because the southernmost corner would hit the lowered ceiling over the bay where the sink and dishwasher were located. The cabinet would have to be shifted north about 3/4" and that would mean shimming out the cavity in the drywall where the south side of the cabinet had been inserted. I would also have to put horizontal supports for the south end of the south cabinet and the north end of the north cabinet. That accomplished, we hung the three cabinets about where they needed to be — leaving about 5/8" between the first and second and second and third cabinets by putting screws through the tops of the cabinets into the beam above. I then drilled holes for the two long bolts that would come down through the beams and through those spaces and then through pieces of mahogany that spanned the space between cabinets and would be snugged up against the bottom of the cabinets to provide support for the middle area. With the cabinets secure, level, and hung in the same plane, we snapped their doors onto the special up-opening hinges Yvonne had installed in the three cabinets some days earlier.

059: Early ferry leaves Wasp Passage heading toward Orcas Landing

Just before full dark, we took the *Huginn* to Orcas and drove to Ruthie's in the Rosario area just north of Moran State Park. We knew Frank and Liz would be there, but only the day before learned that Richard would be there as well, and my first reaction was to be unhappy at the prospect of having to be sociable and polite to him. After each of us spending about 1000 hours — he doing annotations on Jane Austen's six novels and me creating the software to store the annotations and then format them — with the author's original text — into an electronic book we could sell through Amazon and other channels — we had finally published an annotated Jane Austin's *Emma* for Amazon's Kindle ebook reader. After a sustained effort, we had tested the annotation concept and the technology to facilitate it. Now we could experiment with different marketing approaches and adjust the form and content of *Emma* in a second edition, publish the remaining Austen books and then scale the business, bringing in other literature experts to expand the library to hundreds of classics. Using technology not previously available, we would be making the classics more accessible to the modern reader — a worthy goal and potentially financially rewarding. But shortly after *Emma* appeared on Amazon and after we had sold a few copies but not begun the marketing effort, Richard sent me an email insisting the ebook be withdrawn, all his writings returned to him, and the corporation we had started dissolved. I was very disappointed. The corporation was retained, but I returned Richard's investment and after a time of reflection, the remaining three of us interested in publishing annotated ebook classics moved forward, looking for other annotation opportunities to pick up the experiment where it had been interrupted, at the point we could test an annotated classic ebook prototype and the marketing of it. I thought Richard and I were friends; from my point of view, he hadn't acted that way. I didn't want to see him. But Orcas is a small community and it isn't possible to avoid people indefinitely. Ruthie, probably not knowing what had happened, had invited both of us, assuming we were still friends. Yvonne and I would go, and I'd be polite.

Ruthie, a retired high school art teacher and potter whose engineer husband had died years earlier, was always a pleasure to be with — good-natured, spirited, smart, informed. Frank and Liz had had a house on Orcas for 31 years after retiring from southern California. Ruthie, Frank, and Liz were all Unitarian sympathizers and we'd gotten to know them there. I knew Frank had grown up in Prague and escaped the Nazis when they took possession of Czechoslovakia in 1939. I was curious about what he had known about Kafka then, who had died of TB in 1924. He said that Kafka was a recognized author in Prague and he had visited the house Kafka was born in, now a museum, on Old Town Square with its statue of John Hus, an early Protestant. In the 20th Century, Prague was an important European home of Unitarianism, imported by Norbert and Maja Capek from the U.S. — to a responsive Czech group.

I asked Frank how he had escaped from the Nazis, and he gave a long, detailed account, with names, places, and quotations. He had left Prague in March 1939 at age 23, an aeronautics student and pilot. Frank was now 94, handsome, active and still played tennis. After the Nazis closed his university and denied him an exit visa, without telling his family so as not to compromise them, he left Prague by train carrying only an extra pair of socks, a toothbrush and a little cash, getting off just shy of the Polish border and then traveling by foot through areas he knew well having skied there and confident that part of the border would be unguarded. Accepted into the Polish Air force, he had to flee three weeks later when the Nazis invaded and overran

Poland and he began walking south, eventually reaching Turkey three months later. He joined the French Foreign Legion and was deployed to Algeria but ended up in France after the Czech government in exile was established in Paris with the provision that Czechs in the Foreign Legion could join the French armed forces. Not long after getting to France, the Nazi's invaded, France capitulated, and the Vichy government was established with chaos in the cities and countryside. Frank started walking to Spain, preferring Franco to the Nazis but near Biarritz became aware of a British ship docked to take its citizens, now in danger, back to England. Seeing it as a source of deliverance, he managed to board her and hide inside a coil of docking lines until the ship departed. Later on deck, he was taken into custody, and when arriving in Liverpool questioned by authorities. They listened to his story and his request to join the RAF through an officer who spoke German, Frank's second language, but he had no papers; he might be a spy. In Liverpool, they continued their interrogation, in a polite and kind way; after all, he might be telling the truth, and when asked for some proof that he was who he claimed and having heard that the Czech exile government was now in London maybe it would be a source. Frank didn't know the President but he had been in a class taught by the Vice President, a former University professor, who had dated his older sister. Confirmation came from London and Frank was admitted into an RAF training program where he would spend half his time learning English. He did well, and within six months was serving as a bomber co-pilot and then pilot, flying 43 missions and then assigned to a public relations role — telling the story of the British war experience to the American public to build awareness and support. Following his six-month tour of the U.S., he returned to Britain to fly antisubmarine missions. Mustered out of the service in late 1945 with a new suit and very little money overnight he went from an admired defender to a redundant foreigner with British soldiers returning home to a ruined economy, little food, and everyone looking for a job. By chance, Frank met an Indian hotel magnate in London who was looking for experienced help, and since Frank had worked summers in Prague in a hotel to earn spending money, he was hired. Because there were no commercial flights or passenger ships going to India at the time, he used his influence as a retired RAF pilot to secure passage on an RAF transport flight to India and there became the manager of a small hotel in the north, in the Himalayan foothills. And that's as far as we got. Wow!

Sixty: Deer Harbor

"The sun shines not on us but in us." — John Muir

The *Huginn* needed gas, and Yvonne wanted to go to the Post Office, so we took the *Huginn* to Deer Harbor, about a mile north of Crane Island, where we used to live before moving to Crane at the beginning of 2007. It was a sunny day in the low 40s with enough wind from the east to cause a fuss on the water east of our house. However, Deer Harbor, protected on the east (and north and west), didn't show much evidence of the wind.

Cayou Quay Marina, on the west side of the harbor, provides month-to-month moorage. Deer Harbor Marina, on the east side, offers transient moorage as well. In winter, it has more vacant than filled slips. I parked at the fuel dock while Yvonne walked down the dock, up the ramp, and then headed east to the Post Office, across the street from the marina and adjacent to the Resort at Deer Harbor, a Wyndham property.

The Post Office, purchased by the Deer Harbor Community Club in 2008 from Wyndham, is a point of contact among Deer Harbor residents. In the holiday season, the Post Office sported an outside Christmas tree and lights, with green garlands decorating the interior, arranged by members of the Community Club. Today, Yvonne would ship out more Christmas presents and look for Amazon packages to wrap and send out. Our grand-nephew, Aelias, 13, would be going to Japan for a while with other 8th graders, and I had ordered a book I thought would be useful and interesting to him. But it wasn't in the mail — or at least Pat hadn't put it out yet. The Amazon order tracking system said it had been received at the Post Office the day before. Pat told Yvonne she had two big bags of packages she hadn't gotten to yet, being overwhelmed with holiday mail.

Sixty: Deer Harbor

060: Snow berries next-door

While I refueled the *Huginn*, I noticed two men on the upper deck of *Apogee*, a large powerboat owned by resident Bill Anders, NASA astronaut, enjoying their lunch in the December sunshine. Having finished fueling, I sat in the *Huginn* cabin, keeping an eye out for Yvonne returning from the Post Office. Reflected sunlight on the rippling water painted changing patterns on the hull of the *Gladiator*. The *Huginn* rocked slightly, and waves patted the *Huginn's* hull. The cabin was warm in the sunlight. I was drowsy and soon asleep.

Waiting until well out of the marina area, I brought the *Huginn* up on plane, and we threaded our way through a field of crab pot floats, traveled the mile back to Pole Pass, and came down off plane just west of Cal's, on Orcas several hundred yards north of the Crane community dock, and in the Pole Pass no-wake zone area. Walking back to the house across our neighbor's meadow and coming through the trees to our house, we could see the old kitchen cabinets lining the covered walkway to the front door. We hope to move them to a space out back under the rain shelter before son James comes home on the 20th or certainly before Christmas when daughter, Jeni and Yvonne's brother, Ron will come up from Seattle.

While Yvonne worked outside on her garden, raking the debris that had fallen on it during the windy days this fall — fir cones and small branches — I worked on mounting Yvonne's pull-down screen television under the cabinets we'd hung the day before and then installing the lighting I'd saved from the old cabinets. The kitchen was now operational again.

Sixty-one: Run to the Lumber Yard

"The price of inaction is far greater than the cost of making a mistake." — Meister Eckhart

In the kitchen, not long after 4:00, I turned my attention to some unfinished details: the power sources for the lighting to be installed under the wall cabinets on either side of the refrigerator. The new sink cabinet would not contain a disposal or an instant hot water maker, so under-sink outlets were free, each having a wall switch on a gang of three that included the south and east counter lights. I'd run heavy-duty extensions from each outlet under the cabinets (on legs) so that switched power would now be available from behind the refrigerator — where we could run the lines for lighting we'd yet to pick out for those areas. To run the extensions, I had to drill holes in the bottoms of the sink and adjoining floor cabinets. Would that noise wake up Yvonne, at the other end of the house behind a closed door? I hoped not, and it didn't. I then installed the under-cabinet heater I'd taken out a few weeks before. We'd now have heat in the kitchen again if we needed it.

Today's project was to cover the three hanging cabinets whose backs faced the dining area and to add a valence under the front of the cabinets to hide the lighting and wiring fastened to the underside of the cabinets. That meant going to Orcas to the lumber yard, a place I hadn't been to in months but always enjoyed visiting. Strong winds from the east buffeted the *Huginn* as I crossed to Orcas and docked, winds that almost disappeared as I got away from the water. On the dock, I looked for the dock section hinge missing a pin that Jason, Crane HOA president, had emailed me about and found it near the *Huginn* where the first concrete float met the new wood float. It would require a 7" x 3/4" bolt. Wind-driven waves were rocking the two floats, separately where the pin was missing, together on the other side where that hinge was functional. Not good for the dock. I'd pick up a bolt to substitute for the missing pin.

Sixty-one: Run to the Lumber Yard

061: Good neighbor Margaret

The lumber yard parking lot was nearly empty, normal this time of year. In the summer, on a weekend, parking can be a problem. Two men were on duty in the yard building. The younger seemed eager to have something to do. Did they have 1/2-inch 4 x 8 particle board? Yes, but only two sheets that were a bit beat up. They did have 1/2" plywood with one smooth side. I'd need the sheet cut lengthwise into two 20 1/2" strips, since the plywood would be hard to carry whole and hard to cut accurately at home. Done. I also needed some 1/2" by 5 1/2" MDF for the valence. Since the 16' length would be difficult to carry and I only needed a 9' section, I had that cut as well. Then I picked out some 1/2" by 3/4" trim to go on the inside of the valence and the inside of the plywood back covering to hold up the egg-crate-like plastic lattice that would go underneath the lights, to let light through but hide the lights. Then I found the bolt I needed and headed back to the Crane dock parking lot.

I was able to slide the bolt into the hinge without too much trouble, timing the hammer taps (I kept a hammer in the *Huginn* along with other tools) to the movement of the two sections as the waves drove them up and down. Carrying the plywood down the ramp had been a challenge as the strong winds tried to blow me off the ramp. The UPS delivery cabinet had a package for Yvonne. I'd bring that home along with the mail I'd picked up — that still lacked the Christmas present book for nephew, Aelias.

After I shimmed the back of the three cabinets, Yvonne helped me hang the plywood, and it went up without much trouble. I'd work on the valence tomorrow.

While Yvonne cooked up a big pot of spaghetti sauce, the phone rang. It was Margaret, our neighbor whose boat we had borrowed while the *Huginn* was waiting for an engine transplant. We expected her back from Ohio the next day and planned to leave her boat on the Orcas side so she could get home. But no, she was still in Ohio. Her cat, Moonie, was ill, perhaps fatally. She couldn't travel with him, and she couldn't leave him; she would stay with him in Ohio. We looked forward to seeing her and including her in whatever parts of our Christmas she wanted to join — but we also understood her connection to Moonie, a big, overweight, white male who I never saw move faster than a slow walk — because our loss of Samantha, the world's best dog, this late summer, had been a sad time. We missed her.

Sixty-two: Elin's Birthday

"We are each other's harvest; we are each other's business; we are each other's magnitude and bond." — Gwendolyn Brooks

My mother's birthday. She would have been 94 today but succumbed to some kind of liver failure five years ago just before her 89th birthday as I flew home from Colorado Springs where I had spent time with her in her final week, and sisters, Marcy and Julie had been looking after her in a convalescent home since September.

At 7:30, sitting next to the warm wood stove, writing, the phone rang — I knew who was on the other hand — our friends in Boulder were celebrating the winter solstice, and after chanting up the sun were having breakfast together, waiting to call us in shared celebration until they were sure the sun was close to rising on Crane Island. (This time of year the sun wouldn't rise until about 8:00 and then set again about 4:15). Because Boulder is on the 40th parallel and Crane is north of the 48th, their sunrise was about 20 minutes earlier for them and their sunset about 20 minutes later. I think they had thought we would have the same sunrise time as they had but an hour later because they were in the Mountain Time Zone and we were in the Pacific.

Yvonne, not quite awake, picked up the phone from our bedroom and reported she'd been dreaming she was talking with them. We missed them — Tessa and Alan, Ann and Dave, Barb and Dean — and they missed us. They'd been talking about coming to see us in the summer — when we would all go to Victoria and Vancouver Island and then Vancouver. They had talked about politics and become discouraged and then at Ann's urging had talked about beauty. Yvonne and I — and with our kids when they were young — began celebrating the equinoxes and solstices with Ann and Dave in 1979, including Alan and Tessa some years later — we were all members of the Boulder Unitarian Church. Then in 1991 we made our first Chimayo, New Mexico pilgrimage walk, with Barb and Dean included from then on the next year. Always laughter, often sadness at loss or troubles, invariably analysis of society and politics, all underlaid with a deep appreciation of the miracle of life and love.

Mary was eager to play piano for the Unitarian Christmas Service but would need a ride from and to the Rosario area. Ruthie, who lived close by, couldn't help because she would be off the island with family. I called Ray and Kathy, but they would be off the island as well. Sheila, back from Florida, reported success in making arrangements for her failing 88-year-old father and that after two weeks with him had found a way to reconcile with him, an at times hurtful curmudgeon. After a typical tirade, she pointed out to him that they were both too old for conflict, their time together limited, and their disagreement ultimately irrelevant. He agreed. His malfunctioning embedded defibrillator had been removed after it had stopped and then restarted his heart unnecessarily several times and a new defibrillator surgically installed. Sheila said that they would be happy to drive Mary home after the service and without having to ask Howard volunteered him to read Dylan Thomas' "A Child's Christmas in Wales" at the service.

Pam called and invited us to their house on the way back from Chris and Lynn's, but Yvonne declined; too much going on. Pam said that her mother's dementia was particularly hard now that Pam's father, her husband, had died. Her mother would wonder where he was, Pam would explain that he had died, her mother would experience the loss, grieving the loss of her life partner, then forget and ask Pam where her husband was.

More kitchen work. After putting on a coat of primer, Yvonne covered the hanging cabinet's plywood backing with textured wallpaper, which she then painted with "Crunch," the light green that covered the particle board beam cover and most of the living room. She went on to pay bills and hang tarps around the periphery of the rain shelter where we'd store the old cabinets now stacked against the studio wall under the overhang of the front walk. I installed a valence beneath the front of the hanging cabinets, Yvonne having helped me rip the 5 1/2" by 1 1/2" MDF to 5" so it would match the cover over the rear of the cabinets. I could now slide in the egg-crate lattice under the counter lighting. Pending some finishing touches, the kitchen was not just operational but looked almost finished, the most obvious deficiency the white contact paper-covered brown-painted plywood that served as temporary countertop.

Sixty-two: Elin's Birthday

062: Ground fog on the landing strip

Just before dark, we took the *Huginn* to Orcas, stopped at the Post Office to mail bill payments and at the marina store picked up the *Sunday Seattle Times* Nicole had held for us after Yvonne called her earlier in the day.

Chris and Lynn were hosting their annual solstice open house, and Cayou Valley Road was almost impassable because of all the cars parked on both sides of the narrow road. More people would attend this year than ever had in the past even though the invitation list remained pretty much constant. More people were staying on Orcas for the holidays. As we walked toward their driveway, Al and Sue, whose open house we had enjoyed two weeks earlier,

Sixty-two: Elin's Birthday

were making their way to their car. The house was ablaze with every kind of outdoor Christmas light, standing out from other houses — usually with a single string to protest the darkness and celebrate the return of the light.

The aroma of the feast inside was palpable before we opened the front door and let ourselves in. Wall-to-wall people, talking, listening, laughing, eating. Chris greeted us as I took off my coat, and I noticed Richard had been invited and was accompanied by a pretty blonde. Gordon came up immediately and said he needed to transfer a coffee pot to me that Sylvia had borrowed from Yvonne, so I put my coat back on and we walked to his car and then mine. He would be dropping Sylvia at the ferry shortly, and she'd ride with Julia and Jay to Seattle where she would again take up her duties as grandma to help Nicole with her new baby. We saw Frank and Liz again, and I thanked Frank for telling me his wartime story and told him I'd written up a condensed version.

Yvonne and I made our way to the food tables: soup, salads, breads, fruit, cheese, pastries, cake, brownies, cookies, wine, cider — a feast. I brought Brian some soup as he sat visiting with Ken. Howard and Sheila came in a bit after we did. Bev brought over her newly married daughter Brandy, from York, England, a historic city Yvonne and I had visited years back when we traveled with Alan and Tessa there and in the Lake District. Michael explained that Cat had stayed home but was continuing to improve. She had been at death's door a year ago from an undiagnosed condition but after a liver transplant was gaining weight and strength day by day. Eric explained more about how he would provide water to his marina by barge and showed me pictures of the water barge he'd bought, would fill and have towed to Deer Harbor, to cope with the failure of the marina well some years back because of saltwater intrusion, the result of over-pumping a well close to the water. Steve and Nancy had rafted the Grand Canyon in May after her sixteen-year-old permit application had finally matured; her third trip — she accompanied the raft in a kayak. Ken and I talked wildlife experiences. I told him about seeing an Eagle fly by our living room windows with a seagull in its talons. Then he told me how he'd seen two eagles pursue a seagull that tried to escape by diving into the water and then emerging and flying straight up only to have one of the eagles fly underneath, upside down, pluck the gull with one talon, turn upright and fly off. Chris and I agreed to talk soon about the Slocum project and reengage David who we hadn't seen for six weeks.

Sixty-two: Elin's Birthday

The Crane dock on Orcas was bathed in the light of a nearly full moon. A lunar eclipse would be visible, if the night was clear, tomorrow. We made our way back to Crane on the calm water. Yvonne would pick up James tomorrow at SeaTac and bring him home — after stopping at Costco — and IKEA to pick up a few more kitchen project item.

Sixty-three: James Comes Home

"Everyone is a moon, and has a dark side which he never shows to anybody." — Mark Twain

Half an hour before dawn, a very high tide, all the beach and some brave grass drowned in the clear cold water of the Salish Sea. Six ducks break out of the shore willows, flapping 150 feet to a refuge next to the breakwater. A Kingfisher scolds me, our solitary Canada goose paddling slowly along the east float. The sky is broken, mostly clouds. I turn the battery switch, start the engine, and turn on the navigation lights while Yvonne unties *Huginn*'s lines from the Crane dock and pushes the boat away from the dock into the east wind. As we bounce toward the dock on Orcas, the *Evergreen State*, the 7:35 Interisland Ferry, makes its turn to pass the south side of Bell Island. Yvonne will catch the 9:15 ferry to Anacortes, pick up paint there, then drive 92 miles south to IKEA, make some returns and new purchases, and then pick up James, our Bub, at SeaTac, stop at Costco, and then return to the Anacortes Ferry Landing.

Coming back to Crane, I set off on my regular round-the-island walk. On Eagle Lane, not far from our house, I saw that someone has dug out the ditch next to the road — who? — and then I saw that a new standpipe had been installed twenty feet up the road. Gary had cleared the ditch to drain the standing water from the standpipe excavation done six months before when he removed the PVC model so he could install a new steel version. Rounding the corner onto Circle Road, I noticed two fallen trees held off the ground by their branches and candidates for slicing up and bringing home, possibly by dock cart since it would only be a quarter mile each way. On the north side of the island, passing Skip's, something small flew across my field of vision, but I couldn't make it out. Farther on, at the base of Old Road, I could see Winter Wrens on the ground and among the fir branches, flitting from place to place so quickly I could hardly follow them with my eyes.

Sixty-three: James Comes Home

063: Ferry docked at Orcas Landing, two miles away

The Crane Island Association bookkeeper had sent me checks to sign and mail, so I made copies for my Treasurer's file and put the originals in stamped envelopes she had prepared. Steve had finally paid his dues, so I made out a deposit slip, endorsed the check, made copies, put the original in an envelope for the bank, a copy for the bookkeeper, and a copy for my file. Fall collections were complete, except for Becky, who promised to make installment payments. I sent out an email invitation to the Christmas Eve Candlelight Service to the Unitarian community and returned to the kitchen project. After a late lunch and a trip to the Post Office to complete my Treasurer duties and pick up mail — three Christmas packages — I continued work in the kitchen, experimenting with door dampers that wouldn't install, drilling holes for and installing handles, trying one toe kick assembly, installing spacers between the three hanging cabinets, figuring out the best way to fill the southeast and southwest corners. Little to show for all the time.

Yvonne called while she and James waited in the Anacortes Ferry line and then when docking at Orcas Landing. The *Huginn* bobbed on waves driven by strong southeasterly winds as I crossed to Orcas to pick them up. James came down the fixed ramp in the dull light of the full moon obscured by clouds, and we hugged. Wonderful to have him back. Where was the dock cart? The smaller, lighter dock cart still sat below the ramp where it had been since midday, so we used the larger heavier cart to move Costco purchases to the *Huginn*. Yvonne was happy to have James within hugging reach.

A tour of the kitchen, some spaghetti I'd left for him — with Yvonne's delicious sauce she'd made the day before — and some visiting, catching up about Keith, the kittens, grad school. Because of the cloudy sky, we'd given up on seeing the lunar eclipse, but when Yvonne and I sat in the hot tub wondering at the peculiar color of the clouds, we realized that we could see the moon though through a gauze of clouds — but it was cold and windy on the deck. When we came in, we told James, and he thought of the telescope collecting dust atop a bookcase in my office. Yvonne then found that the moon was visible through the skylight in our bathroom. James set up the telescope, and for the next half hour, we watched the earth's shadow devour the moon, leaving a dim copper-colored circle. James took photos and video through the eyepiece of the telescope with his iPhone, and I had some success with my small Nikon. Our own heated observatory, perfectly aligned to see a lunar eclipse falling on a solstice — the first time since 1648. A memorable return home for our youngest son.

Sixty-four: Christmas Dinner in a Box

"Courage is going from failure to failure without losing enthusiasm." — *Winston Churchill*

Yvonne and James left for Eastsound about 9:30, and I got back to work on the kitchen. In two places, the new floor cabinets had a different footprint from the old ones, and the plywood subfloor was exposed outside where the toe kick would be, by the kitchen door and at the southwest corner. I'd saved scraps and one full plank from almost two years before when I'd put in a new laminate floor when the cork floor I installed when we moved in accumulated too many scratches and other defects to be acceptable.

Because it was a floating floor, it was easy to pick up the four sections that covered the floor at the kitchen door. It turned out I had what I needed in my scraps collection, and after shimming the inch-and-a-half strip of subfloor that was exposed, I cut and laid down a new arrangement of laminate. I had to patch one small section I'd cut out to go around the extended corner of the old corner floor cabinet by cutting a 1 x 1 1/2 rectangle, using my pneumatic brad nailer to hold it in place. I used a Sharpie to blacken the boundaries of the little rectangle, rubbing it in to soften the lines. The floor, an antique hickory, was brown and black, so it was impossible to see the rectangle without looking for it. I did the same thing in the southwest corner, though the piece was bigger and more noticeable but in a place no one would likely look.

I installed a toe kick under the cabinets along the west wall with a break to allow for the grill of the under-cabinet electric heater in the south cabinet on the west wall. Now working on the south, sink, and dishwasher wall, I pulled out the dishwasher and leveled it, installing a toe kick along the south wall and under the south cabinet on the east wall, finally adding a toe kick under the north wall cabinets, as Yvonne, now home again, hung the pantry doors she'd gotten at IKEA just before picking James up at SeaTac.

Sixty-four: Christmas Dinner in a Box

064: James and Yvonne compare notes

Yvonne and James returned from Eastsound, the Food Bank, and the Market, about 3:00. The Food Bank Christmas Box distribution had been a big success. The ten volunteers had served 136 families — maybe 300 people, six percent of the Orcas population. Yvonne provided turkeys and hams, and James handed out produce — fresh potatoes, yams, sweet potatoes, celery, carrots, dried beans and rice, and frozen corn and peas. What did James notice? People of all kinds — some well-dressed — some bearded, solitary male recluses who might live in a teepee or converted school bus in the woods, mothers with small children, agents for other people who were homebound but hungry — all grateful and polite, some embarrassed, none pushy or demanding. Not everyone took fresh vegetables or turkey or ham, James noticed. One man said he didn't know how to cook a turkey. James, who had cooked Thanksgiving dinner with Keith for friends, wanted to suggest looking up cooking instructions on the Internet but didn't because he realized this man probably didn't have a computer and maybe didn't use what was available at the Library. He was certain that some others in line had no way to cook a meal — no oven and maybe no stove. And still others who had a hard time grasping what it was they had in their hands. A few, he thought, were clearly meth addicts, victims of an insufficiently recognized plague infecting especially rural America.

And that led to discussion of the journal article James had been working on in the late afternoon, sitting by the fire, with papers in piles, arranged around him on the floor. He was making revisions to an article provisionally accepted for publication in which he was the primary author and his two neuroscience advisors secondary authors. It would be his first publication as the primary author. The paper looked for associations between risk-taking personality types and alcohol addiction. A few other studies, with young adults, had found a significant correlation; his study, of older subjects, had found just the opposite: alcohol addiction was associated with lower risk-taking. Why the difference? Maybe young binge drinkers, risk-takers, don't turn into alcoholics. Or maybe addiction to alcohol makes people more conservative because they don't want to do anything that will threaten their alcohol supply.

We talked about meth and what it does to the human brain, destroying the areas important for decision-making and planning and where Gina was living, our one-time addict niece, and how she was getting along. We talked about Natasha's brother Justin's baby mama and brother Seth's baby mama — lost to drugs and their young children. A scourge. Yvonne talked about her attempts to keep in contact with nieces Sarah and Samantha. She could follow them on Facebook — neither had de-friended her yet — but neither would return emails or telephone calls — still mourning the losses of their mother and father — to after-effects of drug addiction. A scourge. Two years ago, Gina, who was on parole and regularly attending AA, had spent Christmas with us. She was joined by her youngest daughter Cressie, who lived in eastern Washington. Now Gina was lost again — to her daughters and to us. Two years ago Sarah and Samantha, Tony's other daughters, had joined us for a holiday brunch at Ivar's on the Seattle waterfront. Now they were gone too, at least for Yvonne and her brother Ron, the two young women having rejected both aunt and uncle. But Yvonne would persist in her one-sided communication. Maybe they'd be willing to return contact sometime in the future. She wanted them to know — and Gina too — that she was there for them whenever they needed or wanted her.

Sixty-five: Signs of Spring

"In the depth of winter, I finally learned that within me there lay an invincible summer." — Albert Camus

James is a night person, preferring to rise after 9:00. So, though he got up at 7:00 to go with me to the Greybeards at Howard's, it disrupted his diurnal rhythm, and he said he might listen more than talk. David was back after two trips off-island and a great deal of time spent as President of the Medical Center Board planning and negotiating new operating arrangements — that are not yet public — but put the Center on more solid footing, expanding from one full-time physician to multiple doctors, some available part-time. Chris, recovering from an intense month of a cappella practice and performance and acquiring a new director — former director Dennis and wife Candy having moved to Oregon — performing ongoing OPALCO President of the Board duties, annotating Slocum's book, and hosting, with Lynn, their annual solstice party. Howard had a mild black right eye and a bruise mark at an angle across his right cheek and nose. A board he was sawing kicked back and almost knocked him over. Brian was on his way to SeaTac to pick up his son, Brad. David and James hadn't met before.

I briefly described the paper James was writing, and James added detail about studying the correlation between risk-taking and addiction, especially alcohol addiction, with the finding that youthful binge drinkers are high-risk takers and older, alcohol-dependent adults are not. Why the difference? Has alcohol changed their brains, or were they never high-risk-taking binge-drinking youth — that is high-risk takers do not become alcoholics. Chris thought some version of the latter was probably the case. Howard opined that drinking may be a way for some people to hide psychic pain, a kind of self-administered general anesthetic. Howard also talked about the binge drinking he saw among the native people he and Sheila lived among for nine years when they taught school months in Alaska near the Arctic Circle, their summers in Deer Harbor.

James talked about his advisor's problems with LA animal rights activists — car bombing, threats on his life — and the general response of the group was that they were people looking for an excuse to justify malicious behavior.

Bob, absent from the group for more than a year, since he and Megan had moved to Eastsound, had been living in the Friday Harbor convalescent center for almost three months, but his benefits would expire on the 27th, and he'd have to move back home with Megan: he was eager, but she wasn't. He couldn't walk now and required a catheter. She was older than he was, probably at least 85, and didn't have the strength to help him move in and out of bed, and since he was a demanding person, she had probably been enjoying her lower-stress life. Their house would need a wheelchair ramp, and Howard had volunteered us to build one — though details about the how and when were scarce. David said that he and Maxine had been talking about what they would do when they needed care, and their current thought was to hire a cook and helper to live with them, on their lower level. That would cost less than some kind of assisted living facility, and they could stay in their Deer Harbor house they loved. What did James think of the Greybeards? Nice. I enjoyed watching him talk with my friends — expressing himself well and being engaged.

After a little "down time," James requested had as relief from having gotten up so early, Yvonne, James, and I moved all the cabinets and removable trash from the front walk to the 12' x 12' rain shelter Yvonne had walled with two brown tarps. With the cabinets arranged around the periphery and drawers returned to their slots, I could now see and eventually use and move the cabinets to my shop-shed — sometime in the future. While Yvonne swept the front walk and then raked the front yard, I loaded firewood and moved two carts-full to the front porch (I'd taken probably a full cart in smaller increments when I'd run out of wood a few days earlier) — Grand Fir — I think — a windfall I'd found lying across Circle Road south of the airstrip Labor Day weekend. Because our pickup was on the island then, I was able to slice it into sections and bring it home — all within a few hours. The wood lit and burned easily — much better than Douglas fir.

Yvonne had discovered that some crocus were showing themselves. Later I pointed out to her the green thickening buds on the hawthorn next to the hot tub. Too, I had seen three tiny ants on each of the two notebook computers and one on me in bed, a sign the dormancy period was ending for these harmless but annoying creatures who create supply lines across the kitchen floor — or other areas — for a few months each year.

065: Our Crane Island-grown Christmas tree

James and I cut a small Grand Fir not far from the house that Yvonne and I had found during a scouting expedition we had mounted earlier while he took a nap. While Yvonne and James decorated the tree, I worked in the kitchen on toe-kicks and spacers between sections. Yvonne put two coats of paint she'd gotten Monday when passing through Anacortes to pick up James, on the wallpaper-covered plywood backing the hanging cabinets and then mounted Corrina's sunflower photo print — with hand-worked Swedish candle sconces we'd bought in Båstad four years before when visiting Kajsa and Ola there. At 3:30 Yvonne announced that all construction would cease at 4:00, and the house needed to be cleaned out, with no more construction until after Christmas. We were on Christmas vacation. A relief for me — I was tired from all the physical labor of the last month. Precision Countertops called to say they couldn't install the new countertop on the 28th — because they needed more time to make an aluminum frame to support the Corian in the gap in the countertop we use/will use as a table. They might be ready January 4th. I'd have to let Gary know and reschedule his barge. So the kitchen would be torn up a bit longer than expected. But we'd also have more time to fine-tune it. That wouldn't be a bad thing.

While I tried to figure out why I no longer could transfer images from my Nikon S8000, Yvonne and James made Christmas cookies. With all the tools out of the dining room and the kitchen put away, it was a great pleasure to enjoy a white lasagna dinner and talk.

Sixty-six: High Water

"Finish each day and be done with it. You have done what you could. Some blunders and absurdities no doubt crept in; forget them as soon as you can. Tomorrow is a new day. You shall begin it serenely and with too high a spirit to be encumbered with your old nonsense." — Ralph Waldo Emerson

Just before 6:00, in the dark, I noticed James' bedroom door wasn't closed — why? — so I pulled it closed so I wouldn't disturb him as I started my morning routine in the kitchen — beginning with cooking oatmeal — and he turned on the light — he was awake or had been sleeping very lightly. After he said it three times, I could, without my ear whistles installed, understand what he was saying. His two-week-old cold had germinated an ear infection — or at any rate, he had an earache he'd treated with ibuprofen during the night. I told him that when he got up we'd call the Medical Center and that it likely wouldn't be any problem to get him an appointment. He went back to bed and turned off the light. I closed his door and then went into my office — where we also watch Netflix DVDs — and saw that he had been watching *Titanic*, a film that he and I had seen together twice, the first time also with Yvonne.

I took my camera — that I'd had trouble with the day before — because I suddenly wasn't able to transfer image files to my MacBook Pro — into the living room to take a picture of the Christmas tree Yvonne and James had decorated the day before. Set into the bay that extends the living room three feet to the east, toward the water not far away, windows on two sides reflected the single string of white lights Yvonne had hung and the glass-walled China cabinet also behind part of the tree created a reflection as well. There were four delicately lighted trees with a dark background — all lovely — where in the day, with backlighting from outside, the Salish Sea, Bell Island, Shaw Island, Orcas Island, and the big world outside were all visible through the sparse limbs of the little Christmas tree, so that it almost wasn't there at all. In the dark, aglow, it was beautiful and full. In the light, it was anemic, maybe even a bit sad. The picture turned out well — capturing the visual fullness of the tree — and adding a sparkle to the lights.

066: High water mess

Later as I walked outside in the dawn light to make my island rounds, I saw that the water in our little cove was brown — where it was usually clear. Wind-driven waves and a continuing extraordinarily high tide were eroding the soil at the head of our cove. The cove was filled with debris — tree trunks and branches of all sizes crowded to the back bouncing up and down on the waves. The huge stump under the heavy ramp to the beach was also lifted by the water and as I saw later on close inspection had pulled the ramp away from its resting spot on the bank. If I hadn't tied the ramp to a willow stump this fall it would have fallen into the cove by this time. The winds had blown for several days, and predictions called for more days of high winds, a feature of the San Juan's at times during the fall. I struck out on my walk, and as I moved inland the wind was less noticeable among the trees though it reappeared in clearings here and there. The tank was now over 13' and had risen a foot over the last week. At 14' it would overflow, and the pumped water would be returned to the ground, perhaps to reenter the aquifer. I'd have to let Gary know. The daily pumping hours would need to be reduced.

Determined to be able to download images from my Nikon S8000 to my Mac, I read through the problem description and solution suggestions I found on the web. The night before on the telephone, Nikon service had suggested I download the latest version of the transfer program, but that made no difference. The camera was still under warranty, but I didn't want to have to send it anywhere — and be without it. Participants in a number of discussion groups suggested using a memory card reader device. Maybe I could get one in Eastsound when James and I went there later in the day. Then I realized my old Averatec Windows notebook computer might have a memory card reader. It did! I took the memory card out of the Nikon, inserted it into the Averatec, and began to transfer images to a folder on the desktop — and then the transfer quit, telling me it had encountered a corrupt file. I found the bad image file — it had a file number much lower than all the other files in the folder on the memory card. What was it doing there? It wasn't one of the pictures I'd taken since I last transferred images and had iPhoto erase images from the Nikon. After transferring all the images to the Averatec, I put the card back into the Nikon and told it to erase all images and then took a picture and found that both the Averatec and Mac with iPhoto found and could transfer this new single image. The transfer problem was caused by the corrupt image file and nothing in the camera or computer transfer programs told me about it; the programs just hung up. And the cause of the corrupt file — with filename out of sequence with the other pictures I'd taken since the last transfer and erasure — was iPhoto, I'm certain. In the past, I'd always erased transferred files with the camera's routine, but after the last transfer I'd let iPhoto do it — but it hadn't done that correctly — probably leaving the first file in the folder empty but the name was not cleared from the folder directory — and neither the Mac nor Windows (XP) utilities had anticipated such a problem and hung up rather than asking whether I wanted to skip the bad file.

Yvonne had gotten out her paint and was now painting the valence on the kitchen side of the hanging cabinets. I told her about my conversation with James and she made out a shopping list for the Market, both of us pretty certain I'd be taking James to town to have his ear looked at. James got up about 11:00, now having had adequate sleep, but his ear still hurt. Dr. Bishop could see him at 1:30 so that became the plan. The ride to Orcas was bumpy as the *Huginn*, heading east, rode up and over the waves coming west, and as we turned north to go into the dock and got into the troughs, the boat wobbled sideways, startling James. We picked up the mail at the Deer Harbor Post Office, including a box from my sister Julie and an association dues installment check from Becky. Steve had paid in full earlier in the week. Other than further payments Becky would make, the Crane Island Association annual billing and collections were complete. I would now turn my attention as treasurer to the expense side of the ledger. We stopped at West Sound Marina so that I could pay the bill for the recent engine transplant and put it on a charge card to delay having to actually pay the $5200 bill a bit longer. In Eastsound, we stopped at Radio Shack to see if they had any digital picture frames since that morning it had occurred to me that it would be nice to give Yvonne one with representative pictures from the year — but they had sold their supply. The Medical Center was quiet, Brian driving out as we drove in, having been there for physical therapy, I guessed. James' UCLA insurance card was well-received and he had no co-pay to make and we took his amoxicillin prescription to Ray's Pharmacy to be filled and went to the nearby Market to pick up groceries from Yvonne's list and then back to Ray's to pick up James' medicine. The wind was still blowing but this time we traveled with the waves. Close to the Crane dock, trying to deal with the crosswind, I scraped the *Huginn*'s stern swim platform against the dock, rubbing off a little of the swim platform corner. Yvonne served us roasted chicken and rice and salad — with dressing James made up and we lingered at the table talking more about James' school and Keith and his two new kittens. A movie, *Eat, Pray, Love* and then Yvonne and I soaked in the hot tub and then retired leaving James in charge. I kept reading the same page of Crane Islander Stuart Kauffman's *Reinventing the Sacred* over and over trying to finish it but kept falling asleep. Yvonne suggested I just go to sleep. And I did.

Sixty-seven: Christmas Eve

"'Call the fire brigade,' cried Mrs. Prothero as she beat the gong. 'They won't be here,' said Mr. Prothero, 'it's Christmas.'" — "A Child's Christmas in Wales" by Dylan Thomas

Another mild and very windy day — driving waves and carrying logs into our cove — which on persistent high tides lap the steep bank, rock on both sides but soil at the head of the cove. Yesterday I noticed that water had budged the heavy cedar plank that serves as a ramp into the cove from a walkway I carved into the bank in May. Now the upper end of the plank had fallen off its perch on the bank and was hanging from a chain connected to a rope tied around a stump, left from removing a willow that had bent over the water and made it impossible to walk safely on the the path. Not long after we moved to the house, Demetri and I had lifted the plank and positioned it where it then stayed for almost four years. I'd have to do something about the plank — but not right now.

Yvonne, Lynn, and Sheila were in charge of the refreshments for the Unitarian Candlelight Christmas service in the late afternoon. Howard would read "A Child's Christmas in Wales," as he had done twice before to the congregation, Dylan Thomas' word picture of a simpler and richer time. I would act as moderator, would say something about Christmas and invite others to comment. We'd sing five carols and Mary would play the piano.

The day before I'd read a number of UU Christmas sermons I'd found on the Internet and two I especially liked were by Gary Smith, minister at the First Unitarian Church in Concord, MA, a church we attended sporadically when we lived part-time in Concord while James was in high school at Middlesex just north of the historic town, once home to Emerson, Thoreau, Alcott, Hawthorne, and other American literary lights. In the sermon he delivered on December 19th, posted on the church website, Smith talked about the Christmas story being about incarnation, of the divine born in each person, a moral ideal to strive for.

067: Christmas Eve cookies coming

This was conscience for Emerson, an intuitive, transcendent sense about what's right, available to all people who are willing to pay attention to it. The recurring celebration of the birth of Jesus, the Word made Flesh, is a reminder of the numinous in each person, of the fundamental equality of all people, of the continuing need to make the world better, of never giving up on the ought and just settling for the is.

Ron had called at 8:30 to tell us that he and Jeni wouldn't make the noon ferry. Jeni couldn't get ready in time. They'd be on the 3:30, so Yvonne would leave the UU service at 4:30, pick them up, and then return to get James and me.

In the course of formulating something to say about Christmas, I consulted Jakob Trapp's poetry. After serving the Summit, NJ UU Church for twenty years he and his wife retired to Santa Fe, NM, and he would make an annual trip north in his ancient VW Bug to deliver a sermon to the Boulder, UU congregation. When James was very little, Jakob stayed with us one weekend and we kept him supplied with whiskey and he us with poetry — that he could recite endlessly from memory. He loved New Mexico as did we and his poetry reflected the influence of that beautiful, holy land, its history, and the centuries-old presence of the Pueblo Indians and Spanish immigrants. His poems introduced us to Chimayo, years before we began our annual pilgrimages there. After having retired as UU moderator, organizing services and needing to speak thoughtfully if only briefly at almost every service and therefore having to read, research, think, and write — over a period of six years — I realized I missed the process. It had been a necessity, a responsibility, but also a pleasure, since I had a reason, an excuse, a duty to indulge a preoccupation I'd had since childhood — to wonder why we're here.

I dropped Yvonne and James at the West Sound Community Hall, counterpart to the Deer Harbor Community Club, venue for West Sound potlucks and the Orcas Island Yacht Club, an organization Yvonne and I belonged to for some years when we, me especially, wanted, in the worst way, to be out on the water. Once on Crane and on the water every day nearly, and after cruising up and down the Salish Sea, Olympia to Desolation Sound, the craving for more subsided and last spring we sold our 33' sailboat, retaining a 20' daysailer.

Mary was waiting for me outside her house in Rosario. She didn't have a car and so needed a ride to the UU service so she could play piano for us. Since Margot had been in charge of music I hadn't much talked with her in the past; now I asked about how she came to Orcas and then details about her life in a Norwegian family growing up on a farm outside Knapp, Wisconsin. She was the second child of two and should have been a boy so she took a boy's role — milking cows, helping hay, mucking out the stables.

About 20 people appeared for the service, more than I expected, seven of them newcomers we encouraged to return in the future. A lovely time together. Howard's reading, in his English accent and sometimes imitating a Welshman, conjured up the experiences and feelings of a small boy in a small town on a snowy Christmas Eve.

Late in the service Howard and I passed out candles with paper tutus to protect hands from dripped wax. As we sat in our circle, Howard rose to light his candle from the Flaming Chalice and then each of us lit ours from the candle on the left, and the room darkened with the setting of the sun behind thick clouds brightened and then brightened further as we sang "Come, O Come Emanuel" and then "Silent Night." The group lingered, visited, drank coffee and tea, retrieving fudge, cookies, and zucchini bread from the refreshments table. And soon Yvonne was back — with Jeni and Ron — and Lola, Jeni's cat, in her travel case waiting in the car. Chairs and tables put away, "Merry Christmases" complete, we drove to the Crane dock near the end of Deer Harbor road, carried presents, luggage, and a small cat down to the *Huginn* and made the crossing — not in complete darkness — to Crane. A delicious dinner of smoked salmon fettuccini and hours of conversation, the wind still blowing outside. Family together on the night celebrating the incarnation, the divine, in all of us.

Sixty-eight: Christmas Day

"Our hearts grow tender with childhood memories and love of kindred, and we are better throughout the year for having, in spirit, become a child again at Christmas-time." — Laura Ingalls Wilder

We heard later in the day that our grandchildren were up by 5:00 or not long after — with parents and other grandparents — to open presents — making for a long, long day. Not long after 6:00, I was stirring oatmeal so it wouldn't stick. The wind had slacked a bit and would drop to near calm by early afternoon. On my post-breakfast walk around the island, I decided I would try to understand the island's evergreen species better and collected Douglas and Grand fir and a species I didn't know — but had cut and split and was now burning in the wood stove. It turned out to be Silver fir. I also plucked a sprig of cedar, juniper, and a pine I didn't know near the community dock. The water was higher at the dock than I'd ever seen it. The breakwater nearly covered its whole length, and the movable ramp pointing upward from the fixed dock to the Y-shaped linked floats. At home, I grabbed the camera and took a series of pictures, showing, for instance, that the water was only a foot or so below the fixed dock. Consulting the tide tables, I could see it was an 8.7-foot tide. The low had been -1.2 feet, about 1:00 a.m. - a difference of almost 10 feet. The easterly wind over the last few days had piled the water higher.

When I got back to the house and was taking pictures of our cove and the now more severely displaced ramp, Yvonne brought the phone out. Sister Marcy was calling from Colorado Springs. In years past when we lived in Boulder and the kids were home, we'd usually drive to Colorado Springs for Christmas Eve, returning late that night to have Christmas day at home and the Holiday brunch at the Boulderado Hotel. Marcy reported that her son Kevin and wife Lauren had driven back from Columbia, Missouri, with their three dogs, Kevin having taken an assistant professor of theatre position there

Sixty-eight: Christmas Day

in the fall. Marcy's grandson Aelias had not gotten his Japan tour book — for his upcoming trip — because Marcy had forgotten to take it out of the closet. Marcy's granddaughter Alana hadn't gotten her Obama picture/poetry book because sister Julie had forgotten to pass it on. Marcy would bring the books with her when she and husband Paul took the train to Iowa to see his mother Elsie. After being unemployed for six months, Paul would start a new sales job at the beginning of the year. His son Chad had made and sent beautiful woodwork gifts to everyone.

068: Christmas Day - Jeni, James, Yvonne, Uncle Ron

I hooked up the Crane Association tabletop speakerphone on the coffee table, and all five of us talked to Julie who was preparing a Christmas dinner for son Cooper, daughter Phoebe, her husband, Alan — who had a bad cold or flu again, Alan's mother, Kiki — who missed her husband this first Christmas without him, ex-husband, Karl, and his brother, Ted. Her map company employer continued to mismanage what could have been a successful business, and Phoebe's employer — a precious metal middleman continued its high purchase and sales pattern, the Colorado Springs "prescient" public predicting imminent failure of the global economy. They thought gold and silver were the only safe places to be — and you should be armed to protect your horde.

A delicious dinner — roast turkey breast, roast vegetables that included potatoes, salad, and homemade rolls. Noah called during dinner, and we arranged to call him back after dinner and a round-the-island walk. On that walk, we visited the B's barn, climbing to the hayloft empty except for strings of lights running joist to joist on either side, left from a barn dance at least 20 years before. Near the N's, I pointed out the osprey nest I'd noticed in the summer when I heard and then saw a large osprey chick in the huge nest at the very top of a 50-foot dead fir and soon a returning parent bringing something good to eat. We did some tree identifying as well, managing to master the difference between Douglas and Silver firs. And seeing the beach pine near the community dock, heretofore unnoticed, was a pleasure.

Talking to son Noah and his family in Olympia and then son, Eric and his, in Los Osos, California, we enjoyed a chocolate mousse soufflé that we couldn't get enough of. Noah reported son, Morgan and daughter, Opal got them all up at 5:00, slowing them all considerably the rest of the day. They too had gone for a walk. Morgan had a new skateboard, a hand-me-down iPod from Auntie Jen, and skateboard-appropriate clothes. He had become a cool almost eleven-year-old dude. Opal was enjoying the new outfits Yvonne had made for her and Crissa, her doll. I thanked my daugher-in-law, Natasha for giving me — as my Secret Santa — the new two-volume set of Emerson's journals — the lively source of his thoughtful essays — that captured or created the quintessential American philosophy or cultural orientation. Son, Eric, his wife, Kristin, and kids had one by one succumbed to a 48-hour flu — or bacterial infection that had laid them low — his son, Jackson first and then Eric when they had driven to the Sierra's to ski. All were well now. They too had arisen early at the urging of Jackson and Maddie, at in-law's Bob and Diane's overnight to celebrate Christmas with a dinner later on.

Sixty-eight: Christmas Day

At our table, we talked about Gina and then half-sisters, Sarah and Samantha, Yvonne's brother Tony's daughters. Gina was living somewhere near Chehalis and, ashamed of her continuing struggle with drugs, missed us but wasn't willing to connect. Her two half-sisters, in West Seattle, hadn't de-friended Yvonne from their Facebook accounts but wouldn't answer emails or calls from either Yvonne or Ron. Ron told us about his Seattle day with his granddaughter, Krystal, and he called and talked to son, Jesse and his wife, Kim and then Sarah, his ex-wife Lucille's daughter he was still close to.

James Skyped his partner, Keith, in Oklahoma with his parents and brother for Christmas. We all talked to Keith for a while and then his brother Andrew, then mother, Susan and then father, John wandered into the room at his grandmother's house to see what Keith was doing. We hadn't met John and Susan before and enjoyed the 30-minute interchange, inviting them to come and see us if they came to the Pacific Northwest. They were very friendly. James, slightly embarrassed, told me I had been too aggressive, too braggy in the conversation. I thought I was being friendly and enthusiastic, but James may have been right. An email from Keith later told James that the Skype conversation had been a success.

After nachos James made, we settled into my office to watch homemade videos — first the Crane Island 50th Anniversary I had made for the July celebration, then a biographical photo and music production James had created for Yvonne's 60th birthday we all celebrated in Walla Walla, Washington and then Moscow, Idaho — honoring both Yvonne and her mother, Opal. And last, we viewed a two-hour video I'd made of Yvonne interviewing Opal in her apartment in October 1997, shortly after we'd bought our Cayou Valley Road house in Deer Harbor. Grandma Opal, gone for more than 10 years, was present again, her grace, optimism, humor, generosity, and capacity for love evident. Ron, viewing the video for the first time, was moved by it, saying he missed his mother Opal every day.

Sixty-nine: Memories

"In every conceivable manner, the family is a link to our past, bridge to our future." — Alex Haley

The wind was back after slacking off for a day, and the cove ramp had sunk lower, having fallen completely off the bank where it had been resting the last four years. It was now hanging by a rope around a stump, the other end connected to a chain around the upper end of the eight-inch thick cedar plank. By 2:00, the wind had almost disappeared, a welcome change.

James served eggs Florentine, having made his hollandaise sauce, eggs, and butter sauce on poached eggs; plenty of cholesterol for those a little short. No interest in a walk but a continuing interest in family memories. Ron, Jeni, and James sat on either side of Yvonne on the big couch that looks out over the water, and Yvonne took them on a tour of the photo albums Opal had created over the years and that Yvonne now curated. Young life on the Idaho farm, a one-room school, Opal's move to Seattle where she met husband, John, then marriage and family and a divorce. Expanding beyond family, Yvonne took them through Seattle Then and Now, a graphic depiction of the ambition of early, rough Seattle and its more cosmopolitan modern form.

Contact — physical and emotional — building memories — introducing James to one side of his family history and something he hadn't known a great deal about. Ron and Jen had to return to Seattle and the workday world that would start up again Monday morning. The car they had rented sat in the parking lot close to the ferry waiting room in Anacortes. The traffic had been light coming up Christmas Eve and would probably be so again, this day after Christmas.

Though the light was falling at 4:20 when we left the house, the water was smooth, so I opted to take them straight to the ferry landing by boat, 15 minutes each way, much shorter than mooring at the Crane dock on Orcas and then driving to Orcas Landing. Lola, Jeni's cat, didn't want to get back in her

Sixty-nine: Memories

portable kennel; she'd enjoyed the expansiveness of our house compared to Jeni's smaller apartment. As we docked at the ferry landing, the sheriff's boat roared away from the dock on some unknown mission. I walked up with Jeni and Ron to pick up the Sunday *Seattle Times* at the Village Store, and the walkie-talkie in my pocket beeped. Yvonne was on the other end, having seen the sheriff's boat and thinking it was me, was concerned I'd forgotten to get the paper — but I hadn't.

069: James makes eggs Florentine

Hugs, appreciations, love — we'd see one another soon — Jeni and Ron walked up the hill to have a coffee and wait for the ferry in the Orcas Hotel coffee shop, and I walked into the market, under construction for the past six months, picked up the Seattle paper and returned to the *Huginn*. Half dark now, a young couple walked along the dock, alternately intertwined and teasing one another, a happy sight, and I imitated the sheriff's deputy, accelerating the *Huginn* away from the county dock, almost due west, where I'd cross the mouth of West Sound — where we'd seen the *Evergreen State*, the inter-island ferry, stalled, drifting slowly north in the high winds while it waited for the *Yakima* to leave Orcas and cross to Shaw Island. No wind now, smooth water, flying across its surface, navigation lights lit, not another boat in sight, a sense of freedom, power, expectancy, perfect balance, where both Apollo and Dionysos reign — or perhaps neither, the boundary between reason and dream, light and dark, memory and imagination, air and water — exhilarating. The *Huginn* was very happy with its new engine, quieter, quicker, surer. Docked on Crane, I walked the two hundred yards back to the house. It was almost dark now, the house lights promising love and warmth in the gathering dusk.

Over a Cobb salad Yvonne had put together, Yvonne, James, and I talked about family cultures, family mythologies, and how they're handed down, often implicitly from one generation to the next. Sometimes those cultures are healthy and positive, helping family members realize their potential and have successful happy lives, and sometimes they're not, crippling children that grow up under their influence. Some of those children escape, and some are doomed to repeat the mistakes of the older generation. Both kinds of family cultures are visible everywhere; we've been consciously seeking the healthy version. Life is a struggle — no matter what — but the struggle can lead to satisfaction or misery. The choice seems obvious once it's visible.

Seventy: Catching Up

"There is more to life than increasing its speed." — Mahatma Gandhi

On my morning rounds of the island, I could see that the community water tank was now at 14 feet, so it was likely some daily pumping was being lost through the overflow pipe at the top of the tank. Water manager, Gary said he would adjust the pumping time. Spilling water on the ground wasn't desirable — another example of why we would benefit from a float in the tank that would shut off the pumps before it reached the top. I had volunteered to reset the timer, but Gary wanted to handle that himself, though he'd have to come over from Orcas. Since the previous month, we'd pumped 26,000 gallons more than we could account for, having an indefinite amount lost to overflow would further cloud the question of whether the system had a leak and if so at what level.

Because we'd sold the *Simrishamn* , a Finnish sailboat, two-masted, motorsailer in the spring, we hadn't had to draw on my IRA — but now we would, and I needed to determine the best strategy — from a tax point of view. The operation of *Huginn* had cost $10,000 more than budgeted, and the new kitchen another unbudgeted $10,000; one a necessity, the other an investment we could also use and enjoy. I'd bought Turbo Tax for 2010 at Costco during my last trip there and loaded it to test the tax implications of drawing various amounts in the 2010 tax year versus later. Yvonne collected all the relevant income and expense information we had on hand, and it was reasonably complete. I decided it made the most sense to draw $20,000 in 2010 rather than wait until January.

Seventy: Catching Up

070: The tank is FULL

Classics Unbound, Inc., our Deer Harbor eBook publishing start-up, had been incorporated in the spring; even though we had no reportable income, we'd need to file tax returns. Since I'd spent an undetermined amount on behalf of the corporation, it would make sense to gather the information together, show the items as corporate assets, and decide whether to record them as contributions to capital or payables to me personally. Three areas made up most of the expenses: software licenses from RealSoftware, domain names through GoDaddy, and books through Amazon. In all three cases, I could go to my account and print out invoice copies for each relevant item from that supplier. Other items included books from Barnes & Noble and Half Price Books. The items totaled about $1850, so including the $1000 I'd paid to buy stock (David had paid $100 and Chris $50), I had almost $3000 in the enterprise — not including the 1000 plus hours I'd already spent working on the software, contracts, training, documentation, planning, and business generally. At $5/hour (what my efforts cutting and splitting firewood reduce our heating bill by), I'd already "invested" $8000. A more reasonable hourly rate given the services rendered would be at least $50/hour, but I had no way or desire to try to earn money by contract programming or consulting. Our version of Slocum's *Sailing Alone Around the World* would be published in January or early February. Everyone we've talked to or shown our prototype to thinks we have a great idea. We'll get some idea of its appeal soon.

At dinner, James told us that none of his friends read books anymore, and they don't watch television either; the internet is their source for information, entertainment, and communication. They're too busy, he says, and read short-form rather than long-form pieces — that is, articles but not books — of any kind. He liked the idea of calling the company eNotatedClassics and the books eNotated versions of whatever, but his report about the low incidence of reading among his peers is sobering. The discussion continued into the way in which the internet and the availability of instant communications were affecting the neuroscience research and teaching community he was part of. Everyone was now informally expected to be on duty around the clock seven days a week. There was no downtime. He could not understand how his advisors had time to do all that they did and would get emails from them written in the middle of the night. I think of the academic and research community being sedate, but according to James, that's no longer true. To succeed you must act and react quickly. His colleagues complain about this change, in process for the last ten or fifteen years probably, but no one knows what to do about it. You have to play this way or withdraw from the game.

Indications are that at least some businesses and professions expect 24-hour involvement. Is that any way to live? On Crane Island, when we choose quiet, we may not see or talk to other people for days at a time — generating or responding to email at our own pace. That's not possible or desirable for many people, young or old, who crave unremitting connection — that the internet, texting, chatting, Facebook, Skyping, tweeting, and other technologies now afford — but when do people have a chance to know who they are or see the quiet world of nature, spirit, or art?

Seventy-one: More Catching Up

"All photographs are memento mori. To take a photograph is to participate in another person's (or thing's) mortality, vulnerability, mutability." — Susan Sontag

Early in the day, I moved two cartloads of split firewood to the porch, nearly exhausting the stack of Silver fir.

I first got a digital camera in 2002, a little Canon I could carry on my belt or in my pocket. Though I could override the automatic setting, I rarely did. I was looking for convenience — in a new version of George Eastman's Brownie. Since taking the pictures was free, I took a lot and then to share them with friends and family, created a family website James came up with the name, thinking it appropriate because we sometimes talked about our family as a Borg, a hive mind, a feature of *Star Trek, the Next Generation* — so a borgian domain name would be a site for a Borgian family.

For eight years, I used a Windows website creation tool, Trellix, developed by Dan Bricklin, inventor of VisaCalc, the first computer spreadsheet. Believing he couldn't patent his invention, he was overtaken by Lotus 1-2-3 and then Excel. Trellix was well-conceived but never developed much of a following. It was very easy to create and manage complex websites and was especially good at handling image files and albums. By this year, my Trellix-created site was looking dated. With thousands of pictures already posted, I didn't want to start over — only add a new home page and do new albums in a more attractive way. Ten years ago, I spent my time in the Windows world; now I was a Mac devotee, so I tried RapidWeaver but found it clumsy and opaque, so I began using iWeb, Apple's website tool that had been improved over the last year or so. As with using Trellix, I could create photo albums very quickly — with a front page of thumbnails and pages for each photo — with a thumbnail ribbon across the top. Why not just use Picasa or some other free online service? Probably just habit — but I wanted control over my albums

Seventy-one: More Catching Up

and was willing to pay a small annual fee to SiteTurn, the host I'd used all along.

Because I'd been so busy with the kitchen project, I'd fallen behind in posting albums, so some of the day was devoted to catching up. I did a large album for Corrina's visit in November before she left for India to plumb the depths of her love for Arjan. I was now using my third digital camera, a Nikon S8000, having given my first Canon to son Noah and my second to sister, Julie. It wasn't quite as small as what I was used to, but it had a 10X optical lens the similarly priced Canon didn't. But in automatic mode, especially in afternoon light, the Nikon color values weren't acceptable. And I wasn't happy with low light automatic settings. I read the user manual, but when Corrina, a serious photographer, had stayed with us, I had asked her to give me a tutorial. She experimented with the Nikon, taking pictures with various settings and showed me the results. So then I experimented, taking many pictures of the sunrise next morning (gorgeous) and then on an early morning walk around the island. I was paying attention, seeing aesthetically rather than practically and the pictures were beautiful. I had also taken many pictures at the Exchange, our re-use center adjacent to the Orcas trash transfer station, when Corrina and I deposited the trash and walked around the Exchange.

I also had pictures from the day the *Huginn*'s engine threw a rod, from Thanksgiving at Noah and Natasha's house, Christmas on Crane, and the ongoing kitchen project. And Yvonne had taken pictures and video during the mother-daughter karaoke session in Seattle in November. Eric and Natasha had posted Christmas pictures that very day with Picasa. I was way behind. Not having done an album since October, I had to remind myself how to do it using iWeb. Yvonne looked at each album as I finished it and pointed out typos and in some cases suggested I not use a photo because the subject wouldn't be happy with that particular shot. A bit more to finish up tomorrow.

James had left for Seattle before noon to meet Keith at SeaTac. They'd stay in Kelly and Tim's apartment — the couple was in Australia for the holidays and a second wedding ceremony for those in Perth who hadn't been to Orcas for the original I'd officiated in July. James called twice, first to report he'd gotten a haircut in Seattle and the second time to tell us he was meeting Rita, his old friend from our Boulder neighborhood now living with her husband in Seattle, at Nordstrom's — and that since she and Jeff would be away over New Years, he and Keith could use their apartment. Though James and Keith might make the 10:30 ferry the next day to come to see us, the 3:30 was more likely.

071: What Corrina saw at the Exchange

Though we don't watch television often, we did tune in to the Kennedy Center Awards — interested especially in Oprah and Paul McCartney. A wonderful presentation — especially for older people who had lived through the last 40 years of American popular culture.

Early Christmas Eve, I had sent out a long note, patterned after and cribbed in part from my journal, to family and our friends in Boulder and included pictures of our solstice eclipse watching. Noah, our family novelist, responded today with kind words for the writing, a response that encourages me to continue my project.

In the evening, I received an email from Chris with a Slocum book cover draft. The main feature, a sketch of the Spray, was tilted at an angle and included a golden star with the text "eNotated Classic." He's titled the book "The eNotated Sailing Alone Around the World" with the text "Written by Joshua Slocum — in 1899" and then immediately underneath "eNotated by Chris Thomerson — in 2011" — a clever way to show both that the book was old and that this version was new and different — without actually having to say that. I'll carry on, putting the book into near-publishable form, and then Chris, David, and I will decide what to change before publishing it in January.

Seventy-two: Keith Comes to Visit

"In seed time learn, in harvest teach, in winter enjoy." — William Blake

The community water tank is still at 14', which probably means that some pumped water is overflowing, and ending up on the ground. A log boom sits off the north side of Crane, the tug facing into the strong northwest wind with hundreds of logs trailing inside a chain of logs that confine them. These booms appear every few months. Where are they from? Where do they go? Why is this one waiting in the Deer Harbor area? The sheet plastic covering new construction on Ilza's house, facing north, is flapping in the wind. Is the carpenter there? The northwest wind bears right down on the Crane Community dock on its only unprotected side. I walk out on the floats, pitching up and down, to retie the *Huginn* and Margaret's boat, switching the spring line to hold for a northwest rather than southeast wind. Lou has tied his boat behind, that is north of the *Huginn*, instead of on the diagonal float as he usually does, perhaps to avoid having his boat banged into the dock by the wind. It's securely tied.

As I walk across the meadow north of our house, the air over West Sound looks smudged with white — it must be snow and will come our way soon. The temperature has fallen four degrees in the last hour. It's now 34. By 9:30 the snow has begun but falters, then returns, then falters again, and the clouds part here and there to show blue sky. Melted snow drips from the eaves. Four miles straight east, meadows on Blakely's flanks, now white and normally invisible, stand out from the dark forest surrounding them. By 2:00 the sky is mostly blue, cotton balls, floating here and there. About that time, James and Keith drove north from a cloudy Seattle to a snowy Everett and then sunny Marysville only to encounter sleet at Mount Vernon and very heavy sleet in Burlington but by the time they were a few miles west on Route 20, the sky was clear and blue in the direction of Anacortes and the San Juans.

Seventy-two: Keith Comes to Visit

072: James, Keith, Yvonne cosy and busy

The *New York Times* reports on the aftermath of the snow that closed the city. Air travelers on the East Coast and in Europe continue to suffer from disruptions to the web of flights that cross the Atlantic and the two continents they connect. Weather has been hard, hard on people, over much of the U.S. and Europe for a month or more — with heavy rains and mudslides in California to subfreezing temperatures in Florida. Though the week before Thanksgiving was cold for us, in the 20s, most of the rest of the time it's been in the mid-40s — cloudy much of the time and sometimes windy — with one stretch of heavy rain — three inches in three days — but it's almost always comfortable to be outside and the cheery wood stove, burning what I've cut and split, supplementing our electric heat, keeps us cozy.

Yvonne works on another sewing project for Opal's coming 6th birthday, pajamas for her doll, Crissa, made from remnants left over from another project for Opal. The pajamas have feet, Dr. Denton's, I guess. Opal will be very happy that Crissa is warm this winter.

I uploaded five videos Yvonne had made at the mother-daughter karaoke session she and Jeni — with Yvonne's childhood friend Julie and her daughter, Katie — and another childhood friend, Kathy and her daughter, Justine, had enjoyed in Seattle in November and made a Borgfam album of the pictures from the session and then proofread the article James is modifying at the request of the editors of the journal he will be published in. I found a few typos and mostly understood the article, except for the statistical sections. Older problem drinkers are risk-averse; younger problem drinkers are more risk-accepting than the population in general. Does drinking change the drinkers or don't young binge drinkers turn into older problem drinkers — it's the risk-averse population that does?

James and Keith appear at the Orcas side Crane dock about 5:30, the ferry having been a bit late so we cross in darkness, the spotlight on *Huginn*'s bow revealing what's immediately ahead. Yvonne has baked a homemade turkey pot pie and we spend the evening talking about the boys' projected summer trip to Europe — starting in Stockholm, seeing our Swedish relatives and then stopping in Berlin, Prague, Switzerland, and Italy. We want to start the process of communication with Sweden so that summer schedules are synchronized. Early in the evening, the winter stars sparkling, James takes his iPhone out on the deck and uses the Star Map app to identify what he's looking at. When he was small, in Boulder, we'd sometimes go out and view the constellations and visible planets and he came to recognize them. And one day we made a scale model of the solar system in the park, with a basketball as the sun and planets proportionally smaller, placing them at distances the right scale from the "sun." It was amazing to see how far away and how small the planets are — massive distances of nearly empty space.

It's a pleasure to have Keith with us on Crane again since he hasn't been to Crane since 2009. He reported that his parents, John and Susan, with his younger brother, Andrew, are seriously considering stopping on Crane this summer. We'd love to have them.

Seventy-three: Kate and Ken Visit

"One touch of nature makes the whole world kin." — William Shakespeare

The sun dallies in its rising, the time passing so slowly from first light to the source appearing, that I become restless and frustrated. I'm ready for the day but it doesn't come. Scattered clouds but no dawn special effects. Out of the kitchen, to the left, movement catches my eye; it's a mink that's crossed the lower deck from the west, probably coming from the area of the community dock, and it now ducks under the upper deck, no longer visible, with the intention to drop into our cove when the coast is clear. Later, Yvonne finds mink scat and urine in the 10' x 20' carport tent we use for storage. They've gotten into the packing foam peanuts, scattering them around the tarp that serves as the floor of the tent. Cute in the water or when they're passing through but not when they choose to stay awhile.

After cat, Lola left Sunday with Jeni and Ron, I put the sand-filled box Lola had used as her toilet out on the back deck, protected by the roof overhang meaning to pour out the sand and reuse the box which had been protected by a plastic bag. Today as I picked up the bag, I could see that some creature, probably a raccoon, had inspected the sandbox overnight, leaving claw scraping marks in the sand, with a pattern too big for a mink, I thought. I should have dumped the sand Sunday evening. After showing Yvonne and taking a photo of the sand and marks, I went back outside and dumped the sand into the salal just south and bordered on the other side by our cove. It was here, last summer that a small raccoon sat patiently, alternatively watching us on the deck above and Samantha, our black mutt, who was circling the raccoon's location without seeing it. Eventually, the raccoon made for a nearby tree and Samantha, alerted by the movement, gave an unsuccessful chase in an attempt to minimize the indignity the raccoon had already caused.

Seventy-three: Kate and Ken Visit

James and Keith make a loop around the island in the fading afternoon light while Yvonne cleans the carport tent and then continues her sewing projects. I begin work on a New Year's letter, searching for appropriate family member image files taken during the year and then writing text to go with the pictures. It's a slow process.

Kate called to say they'd be a half-hour late so I delayed my crossing to Orcas until about 5:15. Not quite fully dark, the remaining light in the sky reflected in the water, Ken's headlamp appears on the Orcas ramp just as I pull in at its base. James has been cooking one of his specialties, French onion soup, and has baked New York Times no-knead bread after mixing the dough yesterday and letting it rise overnight. Keith has created a plate of hors d'œuvre — cheese wrapped in bacon. As we dock on Crane I notice a star moving slowly to the northeast and point it out to Ken and Kate. A satellite surely, reflecting the sun well below our horizon. If it is a satellite, it will eventually enter the earth's shadow and just as I think that it does, fades, and then is gone.

Around the dinner table, the discussion returns again and again to what the world looks like to the two young men, a topic of interest to the older generation. Kate talks about her evolving experience doing training with their three mustangs, rounded up in eastern Oregon to save the herds from their own success in propagating beyond the capacity of the open lands to feed them. Kate has come to understand that training horses often relies on creating a sense of helplessness in the horses, bringing them to a point that their only choice is to submit to the trainer, accept the human's leadership, after showing them that they're powerless or by flooding them with sensations they can't sort out. Kate, perceptive of the personality differences between horses, can see that technique might work for some horses without destroying their spirits, but for many, it sucks their souls right out of their noble bodies. Her approach is to help the horse conserve its dignity, giving it a chance to control the creation and development of their relationship. She's been taking Black Elk on walks through the forest lately, without a lead, and she's been amazed at how much he shows her of what's going on in his mind. He's not likely to run away; he has no desire to. His herd, his two companions, are back at the paddock, and they call to him once in a while for confirmation that he is not leaving them. As Kate describes them, horses are very perceptive, noticing everything in their surroundings in their way, and have a natural tendency and no objection to accept another horse or human being in the right circumstances as their leader and source of cues.

073: Setting sun on Bell Island

We talk about grief and loss, processing emotional changes, and whether the world of Facebook and Twitter, all width and no depth, makes it difficult for young people caught up in a frantic pace to find themselves or become themselves. James and Keith don't know quite what to say. The discussion turns to overpopulation, climate change, the coming collapse of civilization as we know it. I demur. It's not that simple. It's almost 11:00 when I ferry Kate and Ken back to Orcas. It's been a stimulating evening. Their efforts as real estate brokers have paid off recently: they've made two sales. As I wrap the forward line around a cleat on the Crane dock, I look up at the night sky and am overwhelmed. The Milky Way crosses the sky north to south. The Big Dipper is within reach. Orion well above the eastern horizon begins his trek across the sky. The sod crunches underfoot, its surface frozen in this 26-degree night, as I cross the meadow to our house, the walkway to the front door flooded with warm light.

Seventy-four: New Year's Eve

"For last year's words belong to last year's language and next year's words await another voice." — *T.S. Eliot*

Since it was below freezing this morning I decided to walk up to the tank rather than read the tank level from Circle Road, 200 feet away. If there was overflow from the tank, some of the water would have frozen below the screened overflow pipe. Walking along Airstrip Lane, past well house #5 and well house #6 and the airstrip parking area, I noticed a Golden Crowned sparrow, bouncing around in the grass, not far from my moving feet. It was paying no attention to me and was thoroughly absorbed in looking for something to eat. I stop and stood still for a minute or two admiring the sparrow's markings and its self-possession. The Golden Crown has a bright yellow stripe bordered by black stripes the length of its head and its body is a complex pattern of light gray and black. This bird was alone but I'd seen a group of its cousins, White Crowned sparrows, a few days before along Circle Road. Not as colorful but just as elegant, the White Crowned sparrow was just as busy and just as oblivious to me as the Golden this morning.

Reaching the tank by way of the road, the base 112' above sea level and the highest point on the island, I walked around behind the tank to look for ice below the overflow pipe. None. A good sign. The tank was just under 14' so there was plenty of water but we weren't wasting any either by pouring it on the ground. Descending by the path to Circle Road, I climbed over a small, dead fir that had fallen sometime in the last few weeks. Past the south end of the airstrip, I heard a raven and assumed it must be talking to a companion. I'd often heard what sounded like a conversation between two ravens high in the firs that mostly cover our property. Ice covered half a dozen potholes not far from the Osprey nest, the ice displaying concentric circles where new water levels had been established as water leaked out the bottom of what the Crane Board sometimes described as our speed bumps. On the north side of the island I saw a couple approaching, bundled up against the cold and unrecognizable. Dan and Jan, out for a morning walk, apprehensive when driving up the afternoon before about whether their Boston Whaler motor would start and whether their cabin would be unharmed by the cold, were relieved and pleased when everything worked as desired. We talked about New Years gone by, one when they first had their cabin on the island when a posted sign invited everyone to a party at the Reynolds, now our house, on behalf of Tammy and Sarah, they later learned were the two Clydesdales on the east side island farm. Now, Dan, looking west saw Lou and I turned to look. He was out for his morning walk with Rollie his miniature Daschund who was enthusiastically bouncing along the road in front of him, the very Rollie who had survived a fall from the roof after flying out a second-story window in pursuit of a dragonfly.

Back home, I took a series of photos of a beautiful sunrise. James and then Keith joined the vigil after Yvonne woke them and James marveled at the deep red clouds on the horizon, the color changing every second. A bit later the boys and I boarded the *Huginn*, then slowly crossed to Caldwell Point, the eastern end of the No Wake Zone, and passing the buoy went up on plane for the rest of the trip to the county dock at the ferry landing. I dropped them off and headed home. They would take the shuttle from Anacortes to Seattle and then the light rail from the airport downtown where they could check into the hotel room they'd booked for the next two nights, to celebrate New Year's with Jeni and friends and then spend the night before flying back to LAX and return to grad school.

I had been working on a New Year's letter — we hadn't done a Christmas letter to send to friends and family and thought I was done — when Yvonne showed me what some Oregon friends had sent us. I wasn't done. I gave up on Apple's Pages and went back to Word, in this case a much better fit for what I was trying to do — an attractive presentation of photos on one side and text on the other. I called Carol at Rainbow Services. She'd be open until 3:00 and suggested I email the PDF file so she could have the two-sided color pages ready for me to pick up when I came to Eastsound in the early afternoon.

Seventy-four: New Year's Eve

074: Dawn on New Year's Eve

Yvonne reported that the mink had broken into the carport again. She spent an hour cleaning up their mess and then laid pallets against the back of the tent where she thought they gotten through the fence James and I had built a year and a half earlier. We both had the same reaction: Crane wildlife is cute and fascinating except when it violates our boundaries. The deer, raccoon, ants, mink, otters, and seagulls repeatedly push the limits and we have to push back or be overwhelmed — as we do with moss trying to take over the roof and firs trying to take over the yard. On Crane, the struggle between nature and humans isn't even close. Ultimately and in short order nature always wins.

I stopped at the post office to drop off mail, pick some up, and buy postage. I talked with Pat about how 2010 had been for the Deer Harbor Post Office. Though December was very good, volume was down again as it had been for several years now — not just here but throughout the whole system. Whenever rates were raised the volume dropped as people and businesses used the USPS less and used competition more — UPS or Fedex — or the internet. Carol had the New Year's letters ready. She said they looked very good and asked what software I'd used. At Ace Hardware I returned the $30 drill bit Yvonne had gotten for me to make holes for hanging the kitchen cabinets from the beam — because I'd found another way to drill the 8" holes. I deposited a healthy sum at the bank to cover coming credit card bills for Christmas expenses, the kitchen remodel, and *Hunin*'s engine transplant — more capital seeping away. The Island Market was busy, everyone in a good mood, and I carefully followed the list Yvonne had sent with me, making every effort to fill it correctly, something I managed to do only part of the time. How hard can that be? Coming back to the Crane dock I could see Tom returning to Crane from Orcas to his dock a quarter mile south of our cove. He had been gone for a while, perhaps to Sun Valley. James had called; he and Keith were pleased with their Seattle accommodations and were heading to Jeni's to join her — and Kirstin, arrived from Boulder, and Adrienna, on break from international studies grad school at Carnegie Mellon in Pittsburgh. I finished reading Edith Wharton's *Ethan Frome*, — Noah had recommended it a few days before. We had dinner, a big pot of homemade minestrone soup, salad, and James' no knead bread, and then watched, for the second time, Todd Haynes' *I'm Not There*, a creative biography of Dylan, though I napped through half of it. The hot tub, millions of stars, and bed. A very quiet New Year's Eve. Just the way we like it.

Seventy-five: New Year's Meal

"New Year's Day is every man's birthday." — Charles Lamb

Just a fingernail clipping of a moon hung above the forests of Shaw Island as we crossed to Orcas to begin our trip to Seattle for a noontime meal with family and friends at Elliott's on the Seattle waterfront, two blocks west of Jeni's apartment and close to the Bremerton and Winslow ferry terminal in one direction and the Pike Place Market in the other. In the Orcas Hotel coffee shop, sitting at a window seat enjoying tea for me and decaf latte spiked with coffee for Yvonne, with the ferry dock below and the Shaw terminal less than a mile away across Harney Channel, the sun finally climbed the short distance above a narrow band of cloud at the horizon and streamed into the shop, not blinding but perceptibly warm, welcome on a subfreezing morning. Our van was tenth in line, part way down the hill from the waiting lot. There wouldn't be many passengers today, New Year's Day — from Orcas or Shaw or Lopez where the *Yakima* would stop on its way to Anacortes, a 70-minute trip and free when traveling eastbound.

With little traffic on I-5, we were at Elliott's Oyster House just before noon and the first of our party to arrive. James and Keith would walk from the Ramada, Jeni with Colorado friend Kirstin and Seattle friend Adrienna would walk from her Harbor Steps apartment, Noah, Natasha, Morgan, and Opal would walk the short distance from the ferry terminal after walking on at Bremerton, and Ron would walk down from Capitol Hill where he had a studio apartment and was initiating his acupuncture service. Yvonne had also invited Sarah (no reply) and Samantha (I can't come now, try later). Today she orchestrated the seating so those who hadn't seen each other in some time — especially Noah/Natasha and James/Keith would have an opportunity to visit. All the way down I-5, the Cascades in the east and the Olympics in the west, all blanketed with fresh snow, sparkled in the clear air and bright January sunlight. Seattle sparkled too, the ferries making their way across Elliott

Seventy-five: New Year's Meal

Bay, visible as if through telescopes, seeming to float above the Sound on a narrow hull that flared left and right from the bow to support the parking lot above.

075: Jeni hosts new years in Seattle for Kirstin, Noah, John, James, Morgan, Opal, Natasha, Keith, Yvonne, Jeni, Ron

Adrienna had a semester left in Pittsburgh to finish her international studies masters and found international crime an interesting study topic, but she didn't yet know what she would pursue. Perhaps we could provide a connection to the Gates Foundation in Seattle and Oxfam in Boston. Kirstin (Kiki) had been Jeni's partner in crime growing up in Boulder and this week would interview for a publishing job in San Francisco, where her sister and

Seventy-five: New Year's Meal

family lived. We agreed that Boulder was no longer the town it had been. Too precious, too rich. Jeni, now splitting her time between two hospitals since Dr. B had moved his practice to Harbor View Hospital, reported that the doctor had asked her to help him and other doctors — all with wineries in southeast Washington — to help organize a wine-tasting fundraiser in Seattle — a perfect role for Jeni — and one he saw her fill as hostess of the going away party his colleagues had for him recently. Morgan sat on my left and we talked about their two-day ski trip to Crystal Mountain he and his Dad, Noah, had returned from New Year's Eve. Awesome — as was the iPod Jeni had given him for Christmas, unneeded since she got her iPhone. Opal, across the table and to Yvonne's right, worked on a bowl of spaghetti and couldn't make a dent in it. She told Yvonne she couldn't understand how she could eat and eat and more spaghetti kept appearing in her bowl.

A group photo on the west end of Elliott's dock with Elliott Bay and the Olympics in the background and then we trooped to Jeni's where Morgan and Opal would play in the pool and spa a floor up from Jeni's apartment. Lola, the cat, was still hiding, not to be seen, from Buddy, Kristin's two-pound terrier she had carried on the flight with her, unrealistically aggressive as many tiny dogs are, enough to scare mild-mannered Lola into disappearing — who knows where — in the small apartment. Yvonne and I sat with Noah and Natasha, talking while the kids splashed in the natatorium. Back at Jeni's, Keith had fallen asleep on the couch, Kirstin was talking to sister, Amy in Sausalito, and Jeni and Adrienna had taken forty winks.

We had to make the 6:30 ferry to get back home and dropped off James and Keith at the Space Needle so they could enjoy the color and clarity of the coming sunset. We were cruising the I-5 express lanes north by 3:50. The sunset was spectacular and lasted almost an hour. The setting sun illuminated the big green signs on I-5 near Lynwood and the I-405 junction, turning them into glowing brass. At Everett alpenglow tinted the snow-capped Cascades pink, Mt Rainier behind us, Mt Baker in front, and Mt Washington to the east. In the west, the sky over the Olympics was gold and peach with a bright red ribbon of contrail close to the horizon. By Burlington the Cascades had fallen into shadow and only the western quarter of the sky glowed red. Stopping for gas, we noticed the snow James had seen Wednesday when he and Keith had driven north through it. The subfreezing temperatures had conserved it. Burlington looked wintry in a way Seattle hadn't. At the Orcas ferry landing, I'd been struck by how, without going outside, it would have been difficult to know what season it was. The grass was very green, few bare deciduous trees were visible, and the firs, cedars, madronas, and salal wouldn't testify to the season. Very unlike January in Colorado or Illinois. Chicken noodle soup at the Anacortes ferry landing, reading for me, knitting for Yvonne on the ride to Orcas, home, and into the hot tub I left turned up to 102 anticipating our return. A very satisfying holiday month that started four weeks ago. California was in our sights for February. Now, our Christmas vacation was over; we'd have to get back to work — on our projects and duties.

Seventy-six: Gift from the Sea

"The sea does not reward those who are too anxious, too greedy, or too impatient." — Anne Morrow Lindbergh

Three telephone pole-sized logs had made their way into the Crane Island community dock cove, two partly on the beach east of the dock and one to the west, left high and dry by the highest tides of the year. The northwest wind had driven them to the beach, probably escapees of the tug-towed log boom that sat north of Crane for a few days last week. With the beach only two hundred yards from the house, cutting up the logs where they lay and bringing them home in a dock cart to split and use for firewood would begin to replenish our diminishing though adequate supply. Though the logs had been floating in seawater, perhaps they weren't wet to the core. Had they been, they would have turned into deadheads, submerged logs, often with one end pointing up at an angle but almost invisible, that can cut a big hole in a fiberglass hull. Last week I saw one in shallow water a hundred yards north of the Deer Harbor Marina. With one end resting on the bottom, this dull-pointed spear would sink a colliding boat in minutes. On the water, it's what you can't see that can hurt you.I loaded my chainsaw from my shop and gas and chain oil cans from the tool shed into my dock cart and dragged it to the beach about 8:30, the sun well up in an almost cloudless sky. Another sunny winter day. The lowest tide had been overnight, but there would be a short drop for the hour on either side of 9:30, important especially for having access to the logs still mostly in the water. The westernmost log lay three feet above the current waterline on the beach, and since there was almost no wind, only the infrequent passing of boats caused any waves. I imagined I could lift one end, put something underneath it, and cut sections one by one.

Seventy-six: Gift from the Sea

076: Log boom escapees recaptured on Crane beach for our use

The log, about 30 feet long, was much too heavy — maybe it was full of water. I used the saw to cut about 3/4 of the way through at intervals of 30 inches. I wanted to avoid getting the chain into the sand and gravel on the beach since that would quickly dull the chain. I then rolled the log about 1/3 turn toward the water and chocked it so it would go further, and then finished the cuts, loading the sections into the cart I'd dragged down to the beach and then pulling and dumping the loads about 30 feet back from the beach in the grass. Though I wasn't positive, I suspected the log was Douglas fir. The bark was mostly gone, but the grain looked right. The sections were heavy; perhaps completely penetrated by the saltwater they'd floated in for an indeterminate amount of time. I need to split them and let them dry out before trying to burn them.

Seventy-six: Gift from the Sea

The two logs to the east of the dock were a more complex problem. The one closest to the beach rested one end on a rock and the other on the beach. I retrieved an extra dock line from the *Huginn*, tied it around the top end — the one on the rock — and secured it to the dock overhead. I brought more line from my shop and made two separate supports about a foot apart, hanging them and thus the trunk from a dead willow hanging over the beach. I cut the log between the two supports so that I'd have one half on the beach to work on, but it wasn't easy to cut all the way through since I'd risk ruining the chain. Finally, I managed to prop the log up high enough to almost finish the cut, and pulling the beach end back and forth finally completed the break between the two sections. I cut up the beached half and carried the sections to the dock and threw them up on it. By now I'd spent almost two hours on the project and really had little wood and it of doubtful use to show for my efforts. Now lighter, I pulled the top end of the remaining half log out of the water and up into the grass above the beach, securing both ends so high tide or waves wouldn't carry it away. I tied the end of the third log to the overhanging willow skeleton so it would stay nearby. I could finish the job whenever it was convenient. Six cart trips back to the yard north of the house saw the log sections home, piled near what remained of the logs I had brought home in October when we had our pickup on the island.

The log sections would presumably dry over time, and I could cut the 30-inch sections in half and then split them for the wood stove. I'd spent more than two hours, had more to do, and retrieved at most a week's firewood, so I was probably working for $5/hour or less, given the electrical bill savings burning the wood would generate. On the other hand, it was a pleasure working on the beach, the littoral between two worlds. Though the air temperature was a bit below freezing, the water was a comparatively warm mid-40s probably. I had a chance to really see what was on the beach and at the high water mark in the grass — complex arrangements of detritus — deliberate looking — of small pieces of wood and bark set like a mosaic in the grass at the highest watermark. I enjoyed wading in the clear water, sand underfoot, and wrestling with the logs that were five or ten times my weight. Just me and the water birds, the sun, and the occasional lapping of the water on the beach. And the noise of the chainsaw.

Seventy-seven: Final Details

"Details make perfection, and perfection is not a detail." — *Leonardo da Vinci*

Jeff, at Precision Countertops, called and confirmed that Richard, the installer, would be here Wednesday. That worked for Gary and his barge. And we were happy to replace contact paper-covered temporary plywood countertops with bisque-colored (a warm off-white) Corian. Using color sample plastic sacks, Yvonne painted five sets of three colors in strategic areas in the kitchen: two brown and one green. Neither one of us was convinced any one of the three was the right color — but the light green on the kitchen walls wasn't the right color — next to the light birch cabinets that had a bit of pink in them. The brown seemed too dark and the green sample not contrasting enough.

Five areas needed attention before installing the countertop: the floor under the dishwasher needed to be made flush with the rest of the kitchen floor, the southeast and southwest corners needed to be filled with spacers of some kind, the end wall and floor end cabinets needed to be attached, the three-gang light switch near the back door needed to be prepared so that the installer could cut a hole for it in the backsplash, and residual mastic needed to be scraped from the plywood under the windows in the south wall bay so the backsplash could sit flush against the wall.

The day before, I'd raised the floor under the dishwasher by doing what I'd done almost two years before when I made the hall, kitchen, and dining room all one floor — by raising the kitchen floor (it had been cork) and covering all of it with snap-together laminate. I had saved scraps of the 3/8" plywood I'd put down over the kitchen subfloor and cut two pieces to fit the dishwasher area. I had also saved scraps of laminate, using several a few days before to redo the floor area at the kitchen door because the new cabinets had a slightly smaller footprint than the originals, and I used these to extend the

Seventy-seven: Final Details

laminate kitchen floor to the dishwasher area. It was now very easy to slide the dishwasher in and out of the space (I'd attached longer water and power supplies to the dishwasher). Now I could turn my attention to the corner spacers.

Yvonne had bought extra toe kick stock (4 1/2" particle board covered on one side with laminate) with the thought it could be used as corner fill. The southwest corner was easy. I cut a piece with my chop saw the height of the base cabinets (30 3/8") and used my pneumatic brad gun to fasten it to the narrow cabinet next to the sink and then ripped another piece to fill the 2 1/4" from the west wall base cabinet to the extension.

The southeast corner was more complicated because the space from the southeast base cabinet to the plane of the front of the dishwasher was more than 7" so I couldn't cover the distance with one width of toe kick. Yvonne had already anticipated the solution and suggested I use the end panel she'd bought for the southwest wall cabinet. We could get another one or not cover it since it really wasn't visible in the kitchen unless one craned one's head to look. Using scraps of particle board and MDF, I built a 7 x 2 1/4" visible corner (the long side was actually the width of the end cap, 13" but it wouldn't all show) and fastened it to the southwest base cabinet with my brad gun. Since it was hanging from the cabinet and then the narrower side pressed against but not fastened to the dishwasher, I needed to add bracing behind it to keep it the right distance from the angled southwest wall of the bay — occupied by the dishwasher and sink. It looked good — light but rigid enough to do the job. Even with the corner permanently attached, I had access to the corner space — that contained the satellite coaxial cable — by pulling out the dishwasher. After Yvonne and I agreed on how the end panels should be installed relative to cabinet doors and drawers and using clamps, I was able to screw them on from the inside. Visual details are extremely important in making something look good, and we were getting closer to having them complete.

Late in the afternoon, I put together a borgian album for the period from when Keith arrived at our house with James through New Year's day in Seattle. Yvonne requested a change. I'd included a picture of Yvonne holding the aprons she'd made for Opal and Crissa (Opal's doll), and I shouldn't have. They were birthday presents and surprises not just for Opal but her family (and everyone else) as well. I added our New Year's letter to the site as a PDF file, and its pictures looked surprisingly crisp on our iPad even when magnified by a two-finger spread operation.

077: Ready for countertops

Right before dark, I loaded and brought to the house two cartloads of firewood, finishing the remaining stack of Grand fir and starting on the big stack of Douglas fir. Some unsplit sections of Douglas fir waited under a tarp for when I had more time, and I covered the sections I'd brought from the community beach the day before. I'd noticed that the Grand fir seemed to leave more ash and unburnt coals than Douglas fir, cedar, or alder. I don't know why.

Seventy-seven: Final Details

While in the hot tub waiting for Yvonne to join me and looking for tracks of tonight's predicted meteorite shower, it occurred to me that it might be better to move the three-gang wall switch box up the kitchen wall to the level of the outlets we used for the toaster rather than have the installer cut a hole in the backsplash to accommodate it. To have it come through the backsplash meant I'd have to have a 1/2" box extender and I didn't have one and wasn't sure I could get one. We didn't see any meteorites, but, as usual, the warm water felt wonderful and without any wind the 34-degree air didn't matter.

Seventy-eight: Eyes Everywhere

"The world is full of magic things, patiently waiting for our senses to grow sharper." — W.B. Yeats

A pregnant calm in the thickening air. The drooping green leaves on the madrona outside the living room window tremble. Rime crystallizes on grass leaves unprotected by overhanging trees and on new gravel on Circle Road. The weather, clear and cold for several days, is changing. Rain is coming.

On my morning walk, Molly passed me in her VW van and waved, heading for the community dock. I didn't even know she was on the island. Later, at the dock, she's herding a group of workers into the van. What's the project? Her fence. Last year she and Blair had their original fence replaced with a more robust — and more visible — version. The fence was intended to keep out deer and keep in small children and especially prevent them from falling off the cliff that descends 30 feet to Wasp Passage. She'd had a polite letter from the county citing numerous complaints — from people who had seen the new fence as they rode by on the ferry. One irate citizen referred to their property as Fort Crane. She had to agree with them. The fence was too prominent and wasn't what she intended. She was rehiring the people who put it up to take it down. She'd still have a fence but much closer to the house, not visible from the water, but enough to protect a small garden and small children. Molly wasn't annoyed — only confirmed in her unhappiness with how the fence had turned out and now motivated to do something about it. In the San Juans, everything that is visible is everyone's business.

I was curious about the rime on the grass in the meadow north of the house. I could see that it was a build-up of crystals — that looked like salt, so I went home and got my camera to take some pictures. The relative humidity was probably close to 100%. The saturated air would normally have formed dew on the grass but now the air temperature in the microclimate near the ground, a lower temperature than the air above it, turned the former dew into ice. Magic.

078: Real rime

There is something energizing about cold, saturated air that shows you your breath as you exhale and obscures the view — a sense of expectation, something imminent, a promise of change, the pervasive power at work in the natural world — that makes going inside to a cozy fire especially satisfying.

Yvonne left about 9:30 for a Food Bank Board meeting and errands. The final results of the fund drive were in. About $25,000 more than needed to create a home for the operation had been raised than were immediately needed. The two sections of the building could appear on Orcas by mid-January and, pending county approval, be installed and functioning by March. Sixty-six families were served this day — perhaps 250 people. Because it was the first session of the new year, everyone had to sign up again so that the Food Bank could keep accurate statistics during the coming year of how many people it served every week. Almost everyone was comfortable with the sign-up process except for one woman who was embarrassed to be asking for help. Generally, the Food Bank is a calm, even happy place. Those who need food are happy to have it, and those who provide it are happy to serve. One woman, emotionally needy more than physically, grabbed at whatever she could reach rather than being served by the staff.

My two tasks to ready the kitchen for the countertops were to finish scraping mastic from the plywood above the sink and cabinets in the south bay where tile had served as a backsplash and to move a gang of three switches about six inches higher above the cabinet next to the kitchen door so that they wouldn't interfere with the new countertop backsplash. The first task was straightforward, the second more complex but not nearly as much as I made it — my standard approach. First, I called the countertop people to make sure the backsplash hadn't already been cut to allow for the switches. It hadn't. That would normally be done on-site.

The wall already had a power receptacle we used for the toaster, well above where the backsplash would be. The switches were lower. I'd move them to the same level as the receptacles and used a level to find the right elevations and marked it. After turning off the power at the circuit box, I removed one switch at a time, adding wire extensions to the supply lines that exited the wall through the hole I'd just made. The box was full of wires, but I made sense of them, even for the three-way switch for the outside light between the kitchen and studio. I'd saved scraps of 14 and 12 and 10 gauge wire from previous projects and found enough 14 gauge for all the extensions. Because I didn't have another three-gang box, I let the wires dangle out of the hole, attached the switches and put electrical tape around the body of the switches — functional and safe enough for the next couple of days.

Richard, the installer called to get directions to the barge, and I also gave him Gary's cell phone number. Light rain had started about 4:00 before Yvonne got home from Eastsound. It would be raining for the barge trip tomorrow but not so cold. Richard would be bringing an assistant, wanting to be certain he could complete the installation so that the barge could return him to West Sound before dark. Yvonne and I were looking forward to the installation. More to do after, but not nearly so central to the project.

Seventy-nine: Countertops!

"A house is no home unless it contains food and fire for the mind as well as the body." — Margaret Fuller

At 9:30, I called Gary's cell phone. The Anacortes ferry had been late, but by now I expected to see the Mud Puppy, Gary's barge, round Caldwell point heading for Pole Pass with Richard, the countertop installer, and his partner for the day, with their van filled with countertop sections, tools, and supplies. Wilma answered and assured me they were on their way and would be in sight soon.

As the barge approached Pole Pass, I grabbed my camera and put on my raincoat before dashing out the door. Light, wind-driven rain angled down from the southeast, but it wasn't cold, about 45 degrees, a typical Crane January day. At the community dock, I saw the Mud Puppy pushed west, away from the dock by the wind. I took some pictures to document how tradesmen get to Crane and then greeted Wilma as Gary, on the bridge, lowered the barge ramp approaching the beach. I confirmed a good new year, and Wilma did the same. Richard was the passenger, and his partner, whose name I should have learned but didn't, gingerly inched their white Ford van up the incline of the craft and then down the ramp onto the sandy beach, while Wilma and I loudly encouraged him not to stop until he was clear of the sand, or risk getting stuck. I had made a copy of the Crane map so that Richard could find his way to our house by road since when he came for his measuring session, we had walked from the community dock across the meadow to our house. Richard invited me into the van, fitting himself into some space behind and between the front seats. His partner drove slowly, commenting on the singularity of the day, an adventure compared with the freeway driving he does day in and day out around Seattle and Bellevue.

After spending a few minutes reconnoitering, the two young men set up their work area on the lower deck outside the studio, setting up sawhorses and saws. The rain had diminished, and though they began by wearing coats, they were soon in their shirtsleeves as they moved in and out of the house. Earlier in the morning, Yvonne and I had taken everything off the temporary countertops, and I'd pulled them off and put them outside under the eaves on the back deck. Then we'd pulled out the stove, disconnected the power and gas lines, put it on a flattened door front carton, and moved it into the center of the kitchen, out of the way.

079: Richard and assistant do their magic

In minutes, it seemed, they'd laid down most of the Corian panels, putting them in a position to join the seams. The installation had been delayed a week so that a Precision Countertops supplier could fabricate an aluminum frame that would support the counter over the four-foot space between the cabinet on the north side of the stove and the independent wall section that held up one end of the beam from which cabinets over the stove were hung. Richard also made sure that the bookcase facing the dining area, backing up to the stove and floor cabinets on each side, would not be supporting the countertop, an important condition for being able to remove and replace it sometime in the future.

By 1:00, they'd made the section joints invisible — one of the advantages of Corian — and they were working on the backsplashes. About 2:00, Wilma called for a pickup time. Richard said they'd be done and at the beach to return to the ramp at West Sound by 3:30 — and they were — but not until they'd thoroughly cleaned up after themselves. The countertops looked terrific; the warm off-white, Bisque, looked good with the whiter and pinker and more varied-looking birch cabinets. And the built-in slightly whiter double sink was a wonderful improvement over the stainless steel model we'd been using since we moved in four years ago.

Richard had drilled a hole in the corner of the north wall countertop so I could run power and phone cables down through it to wall receptacles behind the drawers in the base cabinet. I began the process of installing the new faucet we'd gotten at Costco into the new sink and then realized that the flexible supply lines didn't fit the sources coming out of the wall at the back of the sink cabinet. I didn't have anything useful in my plumbing supplies; I'd need to get two converters in some form. So, we wouldn't have water in the kitchen for a day or two — but it wouldn't much matter because Molly had invited us for dinner, and the next day we were going to Bellingham and would have dinner before taking the 7:10 back to Orcas.

Much of the day I'd been working intensely to create an Amazon format publishing candidate for Chris' *The eNotated Sailing Alone Around the World* that I could send to Chris and David in anticipation of our Friday meeting to make final decisions on the book and how we wanted it listed in the Amazon catalog. By the time I finished, the ebook looked pretty good on my Kindle and the Kindle Mac software. It wasn't unreasonable to think we could publish by the end of the following week, a milestone and starting point for marketing experiments.

Yvonne and I walked through the rain and darkness, relieved by Yvonne's headlamp, to Molly's, about a mile away by Crane roads. She was on

Seventy-nine: Countertops!

Crane supervising Ira and the crew making revisions to the fencing the county had said was non-conforming. We talked about grandchildren; her first was a few months old, social justice in one area and another, and Crane news, and she fed us chicken curry. A very nice evening.

Eighty: A Date at the Majestic

"Art enables us to find ourselves and lose ourselves at the same time." — Thomas Merton

Today, we were the eighth car in line for the 8:55 ferry, bound not south for Seattle or east for Burlington but north for Bellingham, the last big town south of the border and the setting for Annie Dillard's historical novel of the development of the Pacific Northwest, *The Living*. I was hungry because I hadn't had breakfast, and I hadn't had breakfast because there was no water now in the kitchen. Though I could get water for my oatmeal in the bathroom, I didn't fancy cleaning the porridge pot in the bathroom sink. Besides, I liked the egg, bacon, and cheese croissant breakfast sandwiches at the Landing store. The kitchen countertops with a new double sink were installed the day before, and the feed lines on the new faucet didn't match the supply bibs. One goal for our Bellingham trip was to find a fix. While I ate my breakfast sandwich and drank my strong tea, Yvonne, equipped with a decaf plus café latte, ate a bit more than half a muffin and handed the remainder to me to finish. I ate too much.

On the way out of Anacortes, we stopped at a building supply store to pick up some Devine paint samples, little plastic bags of paint rather than color strips so that samples could be applied to wall areas here and there. Together we picked out two — both tan to brown and both lighter than the samples Yvonne had already put here and there on the kitchen wall. How I qualified to be part of a color-picking project I don't know — but I did have opinions and found myself favoring the warmer samples, and in particular Gilbert and Macadamia, over the cooler — certainly because I thought they would look better in the kitchen with the new cabinets, the floor, the countertops, and the dining and living area color schemes — but also because I'm not as attracted to cooler colors for living spaces as much as I was in the past — if I ever was.

Eighty: A Date at the Majestic

080: The countertops are fabulous

We were in Bellingham, outside the Whatcom County Museum by 11:30, a dark and rainy day outside though not cold, in the upper 40s. Son Noah and his wife, Natasha had both gone to Western Washington University in Bellingham, meeting for the first time at the end of freshman year, and they corresponded through the summer while Noah worked in a salmon cannery in Anchorage, not making much money and not having much fun but collecting a rich trove of experiences he later reported on in his first novel, *Comfort Food*. Consulting her iPad and the museum's Website, Yvonne realized the museum wouldn't be open, so we went to Trader Joe's and then a fabric store, both on Yvonne's list, so we could pass the time usefully. I read while Yvonne napped, just starting Per Petterson's *I Curse the River of Time*, at Yvonne's recommendation, and was, as she had, enjoying the picture of Norway and especially Oslo, a city we had walked endlessly around and thoroughly enjoyed four years before, visiting the Munch museum as does the protagonist of Petterson's novel, and the Vigeland sculpture garden, a fascinating study of the varieties of human life presented via the human body.

Today we would be viewing art as well, paintings commissioned by the Roosevelt administration in 1933 and 1934 and funded through the Public Works of Art Project, intended to provide artists employment as well as create public art that captured the American spirit. The traveling exhibit had originated at the Smithsonian and would be on view in Bellingham only another few days. The art was all representational — none abstract — and even those with discouraging subject matter — people out of work — were energetic and hopeful in their way — in part, probably because that's what the government was looking for. Yvonne's favorite in *1934: A New Deal for Artists* was Ray Strong's *Golden Gate Bridge*, picturing an early stage in the construction, the piers for the south tower finished but bare, and the Marin side tower beginning to go up, and mine was Ross Dickenson's *Valley Farms*, California green abundance visually threatened by massive brown hills. A wonderful exhibit that had come to Bellingham by way of Ft. Wayne, IN, and would soon be moving to Orlando, FL.

The next stop was the Bellingham International Airport, an ambitious name for a small airport, but now that its runway had been extended, it was host to non-stop flights to Los Angeles, Las Vegas, and some other far-away cities, and at least for now, the flights were inexpensive. Though we'd been driving up and down the West Coast for years — first to visit Eric and Kristen and more recently James and now Keith — we'd done that so we could take our short-legged mutt, Samantha, with us — but now she was gone, and it would be less expensive and provide more visiting time to fly and rent a car on arrival. So we were reconnoitering this little airport — much closer to us than SeaTac and much easier to deal with. Then a stop at Michael's while I got gas, then Lowe's for plumbing and electrical supplies — and two new chainsaw chains for the upcoming tree dropping project, and then Target, and return to Anacortes.

Yvonne had been reviewing dinner alternatives via the iPad and decided the historic Majestic Hotel in old Anacortes, with happy hour economies until 6:00, was a good bet — and it was. Packed, mostly with Boomers, a good menu, modest prices, a pleasant environment, and a chance to talk — in a different way than the everyday, commonplace, reminding us of the Friday

Eighty: A Date at the Majestic

evenings we often spent at the Corner Bar at the Boulderado Hotel, when we lived in Boulder, Colorado, after a week of working, me often traveling, away from the kids and home routines, a couple among others and groups happy to be off work — whatever that happened to be — for us a date of sorts at the Majestic.

Eighty-one: Expectant

"No matter what happens in the kitchen, never apologize." — Julia Child

It was still raining, now in its third day, and Yvonne had deputized me to ship a good-sized, fairly heavy carton containing Christmas presents he'd received at our house and other items to James in LA. I found a large clear plastic bag and, using blue painter's tape, covered the carton so it wouldn't get wet as I towed it to the *Huginn* in our dock cart. The Mergansers and Buffleheads were in place on the west and east side of the community dock, and the two logs I had tied up a few days before now floated in about a foot of water over what had been beach when I retrieved a log and a half, cut them up, and brought them home to split for firewood. It was about 8:30 when I walked into the Post Office, and Pat was loading mail into the fronts of a bank of boxes that backed up against one of the other walls. Because it was $12 less expensive, I chose standard parcel post over the quicker express mail. Late morning, I'd be back to pick up our mail, once David, Chris, and I finished our meeting devoted mostly to final details and decisions relating to publishing *The eNotated Sailing Alone Around the World*.

Chris was already at David's by the time I arrived, three minutes after nine. While I fixed myself a mug of Tazo Awake black tea at the kitchen counter, today with an electric buffer lying on it, David described how his waxing project had become frustrating. Because they are porous, concrete countertops should be waxed regularly, and David hadn't for several years, and when applying the wax had put on too much — the countertops now showing swirls made by the buffer. How could he get some of the wax off? I suggested a blow torch. David said he would never choose concrete again, and I admitted I hadn't understood why he had made the choice in the first place, and we talked about Corian for a while as I described how the installation process makes any seams invisible.

Eighty-one: Expectant

081: Front yard — January 7, 2010

David, Chris, and I were happy at the prospect of publishing Chris' version of the Slocum sailing classic, and we picked Friday, January 14th, as the publication date. Before going through the details, we reviewed our current feelings about our nascent business (encouraged, enthusiastic), bookkeeping (we had a bit more than $800 in the bank, we'd spent almost $2000 in 2010 and made $4.20), assigned David the task of filing tax returns and setting up a QuickBooks account, the status of Real Software's Web Studio IDE (it was missing some features their Windows and Mac versions had that we needed), Jens' progress with Kafka (he and Susan would be on Orcas and working in earnest in February), and future book possibilities (Slocum, Kafka, Goethe, Emerson, Thoreau, Austen, the Constitution), agreeing to make a list of prospective Orcas eNotators.

Eighty-one: Expectant

Sailing Alone looked pretty good — with questions on whether ragged right would be better (probably not), whether unique identifiers should be shown after each paragraph (yes — our solution to the problem of how ebook readers can point one another to specific passages across all ebook devices, software, distributors, and versions, copy protection (none on this first book at least), whether "The" should be included in the title (I was a strong yes, Chris a weak no, and David could see both sides), whether the cover design was adequate (no — I'd experiment with what Chris had done so far), the price (all agreed to $4.99), and whether the product description I'd written up early that morning made sense and what needed changing (it did, but Chris objected to my describing him, in part, as an armchair sailor — with its negative connotations — when what I meant was that besides sailing on the salt sea he was a student of sailing literature — and thus could eNotate Slocum with authority). We'd make a list of potential early readers/reviewers, and we'd ignore the ePub format and Barnes and Noble for now (Amazon had most of the eBook business and though its reader software was inferior to most of the competition, the breadth and convenience of its distribution system was the best).

Ominously, Chris reported that the Bonneville Power Authority was preparing for a major arctic event in the next seven to ten days.

Shortly after I got home, Yvonne left for her Friday knitting session at the Deer Harbor Community Club — well attended and much fun for Yvonne and the other ladies. I turned my attention to the plumbing for the new sink, installing the Hansgrohe Metro faucet we'd gotten at Costco — which once Yvonne and I used it, we agreed was excellent — and the drain piping — which, given two sinks and a dishwasher, took experimenting with my plastic pipe parts inventory before I finally had a configuration I could admire. And nothing leaked! At least that's what I thought until cleaning up the dinner dishes and noticed that the drain for the smaller, shallower sink on the left leaked as if not connected. A project for the next day.

The three switches I'd moved up the wall next to the kitchen door so they wouldn't conflict with the countertop backsplash dangled from their wires through a hole I'd cut in the sheetrock. The remodel-type three-gang box I'd gotten at Lowe's the day before went in pretty easily, and I was almost ready to put on the faceplate when Yvonne returned from Deer Harbor. More to go, especially the glass tile above the backsplashes and below the wall cabinets, but functional now and very attractive. We'd have company the next weekend

Eighty-one: Expectant

so we had a week to finish and clean up. I lobbied for putting up a pre-completion kitchen remodel project photo album but Yvonne said absolutely not — until the tile was up.

After a chicken stir-fry and rice leftovers dinner, Yvonne realized she had two chocolate mousse cups in the freezer that needed baking and eating, so we did. Later, on the verge of sleep, I mumbled something about a happy sense of expectancy. The Slocum book, Yvonne said, that's it.

Eighty-two: Break In

"Nature is ever at work building and pulling down, creating and destroying, keeping everything whirling and flowing, allowing no rest but in rhythmical motion." — John Muir

They were back, and we'd have to take more radical steps to keep them out in the future — the mink, that is, in the carport tent we used for storage. When putting flattened cartons in the tent in the morning, I noticed scat and urine on the tarp serving as the tent floor, and white Styrofoam packing peanuts were scattered around the back, southwest corner. I'd alerted Yvonne, who had cleaned the tent twice before, the second time laying pallets against the fence around the tent at that back corner.

These successive break-ins were almost certainly by one or more mink; their leavings were too small, and access too difficult for otters. Later in the day from in front of Margaret's next door, Yvonne saw a group of four otters swimming north toward Pole Pass, cavorting and chatting with one another, and generally having a good time in the afternoon sun. Otters always know how to have a good time and do, sometimes to the detriment of someone's crawl space, but I didn't know whether mink are party animals as well. According to Yvonne, the tent invaders had an M.O; they'd tear open a plastic bag of packing peanuts and then pee and poop all over them. Why? And why did they need an indoor latrine? Couldn't they just do their business in the woods?

I'd had more than one run-in with mink on the Orcas and Crane docks — the mink on the dock or ramp in the process of coming or going, and me doing the opposite — with the mink initially oblivious to my presence. Two days before, Yvonne had met a mink coming up the long wooden ramp that connected the Orcas parking lot with the floating dock — so she stood still to see what the mink would do. She was particularly struck by the beauty of its coat and could now understand why there had been a market for them. After several stops and starts, that mink finally realized that a human being was a few feet ahead of him, and he scampered back down the ramp and hid while Yvonne got in the *Huginn* and pulled away to return to Crane.

082: Becker's barn loft, once scene of island parties

I'd lend a hand to this round of preventive measures. The 10' x 20' tent was surrounded by a wire fence, and in the past inside the wire fence, James and I had packed plastic fencing, the idea being that by making the tent sufficiently difficult to get into, the mink would get discouraged and find some other place to use as a privy. But last spring I'd pulled some of the plastic net fencing out to use to keep the deer out of Yvonne's planting below the deck

Eighty-two: Break In

between the house and the water. The mink had finally noticed the change in the tent's protective ring, had gotten in, and would keep coming back indefinitely. So we put the plastic fencing back into the space between the metal fence and the tent. We'd check again in a day or two to see whether the perimeter had held.

Though I had no problem with the way the tent area looked, Yvonne was appalled. It was a mess — very unattractive and difficult to access. To me, that was the price we had to pay to keep the mink out — but of course, I could have built something more elaborate, perhaps even another shed and gotten rid of the tent. In this and other environments, Yvonne and I had different standards of visual acceptability — mine much lower and with a concern for function over form as well as a laziness to do much more than was absolutely necessary.

Yvonne spent a few hours transplanting flower bulbs from a box the Food Bank had received from a patron, intending to move the bulbs eventually to the new Food Bank building once it was completed in the spring. I spent the day finishing up details in the kitchen — with varying levels of success. I'd discovered the night before that the small kitchen sink was leaking. This morning I quickly found and fixed the problem — the metal drain that holds the strainer had not been snugged down sufficiently on the Corian sink bottom.

The trim for the kitchen door and the doorway between the kitchen and the hall were a different matter. With the new wall and floor cabinets, the vertical trim piece was too wide. It would have to be ripped — but not the whole length — because the space between the top of the backsplash and the bottom of the wall cabinet, about 9", could accommodate the full width of the trim. On the other hand, the countertop itself extended about 3/8" beyond the side of the floor cabinet below and the backsplash above. In both cases, I ended up butchering the trim, but I installed it anyway because Yvonne needed an inside trim edge to apply the glass tile she'd had for a few years to the wall gap between the backsplash and the wall cabinet bottom. But at some point, I'd need to buy more trim and redo at least these two pieces. I went from that debacle to trying to find a way to deal with two irregular areas — at each end of the cabinet row hanging from the beam over the stove. I managed to cover the cracks, but the results weren't pretty — so once Yvonne paints them, I'll see whether some of it needs to be pulled off and redone. I put in some other

Eighty-two: Break In

small trim pieces and found a way to fill in around the Sony flip-down screen TV hanging under the cabinets to the right of the stove. That solution once painted will probably be acceptable.

Yvonne has put a selection of Devine paint samples on the kitchen walls here and there and has decided on a color — something that looks like coffee with a little bit of cream. Her tentative goal is to have the tile and painting done before Tim and Kelly arrive on Saturday.

The wind was now out of the northeast and was predicted to be for the next five days. As we walked outside on the way to the hot tub, the frozen sleet crunched under our bare feet, making the 102-degree water even more pleasant than usual. We had plenty of firewood on hand. Let Boreas blow.

Eighty-three: Moving Day

"Home is the nicest word there is." — Laura Ingalls Wilder

Four years ago on this day and the one following, we moved out of our house on Cayou Valley Road in Deer Harbor and began living in this one on Crane Island. The actual process of moving took much longer both before and after, but on these two days, we hired Gary and his barge to move a 24' U-Haul truck back and forth from Crane and then our pickup towing a U-Haul trailer. It was a very big job, but we had lots of help.

We'd sold our Deer Harbor house in November but were renting it back through the holidays so we could enjoy them with our family without complete disruption. On January 8th, I picked up the U-Haul truck in Eastsound — Orcas finally had a truck and trailer rental service — and the whole neighborhood helped us load it with what we'd stored in the boathouse down by the road. The 9th Yvonne and I drove the truck to the barge ramp in West Sound, and helpers Dave and Demitri met us there and went with us on the barge. Because the truck body extended so far over the rear wheels and was as low as possible so that it would be easier to load, it was difficult to back the truck onto the barge; its tail would scrape the barge's ramp. By strategically placing planks on the ramp for the truck to back up onto, Wilma's efforts finally paid off, and the truck cleared the hinge where the drawbridge loading ramp is attached to the barge hull.

The weather had been stormy, and though we had wind, we avoided rain on the 9th and the 10th. By the time the barge reached the beach at the community dock, Howard and Sheila had already arrived to help with the unloading. Tom, representing the Crane community, met the barge and had cleared a fallen tree on Circle Road that morning so that I could get the truck to our new house.

Not having driven on Crane before and not having a map handy, I missed the left turn onto Circle Road and ended up going around the whole island

and then mistakenly turned right on Rocky Road, which I thought was Eagle Lane — at that time there were no street signs on Crane. Rocky Road has a tight turnaround at the end, and I barely got the truck around it and coming back to Circle Road I continued around the island until I came to the next right turn — Eagle Lane. At the house, everyone was waiting for me and the truck and couldn't understand what had happened.

083: Yvonne's crocus flower

Yvonne directed the unloading, and what didn't belong in the house was packed into the two-car garage, finally filled to the point that it wasn't possible to walk through. We moved the existing electric range out and moved in the hybrid electric oven and propane cooktop we'd brought from Deer Har-

Eighty-three: Moving Day

bor. Earlier I'd run black pipe down through the kitchen floor and then out the side wall of the crawl space to a three-position valve and two 10-gallon propane bottles to supply gas to the new stove.

With Gary, Wilma, and their daughter, Ruby lending a hand, the truck was cleared in less than an hour, and I managed to get it up our steep driveway and the even steeper section of lower Eagle Lane. Some months later, the truck bringing us lumber from Island Hardware and Supply got stuck on Eagle Lane and didn't get off the island for several days. Though we were now operating from Crane Island, the move wasn't complete. We had another day to go.

Prior to the move, we'd made about twenty trips to Crane bringing over whatever would fit in the *Huginn* (which we'd bought from the new owners of our Deer Harbor house), especially what belonged or could be outside, such as scores of potted plants, many of which Yvonne would transplant into her Crane garden as she fenced and organized it that spring. Since many friends wanted to see our new house even before we moved, we offered to give them passage and a tour provided they helped carry something or haul a dock cart to the house. The path across the meadow, ankle-deep in the runoff of winter rain, turned to mud with all the cart runs and foot traffic. Covering the end nearest the house with fir boughs made it possible to walk up a little rise without slipping but generally speaking, the path, grounds, and house were a mess to begin with. No trees or bushes had been cut in 20 years so they grew everywhere, filling in what had been clearing.

Back to the present — and a bit more work on the kitchen project. The day before I'd been unhappy with my efforts to put the finishing touches on the north and south ends of the hanging cabinets facing the kitchen, but this day saw what I could do that would be simple and visually acceptable. And then I began the process of moving my tools back where they belonged and materials to where they would be out of the way, safe from rain and ground damp and accessible. My inventory of tools and materials — including lumber scraps has been extremely useful and made innumerable trips to Orcas unnecessary. Yvonne did some touch-up spackling and painting but would need more paint in the new color she'd chosen to do the kitchen walls. She'd laid a sheet of glass tiles on a newspaper and then filled the interstices with brown grout she'd bought at least three years earlier for this purpose and was pleased with the results. She later continued her current knitting project — ponchos for Opal, whose birthday was imminent, and her doll, Crissa.

With my work on the kitchen complete for now and my mess cleaned up, I could now devote my time to eNotated Classics and the imminent publication of *The eNotated Sailing Alone Around the World*. While I sat by the woodstove with my Powerbook on my lap, Chris and I had a productive meeting via FaceTime on the corrections for the Slocum book and his latest cover design. Before dinner, I made a revision and sent it to Chris to consider. Yvonne cooked a stir-fried Indonesian, tofu-based dinner that included soba with onions and celery. Delicious. We'd been in our house now for four years, had made many improvements, and established efficient systems and habits, and both felt more at home and content with our lives than we ever had at any time before.

Eighty-four: The Father of Invention

"Necessity is the mother of invention." — *English Proverb*

For more than 48 hours, the thermometer hadn't moved from a few degrees around freezing, and the ground, where wet and exposed to the sky, was crusty. Some of the corn snow we saw last week formed a thin blanket around the base of a big fir and over patches of grass. Our roof was a gray and white plaid, gray where the beams underneath let more heat through to melt the thin coating of ice that covered it. Though the predicted major arctic event hadn't materialized, for us at least, the cold air seeping down from the Fraser River Valley on the northeast wind discouraged us from doing much outdoors.

We'd been using two dock carts of firewood per week, about 14 cubic feet, and I'd been splitting it as I needed it rather than deplete our stacked and tarp-covered supplies. But for the last month, with the holidays and kitchen work, I had drawn on one of the stacks, cut and split from a grand fir that had fallen across Circle Road in a still wind over Labor Day weekend, leaving a 15' high stump — why it fell, I haven't the foggiest. But now I had some time again, the wood supply on the porch was almost gone, so I put on my Carhart jacket and knit cap and went out to the pile of sections from the wind-pushed-over Douglas fir I'd brought home in October. Most of it was gone now; what was left was a variety of sections 8" to 24" in diameter, probably enough for two cartloads, maybe a bit more.

The smaller diameter sections split easily, in one whack from my splitting maul, assisted perhaps by the cold temperatures that may have created ice crystals here and there inside the wood. What I'd done with the larger sections in the past was to smack the back of the head of the maul with a 10-pound sledgehammer, using the maul as a wedge. Anyone who knows would have told me not to do that, I suppose. The result was to begin to crack the head of the maul. So what I'd started to do a few splitting sessions back was to pull the maul out after that first, unsuccessful whack and substitute an older but stouter maul with a cracked wood handle held together with hose clamps. The newer, fiberglass-handled maul would be the axe, and the wooden-handled maul the wedge. But even used this way, the wooden handle was deteriorating.

But I had another maul, a short-handled one I had bought at McGucken Hardware in Boulder 25 years ago, thinking it was a hand axe. At the time, I bought a huge two-man saw I imagined I'd use to cut down dead trees somewhere to use for firewood for our Vermont castings soapstone stove. However, Boulder County had then forbidden burning wood, and we'd replaced the wood stove with a natural gas model, son, Eric doing the gas plumbing for us. On Crane I'd used the small maul sparingly, mostly to split kindling, especially cedar. But maybe the small maul, with a very heavy, strong-looking head like the larger wooden-handled maul, could serve as a wedge as well — and as it turned out it could. On those occasions it was inadequate to the task of splitting — because the diameter was too large or the grain too convoluted — I'd supplement that maul-as-wedge with the larger wooden-handled maul. Improvisation to make do rather than do the job in the right way from the beginning or at least to repair the tools I'd injured. I did neither. My pattern was more to push until I broke something and then figure out a way to carry on — a form of laziness. After all — necessity may be the mother of invention, but laziness is the father.

The Slocum book project continued to move forward, and I created some alternatives to the cover Chris had created. In the process, I learned more about Apple's Mac Pages software, realizing that it was competitive with Microsoft's Word for anything I needed to do but, in some ways, more straightforward. My thought was to include an example of how eNotation worked by excerpting a text passage with a link and the note it pointed to, but Chris thought the result too busy. I also experimented with using the picture of Slocum's boat, the Spray, as a background for the cover, with text on top. I also pointed out to Chris that he had created an 8 1/2" by 11" cover and what we really needed was something 6" by 9" or perhaps 5" x 8" — in any case, with the right proportions and small enough to have good display quality from a compact JPEG file. Chris had found a few errors and also wanted to make a few changes to his eNotations, so I fixed that as well.

084: Sailing Alone cover

Eighty-four: The Father of Invention

Four years ago this date was the second of our two major moving days to Crane, and it had been a challenging one. The first day we had rented a 24' U-Haul truck. I had taken that back to the rental office as soon as I got it back to Orcas and picked up a trailer. Hired helper Demitri and I then loaded the trailer with what we'd put in a storage locker and then brought the truck and trailer back to the house for more loading — and found that we couldn't fit everything — so the next morning — the second day of the move — I got up very early and in the dark drove our pickup to the barge ramp and unloaded it on the beach and then came back to reload the bed of the truck and pick up the trailer, making it to the ramp by 8:00. When it was obvious I couldn't figure out how to back the trailer onto the barge, Gary did. All of us then picked up what I'd stacked at the ramp and then packed it around the truck and trailer on the barge and headed for Crane, where I took the trailer to the house and had more luck backing it down the driveway. We unloaded, stacking even more in the two-car garage somehow and made the return trip to Orcas where I dropped off the trailer. We were now living on Crane — but in the midst of a disorganized mess. The house needed painting, and the living space expanding so that we could house the whole family and other groups for Borgfest and other gatherings. We were exhausted by the months of preparation at both houses and as a break soon left for some time in California with Eric, Kristin, and baby Jackson.

Eighty-five: Water Policy

"A healthy social life is found only when, in the mirror of each soul, the whole community finds its reflection, and when, in the whole community, the virtue of each one is living." — Rudolf Steiner

The temperature rose a bit during the day, from 32 to 34, but by evening, the east wind had picked up with rain and sleet blowing against the living room and dining room windows and along the deck on the south side of the house, so going outside and getting into the hot tub was an adventure. As usual, I went first and opened the lid and got in. Yvonne came out a few minutes later with a big umbrella that served to protect us as we sat with our backs to the wind in the east half of the hot tub I'd opened. The pleasure of the warm water is increased by the discomfort in reaching it.

The Crane Island Association Board meeting was scheduled for Saturday at our house, and I was responsible for two areas — Finance and Water. I'd gotten the year-to-date financials (August to July) as email attachments from the bookkeeper on Friday and forwarded them to the Board Secretary for distribution. The previous meeting, in December, I reported on income — since it came almost entirely from association dues and service charges billed in September — and it looked like collections would meet what we'd budgeted. This coming meeting I'd report on how expenses were unfolding relative to the budget, and so far there aren't any surprises.

The financial area is important certainly but wouldn't require any new action — but the water area would. Dave, with a background in water systems, had modified the Washington State Department of Health community water system cross-connect policy template to fit the Crane situation, and the Board would need to approve it — so an implementation and ongoing monitoring plan could be created — having a policy and operational plan being mandated by the state. The cross-connect focus is on preventing water flowing the wrong direction — into rather than out of the community system. The community system is constructed, chlorinated, and tested to deliver safe water. Private systems aren't and could contaminate the community system should private water enter public pipes.

092: How to read a Crane water meter

We'll also be talking about the implications of island growth on the water system. We've got 44 houses now — with the potential for 59 with a complete build-out. We've had two new houses completed in the last four years, with one providing nearly all its water via a catchment system. How many new houses should we expect in the next ten years? How many major remodels or scrape-offs and rebuilds? Will we have more full-time residents? Will we need another tank, well, main? The point is to have adequate money put away to cover major water projects (and dock, road, and other projects) so that they can be completed without requiring special assessments — so we need to know what we'll probably need to do, what it will cost, and then what dues we'll have to collect to have adequate funds set aside.

I'll also be reporting on the system leak that appeared in October, probably about the 17th, and which isn't on one of the four spurs because the spur meter readings match the sum of the individual readings on each spur. The leak, less than 1/2 gallon per minute totals about 20,000 gallons over the month, considerably more than the metered water being delivered to households. We've had problems with fire standpipes (hydrants) before. They're not metered, and as they age, some begin to leak, and the leaks aren't visible because the hydrants are capped, and the leaks exit the standpipe through a weep hole — which probably allows about 1/2 gallon per minute. Maybe a standpipe is capped but not fully turned off.

Yvonne went to Eastsound to the Tuesday Food Bank session and reported more new people, some embarrassed, who registered and are seeking help providing food for themselves and their families. She continues to work on her knitting project for Opal's birthday coming up soon and booked our February flights between Bellingham and Los Angeles — about the same price as flying out of SeaTac but presumably without the hassles. I began research on booking return flights from Rome this summer for James and Keith as our contribution to their trip. James was hearing back from our relatives in Sweden, and they were eager to provide their hospitality. My guess is that Sweden will be the best part of their trip.

After spending some time with the new Real Software Web Studio, an Integrated Development Environment that makes it possible to write Web applications like desktop applications (potentially very useful for what we're trying to do with eNotated Classics) and finding some hurdles (though no show-stoppers), I began experimenting with the design of an eNotated Classics Website — something we'll want in place when the Slocum book is published a few days from now. The thought is to include a sample of each book we publish a visitor can read online.

Eighty-six: Water Streaming Down the Walls

"The ultimate test of a moral society is the kind of world that it leaves to its children." — Dietrich Bonhoeffer

In the morning darkness, when I went into the living room about 5:30, the walls, from floor to the vaulted ceiling with its long skylight straddling the peak, were streaked in a complex pattern of woven ribbons that, when I looked closer, were alive, moving steadily downward. Here and there bright spots, pearls, streamed irregularly down. Even the dining room walls were in motion.

When the light from the white Christmas lights strung along the deck railing outside passed through the rainwater streaming down the windows, it cast moving, streaming shadows on all the walls and here and there a big drop of water, focusing the light like a lens, cast anti-shadows, bright orbs on the wall. Magic. Four years in the house and I'd never noticed. How was that possible? Well, it would only happen when the lights were strung, and there was enough rain and wind outside to create the right flow on the windows. Since the lights were up maybe six weeks a year and the right rain ten percent of the time, that meant I'd had maybe a dozen chances to notice it in the past. Not a lot or not very observant? I was tempted to wake Yvonne but I didn't. Later she was happy to hear about the phenomenon but happier still to have snoozed through it.

Several years ago, the county power utility coop, OPALCO, in order to accommodate both green power and power-at-the-lowest-cost member factions, created a program to allow members to sign up to be billed at a higher rate with their "donation" to be used to buy green power through the Bonneville Power Authority, the Island's power source on the Columbia River. But Bonneville would no longer buy and pass through wind and other green power, so the OPALCO Board either needed to shut down the program or find local green power sources. The MORE committee, with representatives from each of the island communities and from the green power installation business interests, was tasked by the OPALCO Board to figure out how a new, successor program could work. I had run for election to the OPALCO Board in the spring and been soundly defeated, but the Board knew I was interested in OPALCO, so I was asked to join the committee.

086: Front yard promise

I'd been to two MORE committee meetings months before but then found myself too busy to continue to attend. The committee was now making its final recommendation to the OPALCO Board and I was encouraged to rejoin the process so it would represent not only the interests of the people whose business it was to install photovoltaic systems but OPALCO customers as well. Driving to Eastsound, I was surprised to see snow on the ground and evidence that the plows had been at work. On Crane, we'd had flakes and sleet but it didn't stick. The meeting was conducted via a nifty video conferencing system with a huge screen partitioned into four sections. Our group appeared in one, and groups from San Juan and Lopez Islands in two more. Though San Juan County is physically compact, maybe 15 by 15 miles, because our roads are ferries a 10-mile trip, with waiting and passage, can require hours, video conferencing among the islands is a good fit for our needs.

The committee had done a great deal of work during my absence, proposing basically that the green power donations OPALCO had been collecting go toward bonus payments to coop members who were attached to the OPALCO grid and generated green power they would use rather than consuming OPALCO Bonneville power. The bonus would be high for early adopters, falling in stages during the life of the program. But the Board had returned the proposal to the committee to fine-tune — without clarifying what that meant. The green power installers were adamant about the plan they'd put together and did not want to compromise. My role, in part, was to help them understand that the Board had many constituencies they had to pay attention to, and one was opposed to OPALCO being involved in anything at all other than delivering reliable power at the lowest price — considering any investment in or expenses generated by green power involvement irrational and unbusinesslike. According to them, green power technology just wasn't ready and didn't make practical sense. The installers' faction finally agreed to modify the plan, reducing the early and ongoing subsidies to members who installed green power generation. The struggle playing out at OPALCO between members who believe it important to invest in and pay more to have green, sustainable, non-carbon power and those who think those technologies are premature at best and irrelevant at worst, is playing out across the planet, and all the points of view have some merit. OPALCO is particularly interesting because it's a well-run, small rural co-op that supplies a well-educated and informed base in an environment where power costs about one-third of the national average.

Eighty-seven: Publish or Perish

"All growth is a leap in the dark, a spontaneous unpremeditated act without the advantage of experience." — Henry Miller

The plan was to meet with Chris at his house at 10:00, finish whatever needed doing with the Slocum book, upload it to Amazon, and publish it. I'd been working on the enotatedclassics.com website — that would play some evolving marketing role — and I was pleased with the progress I'd made. The site included the first chapter of Slocum's book in our format so those interested could try out what we had to offer.

Yvonne had already taken the 8:55 ferry to Anacortes. She would buy paint for the kitchen, a chocolate brown, and also large-sized switch and outlet plates that would cover the spots where it had been difficult for her to attach glass tile above the backsplashes. And she'd stop at Costco to stock up for Kelly and Tim who we expected to arrive on Orcas on the mid-day ferry.

Click-click-click. My pickup had been sitting in the Crane parking lot on Orcas and the battery was dead — or at least didn't have enough juice to start. Both the Orcas and Crane dock parking lots have portable battery jumpers available for cases just like this and I was able to start the truck and head for Chris' house. We spent about 90 minutes going over the book and decided to post it to Amazon's catalog. We weren't aware of any specific problems, we spent a good deal of time reviewing our work, and we can make changes later on if needed. Why wait?

On the way back to the dock, I stopped at the Post Office to mail a box Yvonne had prepared for Opal for her birthday — including the poncho knitting project (for Opal and her doll) she had just finished. I was also mailing a check to Cresi — Yvonne's niece Gina's daughter — now 17 and living with an uncle's family in central Washington. Cresi had written to say that her mother was gone from her life, her father and grandfather wouldn't speak to her, and she was determined not to fall into the holes her two sisters had. She didn't want to start having babies; she wanted to go to college — but she had virtually no money and was asking for help to get through high school — the next year and a half. Yvonne and I talked about her problems and her hope and decided we'd promise to send her something every month through graduation and Yvonne would help her with planning for college and the application process, but we didn't have the resources to subsidize her college study.

087: It's a private island

Dave was arriving at the Post Office as I was leaving, so we drove over to his house so that I could sign stock certificates he'd prepared and look at the 2010 financial reports he'd prepared for Classics Unbound. On the way to the Crane dock, I stopped to chat with Kate and Ken, on a long walk along Deer

Harbor Road. Kate wanted to talk about publishing — a topic I'd encouraged her to consider since I thought her experiences with a new way of training horses would be very interesting to the equestrian demographic. I couldn't come to lunch right then, I had work to do at home, but we'd see each other at the Friday Deer Harbor Community Club potluck and maybe we could get together next week. At the dock, I decided I had time to bail the *Pronto*, the very heavy and slow rowboat that serves as a transportation alternative for getting from Orcas to Crane. We'd used it twice in the first year we lived on Crane when we had problems with *Huginn*. *Pronto* had at least 100 gallons of rainwater and was riding low in the water. The plastic life jacket container had been standing open for a month at least with the three life jackets floating in the pond in *Pronto*. For whatever reason, the life jackets were always scattered around the boat, no matter how often they had been put away — Otters perhaps?

Once I got home, I began to receive emails from Chris about problems he'd found in the Slocum book. Then I started to look, and I found a number as well. Had I been too impatient about publishing? Should we have done more intense proofreading? Maybe — but we could pretty easily fix whatever was wrong. Chris and I separately spent hours scouring the Slocum book, and I made the required changes to the database as we each discovered and reported on problems. But I was reluctant to upload to Amazon too quickly — or I'd have to do it a third time. It made more sense to me to let more errors emerge and when they trickled to a stop, republish.

I sat by the wood stove with my Mac Powerbook on my lap mostly using the Annotator program I'd written to find and fix the problems and overall I was delighted with its usefulness. A good tool we'd need to improve as we recruited more eNotators.

By evening The *eNotated Sailing Alone Around the World* had appeared in the Amazon Catalog. We were on our way. A false start in June when one of our partners bolted — insisting we pull the book he'd annotated from the Amazon catalog. Now we were there again, and we could begin to experiment with marketing and recruiting. Jens would be on Orcas about the 25th and intended *Metamorphosis* be ready by the end of February. We had ideas for other people and other books. Looking up.

Yvonne's ferry was on time and I met her at the Orcas parking lot a bit before 5:00. It had rained most of the day and the air was mild, if not quite the

Eighty-seven: Publish or Perish

balmy 58 it had been in Burlington, and Yvonne commented on how good the air smelled as we walked down the ramp to the *Huginn*. She was right. The scent of something growing or decaying but lovely. As we crossed to Orcas, some clouds in the western sky were purple — a color neither of us had seen in the sky before and for a minute or two the purple clouds parted and far behind and above them a cirrus cloud glowed orange — like the fir logs in our wood stove. As I'd left the Crane dock in the falling light, mild, still air, to pick up Yvonne, with the Canada goose pair on the breakwater, the Mersangers to the east and the Buffleheads to the west, I was aware of how right this place, this time seemed for me and I knew for Yvonne. Not simply because it was beautiful. There was something else — a deep peace — and a sense of being in a holy place that filled and, I guess, comforted me. How could I be so fortunate? This is where I was born to be — and Yvonne felt the same. The green, the water, the moist, clean air, friendly wonderful people, the four-leggeds, and creepy crawlies, and the feathered, winged creatures. Miraculous.

Eighty-eight: Piping in the Haggis

"Food is not just fuel. Food is about family, food is about community, food is about identity." — Michael Pollan

When we drove into the Deer Harbor Community Club in the dark, we could see and then hear a bagpiper warming up at the bottom of the front stairs. Though the club was more than a week early, this evening we'd celebrate Robert Burns Night at our potluck (second Friday of the month) — a four-year-old tradition here encouraged by Jim and managed by the club president, Howard, an English emigre who had taught in Scotland for several years before finding his way first to the Dalles in Oregon as a teacher on the Columbia River and finally to Deer Harbor as a retiree after a nine-year stint with wife, Sheila teaching in Alaska just south of the Arctic Circle.

Inside in the light, warmed by friends, neighbors, and the propane heater that two years ago replaced the huge iron wood stove Bob and others brought in to replace an older smaller stove, Yvonne and I found ourselves in a series of separate conversations with people we'd known for more than a decade. At about 6:40, Howard asked guests to identify themselves — several were men dressed in kilts — and then asked everyone to rise for the piping in of the haggis, and the burly, kilt-wearing piper we saw in front came in piping through the back door to rhythmic clapping, smiles, and laughter. Howard positioned the haggis on a table in full view of the crowd, read Burns' Address to the Haggis, in a Scottish brogue and then ritually sliced it — making it ready for serving. A generous, varied serving of tasty and interesting casseroles — Yvonne had made Hawaiian chicken — salads, soups, breads, and desserts waited on tables at the south end of the big room, years ago two rooms that served as the Deer Harbor school.

Eighty-eight: Piping in the Haggis

088: Frost on the *Huginn*

After almost filling my plate and paying special attention to David's bratwurst and sauerkraut, I moved to the dessert table and scooped up a piece of lemon meringue pie Cal had made — fearing it would be gone by the time I'd be ready to go back for dessert — encouraged by Yvonne who said she'd take half my serving. We were seated across from Sheldon and Dawn, and he told me about the plans the A cappella choir had for performing in Florence the summer of 2012. Sheldon had also joined the Orcas Choir and wanted very much to become part of the Rock and Roll Choir Yvonne had sung with over the last 18 months. Then Sharon, with her beautiful operatic voice and guitar, and Michael with his bass, arco-played and sang two Burns' songs — "My Love is Like a Red, Red Rose" and then "MacPherson's Lament." At the end of the evening with the tables pushed against the wall, Howard led some circle dancing that Yvonne and I enjoyed. Howard's view is that every successful culture is marked by communal song and dance.

Eighty-eight: Piping in the Haggis

The day began with an email from David saying he had seen Richard at an event and asked if he wanted to publish through us — under any arrangement that suited him — thinking that when Richard had withdrawn from our publishing project, he would have left his six sets of Austen annotations lying idle. Richard's reply was that he expected to publish all six books in a few days and was very happy with his website. So, I grimaced, he has gone into competition with us. I'd had the idea and worked out the product concepts and software, the structure of the books, and so on, and apparently he was now going to steal and build on what I'd done. A sorry situation — with someone I'd once considered a good friend. Richard had betrayed others and I knew that. Why did I imagine it would be any different with me? It happens every day.

Yvonne was ready to apply grout to the glass tile she mounted to the kitchen walls above the backsplashes and under the wall cabinets — but the switches and receptacles had to be shimmed to the level of the tile so that they'd protrude through the faceplates properly. I had imagined using 1/4" wood strips to do this but what I found in my box of scraps was too thick or too thin so I decided to use pieces of the 1" by 1" tile as shim. Yvonne had a small tile cutter she showed me how to use and once I shimmed the switch on the north wall, she began to apply grout as she'd seen done in a YouTube video she'd consulted the day before. As I moved along to the other wall sections and shimmed the switches and outlets, Yvonne followed with the grout. At my urging, Yvonne had bought new, larger faceplates at Lowe's in Burlington and longer switch and outlet mounting screws, the former to cover the areas around the boxes where she hadn't put tile (she hadn't cut any) and the latter to account for the shimming. In two places the covers left visible tile gaps, so I cut some tiles and once Yvonne showed me how to do it, mounted the tiles to the walls. Late in the day after she'd wiped the tiles a number of times to clean off any excess grout, Yvonne told me I could mount the outlet and switch covers. The kitchen was nearly finished now — a bit more painting and some door and drawer tuning — but it looked very good. Then Yvonne noticed that because she'd used tile from two different production runs side by side in two places, the colors weren't quite the same — but I assured her I hadn't seen this subtle difference until she'd pointed it out. No one would notice.

Eighty-nine: Kelly and Tim Come for a Visit

"A happy family is but an earlier heaven." — George Bernard Shaw

We had followed their doings from Crane — through Facebook, email, and reported sightings — but we hadn't seen them since their wedding at the Orcas Hotel in July. I had officiated, and Yvonne had helped manage the service (the entrance of the right people at the right time). Now Kelly was pregnant, a little boy due at the beginning of June, and they'd spent the holidays in Perth and Sydney with Tim's relatives and friends, where their marriage was again feted, and they were showered with love. In early December when she volunteered the use of their Seattle apartment while they were gone, should we need it, Kelly made arrangements for them to visit us on Crane in January. They'd arrive about 1:40 from Anacortes and I'd pick them up with the *Huginn* at the ferry landing.

The Crane Island Association Board meeting was to convene at 9:00 at our house so I'd set out the conference phone on the dining room table and collected all the agendas, minutes, statements, and reports I thought we'd need for the meeting. Jason, Board president, had sent me an email asking me to chair the meeting. A death in the family required him to be in Idaho. I liked running the meeting because I thought I could make the process more effective and of shorter duration but I was treasurer and water chairman, not vice president, Dan was, so shouldn't Dan run the meeting in Jason's absence? By 9:00 I hadn't heard from Jason and Dan hadn't shown up yet so I called the meeting to order and continued to run the meeting even after Dan appeared. Martha and Dave were also on Crane for the meeting; Tim, Cate, and Pat called in through the conference call service.

There were two things I wanted to accomplish: adoption of the cross-connect policy Dave had drafted (mandated by the state) and adoption of an orderly and appropriate set of water policies Dave had worked on two years before and which I'd thought about and added to. We adopted the cross-con-

Eighty-nine: Kelly and Tim Come for a Visit

nect policy and could now work on the implementation plan we'd announce at the Annual Meeting in August and we came to an agreement on the other water policies, though Dave would have to work on the wording and submit them to the Board for final approval at the next meeting at the beginning of March. Yvonne made coffee and drop biscuits and when she served them, we made the absent members aware of what they were missing. We were done before 11:00. A good meeting.

Yvonne needed coffee, so I was to pick some up at the market at Orcas Village Store at the Landing. Ron and Mary were adding on to the store, to the north next to the road, a two-story structure now framed with a plywood roof. They'd opened the store about eight years ago and it's hard to imagine the Landing not having a market. I was to buy espresso-style ground coffee and if I couldn't find some already ground, I was to open the bag and use the grinder there — and I was to pick up the Saturday and the *Sunday Seattle Times*. I insisted Yvonne write me a note, and by the time I got to the store — the *Huginn* to the county dock and then walking up the ramp to the nearby store — I couldn't find the note — but then I did. Good grief! By the time I figured out how to open the coffee bag (Perugia) and grind it without spilling all of it and then paying for the coffee and two issues of the *Seattle Times* and then leaving the store, the *Elwha* had already docked and the walk-on passengers were coming up the ramp — but no Kelly and Tim in sight. Finally, they appeared and were ready to go — no need to go back to the store.

Before dinner, the four of us sat in the living room and caught up on their trip to Perth and second wedding. We told them about how Noah's back had gone out the afternoon of the rehearsal and how he had finally treated it using a hangboard. And about how the house sewer system had backed up when twelve of their guests were staying with us and how I figured out what to do and then fixed it. They'd had a good time in Perth and would consider living there sometime but didn't get enough time to themselves to get a feel for it. Yvonne cooked Alaskan halibut with rice, salad, and no-knead bread — a delicious meal. More conversation — about their opportunity to live in Paris for a while where Google, Tim's employer, is opening an office. We recommended they go if Tim is offered a position — a different response from most of the people they talked to who recommend staying in Seattle — and I suppose settling down (Huh!). They were more grown-up, more adult than when we'd last seen them; they had taken another developmental step or two — maybe because they'd be parents in early June.

089: Tim and Kelly at Orcas Landing

Kelly was winding down her work with Erica in Seattle and showed me the Claxon Marketing Website — focused on helping not-for-profits market for donations. Tim and I talked about Google's current inability to counter Facebook in the social networking space, maybe because the company was involved in so many projects. A pleasant evening and by 9:00 Kelly was falling asleep so we all retired for the evening. The day had warmed to over 50 and because I had continued to put wood on the fire, the house had warmed to 77, uncomfortable for Yvonne and perfect for Kelly. Yvonne and I talked for a while. She reported on her conversation with Jeni, and we both remarked on how much fun it was to visit with a young couple getting started who actually wanted to spend time with us old people and were interested in what we had to say. I managed to stay awake until almost 10:00.

Ninety: Let the Chips Fall

"Chop your own wood and it will warm you twice." — Henry Ford

Piles of sawdust littered the ground, especially around three stumps almost level with the ground and in parallel lines about 16" apart in three locations in the yard south of the house, amidst a dense stand of 50' Douglas firs. A few days before Kelly and Tim arrived, I wrote to Tim, suggesting that if he wanted to help me cut down and chop some trees during their visit, he should bring some old clothes. I guessed that this energetic Google software engineer and city boy would find the prospect of handling a chainsaw very attractive — and indeed, he did. I gave instructions and watched while Tim did the work.

Our property has hundreds of trees; they grow like weeds here and will take over everything if you let them. The stand south of the house, which we thinned last year, continued to cast too much shade on Yvonne's raised bed garden. Last summer's crop had been disappointing, and inadequate sun may have been part of the problem. Yvonne had mandated that ten specific trees had to go and applied blue painter's tape at eye level to their trunks to identify the doomed trees. With our kitchen project (almost completely) behind us and the length of the day and intensity of the light increasing, it wasn't too soon to begin to take the trees down, cut them up, and stack them to dry out in readiness for the next heating season. Tim was coming, he was strong (he played Australian football, didn't he?), he liked technology, and even if he actually wasn't one, he had the character of an Eagle Scout (coming from me, a compliment of the first order).

Saturday afternoon and evening, Tim (a native of Perth), Kelly (a Pennsylvania friend from Corrina's childhood), Yvonne, and I caught up on each other's doings since their July wedding. Sunday would be a workday, and we got started about 10:30 (both happy to sleep in, and Kelly logging 12 hours, perhaps in part as a response to her pregnancy and early June due date). Tim and I retrieved my Craftsman 18" chainsaw (a Poulan), and I showed him how to check and fill the gas and chain oil reservoirs, and to check and tighten the chain. As I found during the day, he watched carefully, learned, and later applied what he knew to the tree-cutting project.

090.1: After a little instruction Tim goes at it

We picked a 40′ tree as a starting point. It was rooted near the driveway, and we could see how we could drop it in a way that wouldn't get tangled up in any of the nearby trees. I took the 20′ extension ladder from the back porch where it was waiting to be used for doing the high painting in the kitchen Yvonne hadn't yet had a chance to do, and set it against the tree to be cut, asking Tim to hold it while I climbed as far up as I could safely go to attach a yellow polypropylene rope I'd untangled from the prop of Gumption, our pocket trawler, some years before after Yvonne accidentally ran over a crab pot line. Climbing down, I uncoiled the rope and tied it to a Douglas fir about 40 feet away where Margaret's driveway branches off from ours. I then explained to Tim about cutting and notching the tree on the fall side and then finishing up on the other side just above the first cut. We talked about the need for level cuts and how far he could cut without the tree immediately falling — and surprisingly, I think, to know that you could cut halfway through the tree without it toppling (at least in calm air and for a while).

090.2: Yvonne and Kelly feed the burn pile

He started his first cut, and it was obvious the chain wasn't sharp enough. It had felt sharp to the touch, but it wasn't, so Tim watched as I

Ninety: Let the Chips Fall

mounted a new Oregon chain and talked about how new chains stretch after a bit of use. Back at the tree, Tim finished the two cuts on the fall side and took out the wood wedge we'd use later when cutting the tree into sections. I went over how he should do the final cut, and then walked to the end of the rope, untied it from the tree, and prepared to pull it in my direction. Tim cut while I put some pressure on the rope, and as he cut further and I could feel the tree begin to yield, I pulled harder and then the tree came in my direction. Timber! Thump! Crash! Branches hitting the ground and shattering.

After Tim used the chainsaw to remove any remaining branches (and being a Douglas fir, they were all at the top), Yvonne and Kelly began to pick them up for the burn pile they had prepared. Yvonne had gone online to the county offices to buy a burn pile permit ($15), and she and Kelly had pulled a safety hose to the burn pile area, stacked branch cuttings, applied some gasoline, and then started the fire. It sputtered, so I added some used motor oil I'd been saving for the purpose, and when that proved inadequate, carefully added some more gasoline. Yvonne and Kelly piled on more needle-covered branches, and they sizzled and popped as they caught fire — surprising the first time you see it and then frightening once you understand the implications: green, wet trees burn just as well as brown, dry trees in a hot enough flame so the risk of forest and brush fires is, to some extent, always imminent.

A fire of cut green fir boughs gives off dense white smoke, and Yvonne and Kelly were careful to keep out of its path, this day north to south on a very mild breeze. I showed Tim how to shim the supine trunk to cut sections without also cutting dirt and rocks, and he moved systematically along the trunk cutting more or less 16" sections, and I loaded the sections into the dock cart and took several loads to the north side of the house to stack and cover so they could dry out and be split for use next winter. Tim downed two more trees, these about 50' high with a 12' diameter, and we used the same technique of tying a line about 15' up the trunk I would pull to help the tree fall in the right direction. In this case, we had the third tree fall on the second, making it easy to cut up the third tree since it was elevated but in easy reach. Yvonne and Kelly continued to collect greens Tim had cut from the top part of the trunks, and I moved sections to the wood storage area. And then it was time for lunch.

Tim made himself two sandwiches, and we talked about how many calories lumberjacks (used to?) burn, Yvonne's Scandinavian grandparents, as young adults, having both cooked in lumber camps. Then Yvonne went back out to tend the fire, and Tim and I went to the north side of the house where I showed him the sawbuck and the log sections I'd brought to the house from the south side of the Island in October and that now had to be cut into 16" lengths and split for firewood. After he cut the logs into sections, I showed him how to use the splitting maul and the stump I used as a ground, and he went to work — at first being a bit too tentative and then getting the idea and splitting about 10 days of wood, most of which we brought to the front porch for stacking in two cartloads, and then Tim stacked the rest with the main firewood pile. Along the way, I cut the logs I had brought from the community beach the week before and then split one of the sections as an experiment to determine whether it was promising as firewood. I decided that it was.

Kelly and Tim made dinner for Yvonne and me — a rare luxury in our house — a braised chicken with ginger that tasted very good, rice, broccoli, cold fresh bean salad, and a dessert of grapefruit sections and chocolate. While they cooked, I talked to Noah on the phone about the doings at their house and, in particular, about whether he thought Morgan would want to read Heinlein's *Red Planet*, the book I read when I was Morgan's age that eventually led to reading literary classics late into the night during high school. Another pleasure of my youth was B-grade movie serials. I'd given Morgan the complete *Flash Gordon* with Buster Crabbe, and Noah said he'd watched it 50 times. I now had in mind Clyde Beatty's *Lost Jungle*. Noah told me that given the film's association with animals, Morgan would probably love it — especially if I introduced it as being fascinating to me at his age.

After dinner, the four of us sat and talked for two hours about the settlement of Australia, Tim's roots, Perth and the coast south of it where his family has property they plan to build on, the cultural connections between Australia and the US, and why young people choose to emigrate from Australia to the US. Kelly has been reading Australian fiction and Yvonne and I suggested she read Colleen McCullough's *Thorn Birds*, a 1977 best-seller we both found fascinating. An enjoyable evening Yvonne and I retired from about 9:30, warming up in the hot tub and then reading until sleep overcame first Yvonne and then me.

Ninety-one: A Return to Our Routine

"There is no substitute for the comfort supplied by the utterly taken-for-granted relationship." — Iris Murdoch

Tim was particularly pleased that he'd served himself a piece of cowboy coffee cake with a generous portion of melted brown sugar. He was surprised that Kelly, Yvonne, or I hadn't seen and snagged it before he appeared at the table. Everyone loved cowboy coffee cake, especially when served warm with melting butter on top. It was an old family recipe and it has become part of our ritual breakfasts with our Boulder friends. Kelly looked beautiful this morning in a green knit dress, flawless pale skin, dark hair, and today, red lipstick. When asked why she was so dressed up, she smiled and said she wanted to look good on the return trip on the ferry.

At around 10:00, we got out of the house and went for a walk around the island — a pleasure for me, even though I had already made my rounds before dawn and startled a pair of mallards that took flight as I walked down Dock Road to return home. Everything was soaked after several days of intermittent rain, the ground saturated with water until it could hold no more. Low places now cupped water until it could seep away or evaporate. Though hard to believe, by August, the ground would be bone dry, with the sky's spigot mostly turned off from the beginning of July through mid-September. I pointed out the three-foot diameter osprey nest perched impossibly at the top of a 60-foot dead fir. Tim and I began to talk about technology, and Kelly and Yvonne talked about family.

We discussed the evolution of what Tim called multi-core processors — computers that may eventually have a hundred processors in one integrated circuit, each executing instructions and processing data in parallel with one another. Traditional programming, even multi-threaded, cannot take advantage of the power of these computers; the program needs to operate more like a network, requiring new programming techniques. The upcoming replacement of mechanical mass storage (hard drives) with solid-state drives calls for new techniques as well, given that current I-O data access optimization is based in part on the physical characteristics of spinning drives. Having begun my experience with computers with a deck of punch cards in 1962, the changes of the last almost 50 years have been amazing and stimulating. We also discussed the integrated development environment, a programming tool I was using that had recently released a version that could create desktop applications running in browsers. This allows Mac and PC software to migrate to the cloud (operate on remote servers) but still be written in the same way programmers were familiar with, instead of adopting a whole new world of HTML, Javascript, PhP, CCS, and so on. The vendor was calling the approach Web 3.0.

During our walk, Yvonne and Kelly talked about their family backgrounds, both sharing some French ancestry. The topic of family wove itself in and out of our conversation over the weekend — family being a source of great joy and a connection to the past and the future but also sometimes problematic when people who love one another struggle with their foibles and those of others.

Around noon, I took Kelly and Tim to the ferry landing for their trip back to Seattle. The sun was bright on the rippled water, and the sky a jumble of blue and white. On the county dock, they thanked me and talked about how much they enjoyed having friends that were not their age. "Old, you mean," I teased. Yvonne loves to have friends that are young.

Back at the Crane community dock, I checked Margaret's boat since we hadn't used it in a month. We'd need two boats the next day so Yvonne and I could have our own schedules. The Yamaha 50 started up right away, and I turned it off, raised the prop out of the water, and refastened the runabout's canvas cover. The two logs that had escaped from a log boom and had ended up on the beach were now close together and high on the beach. I retied their tethers to keep them from floating lower in the next high tide. The day before, while Tim split wood, I cut up the longer log sections I had scavenged from the beach the week before, bringing them home to cut into 16" lengths. I interrupted Tim's work to split one of these sections to get a sense of how easily they split and how wet they were. This information would help me decide whether to go to the trouble of bringing more home. I decided it would, and

Ninety-one: A Return to Our Routine

thus the attention to the logs at the beach today. I wanted them to be as convenient as possible to split.

As I worked with the logs, Martha and Stuart came up, on the island so Martha could attend the Board meeting Saturday. They were curious about what I was doing, and Martha told me that someone in Deer Harbor would come and get the logs, and she could give me his name. But I intend to cut them up and use them as firewood. "Oh, well then have at it," they said, and they walked away down Dock Road.

091: Foggy sunrise

I took Yvonne to Orcas so she could attend her Master Gardeners meeting at the Library, where Michael would do a presentation on catchment systems

— increasingly popular in the islands and a business he managed in parallel with his boat repair service. Attendance was sparse, as Yvonne reported later, a frustration to her since she organized the meeting presentations. She was disappointed with most of the Master Gardeners' lack of interest in becoming better informed. The Orcas group liked manning the question and answer table at the Orcas farmers market but not attending meetings.

Son Eric called while heading home on The 5 near Santa Maria, having come from San Diego where they helped celebrate Lauren and Dave's engagement. They'd stopped at a beach south of Santa Barbara so the kids could play. It was a beautiful sunny day there. Everybody was fine. The big excitement was that Oprah's crew had visited San Luis Obispo over the weekend for a broadcast Thursday, planning to cover SLO and why it's been described as the second-best place to live in the U.S. Because they had been in San Diego, Kristin (and maybe Eric) had missed being part of the taping that involved the Chamber, Kristin's employer. They finished the process of refinancing their house, which happened only because they could pay down the mortgage a bit, as their house had lost value since they'd bought it, a common problem in California over the last few years and in the San Juan Islands as well.

As it got dark, I realized Yvonne might be calling for a pick up from the Orcas dock, and I had to tell Eric goodbye. He was happy; their complicated life was increasingly in order.

Ninety-two: Bad News from La Jolla

"Don't walk behind me; I may not lead. Don't walk in front of me; I may not follow. Just walk beside me and be my friend." — Albert Camus

I was late for our 9:00 meeting. I had left home too late, as usual, and the extra time it took to unzip, unbuckle, and unhook the canvas on Margaret's boat at the Crane dock, and then reverse the process on the Orcas side, took an additional six or seven minutes. So, I knocked on David's door around 9:12, noticing that Chris's car wasn't in the driveway, and he's usually early everywhere he goes. David opened the door and was temporarily befuddled because he hadn't put the meeting on his calendar. David called Chris, who then came right over, acknowledging that he had entered the meeting into his iPod for 10:00 instead of 9:00. No matter.

I had gotten up early and was at my desk before 4:00 to run through the list of errors Chris and I had found, to look for more, make the corrections, and then upload the revised book to Amazon. I finished around 8:00. It could take 24 hours before the new version was posted to the Amazon delivery system.

We reviewed the changes and corrections I had made to the Slocum book and decided we needed a few more — some structural ones so that, for instance, turning the cover page would go to the general Table of Contents rather than the Chapters Table of Contents. We also agreed that it would make sense to have a help section. Chris had taken steps to have us interviewed for the local news blog, orcasissues.com, and I was working on getting an article published in the weekly newspaper, the *Islands Sounder*. The next step was to talk and write to people we knew who might be interested in reading the book and doing a review on Amazon. Since many of these people didn't have a Kindle, we'd need to provide a way for them to read the book online through their browser. Thus, I would have to put the book online as a website not publicly visible and make improvements to the enotatedclassics.com website so that readers, reviewers, and potential eNotators would have somewhere to look to understand what we were trying to do. We also went through a list of potential eNotators, noting that the character of a prospect counted as much as their expertise. Chris was eager to begin work on Slocum's *Liberdade* and *Destroyer*, so I'd need to load the text into a database for him to work against.

092: Circle Road at Becker farm

Back home, I spent most of the afternoon putting up a version of the book as a website for Kindle-less reviewers, and then I added to the marketing website. I found myself frustrated by a bug in Apple's iWeb that wouldn't let me make certain changes to text fonts, sizes, and colors. It seemed better to code the HTML directly.

Ninety-two: Bad News from La Jolla

Late in the afternoon, I noticed what looked like a Christmas card on the counter with a half-page note inside. Yvonne must have brought it home the day before. I recognized Nora, Sarah, and John in the mosaic of pictures but didn't see Alan. Foreboding. And there it was. Nora acknowledged that her news might shock: Alan had died in July after years of suffering from agitated depression. She missed him but was grateful that his torment was over. Her daughter and son and their families were nearby, and her friends and larger family had been supportive and loving.

I had last seen Alan about eight years ago. Yvonne and I were in La Jolla visiting Kristin's family and stopped at a bakery we'd enjoyed — and Nora appeared with her dog. We hadn't been in contact with them for a few years because I no longer felt comfortable with Alan. In my view, he'd become too much of a curmudgeon. Nora was curious why we were in La Jolla and hadn't called them. I told her the truth, and she asked if I'd like to talk to Alan and tell him about my concerns. I reluctantly agreed, and he was there in a few minutes. I told him I thought he had lost some of the humanity I'd seen in him when we first met in 1971, and I talked about why I thought that. He was hurt and said he didn't understand why I saw things the way I did. We went on with our day, and he and Nora went home. Alan was the most energetic person I'd ever met and maybe the friendliest. He was also gifted with an intuitive and studied understanding of planning, real estate, construction, and investment and had become very wealthy. He was also never at peace — with himself or with his family.

I had walked away from something more than an acquaintanceship and something less than a friendship without thinking much about it. I suppose I was a bit self-righteous. Now I understood something I hadn't known or understood before. Agitated depression is the combination of a depressed mood with hyperactivity. Alan's energy had a dark side, a kind of hell that expressed itself positively and creatively but also in anger and frustration. He had suffered, and I hadn't had a clue. Everything about him, everything I'd admired and criticized, now looked different. My story of Alan and how I told him my truth and walked away was mistaken. I was wrong, and I felt guilty. And I did feel bad for Alan and Nora and their family. Alan had been a remarkable person who had changed the world he walked and talked and loved and worked through.

What's Next?

Crane Island Journal is a four-volume memoir covering October 19, 2010 through October 18, 2011.

This is **Haust (Autumn)**, the first volume of Crane Island Journal.

Find information about **Vetur (Winter)**, **Vor (Spring)**, and **Sumar (Summer)** on the Journal's website, www.craneislandjournal.com.

www.ingramcontent.com/pod-product-compliance
Lightning Source LLC
Chambersburg PA
CBHW070419010526
44118CB00014B/1815